Praise for John Feinstein's

The Punch

ONE NIGHT, TWO LIVES, AND THE FIGHT THAT CHANGED BASKETBALL FOREVER

"Every NBA player, if not every pro athlete, should be required to read *The Punch*, John Feinstein's chilling book about how a 1977 fight in a Lakers-Rockets game changed the lives of Kermit Washington and Rudy Tomjanovich. If current NBA players read this book, maybe they'll realize the potential physical and psychological consequences of the fights that occur in NBA games every so often between these huge, powerful athletes. Maybe they'll realize that they could be haunted for the rest of their lives by one punch, as Washington and Tomjanovich have been. . . . Maybe if enough NBA players read *The Punch*, there won't be another punch like it."

—Dave Anderson, *New York Times*

"Just when you think John Feinstein couldn't possibly top himself, he goes and does just that. In *The Punch*, Feinstein offers a behind-the-scenes look at how one of the most infamous fights in modern professional sports annals affected the lives of the combatants, onlookers, teammates, and ultimately the National Basketball Association."

—Steve Goode, *Hartford Courant*

"*The Punch* delivers an incisive look at a critical moment in sports history."   —Rodney Price, *Rocky Mountain News*

"Feinstein has carefully documented one of the key events that helped civilize professional basketball. . . . He spends the first chapter setting the stage and then delivering a literary punch of his own with a captivating account of the incident. The story, already compelling on its own, sinks its hooks deep into the reader with the author's wonderful fast-paced narrative. . . . The tale is rich with quotes and impressions from many who were present at the fight. . . . Expertly telling the story of two men, Feinstein is also chewing up a good bite of NBA history that offers insights into how the league handles on-court conflict to this day. *The Punch* will probably race up sales charts and find a wide audience among those who love sports, but those who don't share that passion will find the book equally engrossing. Feinstein hasn't delivered a 'sports book' but rather has used sports as a way to examine the human experience in what is truly a fascinating read."

—Larry Curtis, *Salt Lake Deseret News*

"Feinstein is a fluent, facile writer. For the most part the pages go by quickly. . . . Feinstein is one of the country's most respected sports journalists."   —Fritz Lanham, *Houston Chronicle*

"Exhaustively researched and straightforwardly written."
—John Powers, *Boston Globe*

"Instructive and likeable. . . . Feinstein, who intuitively understands the bonds of teammates, skillfully draws the repercussions of the Punch."   —*Kirkus Reviews*

"It remains the touchstone for any discussion of violence in professional sports. . . . Feinstein captures not just the immediate aftermath of Washington's thundering punch but also the years of pain, anger, and sideways glances that each man endured because of the episode. . . . In an odd way, it may be Feinstein's thoughtful, detailed examination of each man's life—before and after the punch—that finally gives Washington and Tomjanovich the peace they both deserve."   —Mark Luce, *San Francisco Chronicle*

"*The Punch* is a story of how men build and rebuild their lives in the spotlight's glare. . . . It's about how bad things happen to good people. . . . Feinstein tells a television-age fable of how, in a split second, two strangers became linked in a way that's possible only when that moment is captured on videotape."
—Allen St. John, *Washington Post*

"*The Punch* has all the hallmarks of a John Feinstein special—the candid interviews, the touching nuances that personalize public people, the friendships and feuds that fuel the inner workings of a team."   —Katherine Pushkar, *Newsday*

"Feinstein's approach is utterly thorough regarding the event and painstakingly fair to both parties involved. . . . He convincingly proves his point that one punch in 1977 changed things for the men and the NBA."   —Susan Ellis, *Memphis Flyer*

"A compelling, detailed account of a terrifying incident. . . . Feinstein is a reporter at heart and this, his 13th book, is a fine display of his curiosity and tenacity."
—John Wilkens, *San Diego Union-Tribune*

"If you like sports, you'll love this book. If you like psychological studies, or great character development and strong subplots, you'll love this book." —John Burr, *Florida Times-Union*

"With his superb reportorial skills and layered insight, Feinstein has reigned as one of our nation's top sports storytellers for nearly two decades." —David Davis, *Jewish Daily Forward*

"*The Punch* is a wonderful piece of reporting that is required reading for anyone who loves sports, or sports history." —Mike Lupica, *New York Daily News*

"Feinstein does a respectable job of reporting the details of the punch and presents competing evidence conscientiously . . . The biographies of Washington and Tomjanovich are the most interesting sections of the book. . . . Washington's story is particularly engrossing." —Hugo Lindgren, *New York Times Book Review*

"An excellent and engaging book. . . . Feinstein's latest tears the scab off one of the deepest wounds in the history of professional sports. . . . He tells a moving story. . . . His research is sharp, and his time line jumps around effortlessly, like a good Quentin Tarantino film. . . . His portrait of each man is compelling." —*Publishers Weekly* (starred review)

"*The Punch* chronicles how this single, horrifying event forever changed the lives of the two men most directly involved. It also sheds light on how the NBA—and, indeed, all professional sports— has been affected as a result. . . . *The Punch* is more than a 'sports book'; it raises questions about race, violence, and, ultimately, redemption. Gruesome at times, but always engaging, Feinstein's latest book is a knockout." —Todd Tobias, *IMM*

The Punch

Also by John Feinstein

Open

The Last Amateurs

The Majors

A March to Madness

A Civil War

A Good Walk Spoiled

Play Ball

Hard Courts

Forever's Team

A Season Inside

A Season on the Brink

Running Mates
(A Mystery)

Winter Games
(A Mystery)

The Punch

ONE NIGHT, TWO LIVES, AND THE FIGHT THAT CHANGED BASKETBALL FOREVER

John Feinstein

BACK BAY BOOKS

Little, Brown and Company

NEW YORK | BOSTON | LONDON

Back Bay Books / Little, Brown and Company
Hachette Book Group USA
237 Park Avenue, New York, NY 10017
Visit our Web site at www.HachetteBookGroupUSA.com

Originally published in hardcover by Little, Brown and Company, November 2002
First Back Bay paperback edition, November 2003

Library of Congress Cataloging-in-Publication Data
Feinstein, John.
    The punch: one night, two lives, and the fight that changed
basketball forever / John Feinstein.—1st ed.
        p.   cm.
    Includes index.
    ISBN 978-0-316-27972-2 (hc) / 978-0-316-73563-6 (pb)
    1. Violence in sports—United States.   2. Basketball—United
States—History—20th century.   3. Washington, Kermit, 1951–
4. Tomjanovich, Rudy, 1948–   I. Title.
    GV706.7 .F45 2002
    796.323'64—dc21   2002016210

10   9   8   7   6   5   4
RRD-C

Book design by Victoria Hartman

Printed in the United States of America

This is for Dick Hall and David Sattler
Neither is a relative by blood
Both are brothers in my heart

Contents

Introduction

It was a comfortable June afternoon and I was in my car en route to a meeting in downtown Washington, D.C. I was listening to my friend Jim Rome's syndicated radio show when I heard him introducing Kermit Washington.

Like anyone who follows sports, I knew the name well, and as with most people, the instant I heard his name one image came into my mind: The Punch. I don't know how many times I had seen it on tape, but it was right there in my mind's eye, Washington turning and punching Rudy Tomjanovich with such force that Tomjanovich appeared to fly backward through the air.

The date was December 9, 1977, the place was the Los Angeles Forum. Washington was in his fifth year with the Los Angeles Lakers at the time. Tomjanovich, a four-time All-Star, was in his eighth season with the Houston Rockets.

I probably knew a little more about Washington than most people, even though I had never met him. He was a graduate of American University, and a number of people I had worked with at the *Washington Post* knew him well. Mike Trilling, the *Post's* late assistant sports editor, had worked with him at AU, and a number of the guys I had worked with at the paper had written about him through the years, since he was a local hero in the early 1970s. All said the same thing about him: "Sweetheart of a guy."

As Rome introduced Washington, talking about his accomplishments—two-time academic All-American; last player to average 20 points and 20 rebounds in a college season (1973); nine years in the NBA; charity work in Africa—and then brought up The Punch, I remembered reading a piece in the *New York Times* a few weeks earlier written by Washington, about how the night of the Tomjanovich punch still haunted him. I also remembered interviewing Tomjanovich on the subject for the *Post* during the 1981 NBA playoffs. He was very polite, but it was clear he didn't want to talk about what had happened. Who could blame him?

Rome had read the same piece in the *Times*, which led him to book Washington for the show. He began walking Washington through what led up to the fight and then the fight itself. As he talked, two things were apparent to me about Washington: he had done this before, and he was still in a lot of pain. By the end of the first segment, I had reached my destination and parked my car. I was a few minutes early, so I stayed in the car and listened to the second segment. When I heard Rome saying he was going to keep Washington for a third segment, I was surprised but not surprised. Rome almost never keeps a guest two segments, much less three. But there was clearly more to ask, and he knew it. By now, I was late for my meeting. I stayed in the car.

By the time Rome finished, I was convinced there was a book to be written about Kermit Washington and Rudy Tomjanovich. Clearly this moment had changed Washington's life and, I was willing to bet, Tomjanovich's life too. Clearly it was a watershed moment in sports, because it has become *the* symbol of what can happen when fights break out among very strong, very athletic young men.

"What this event told us," NBA commissioner David Stern told me later, "was that we could not, under any circumstances, allow men this big and this strong to square off and swing at one another. We sometimes get criticized for the rules we have, especially when we have to suspend players for wandering off the bench during a fight in the playoffs [see New York–Miami, 1998]. But I would rather have that happen than have bench-clearing brawls that lead to serious injuries.

"People forget, that was a tough time in the league. This was a monumental event when it occurred, because it appeared to symbolize everything people were saying about us. And it got *so* much attention at the time, which only made it more difficult for everyone."

I was fairly convinced that Washington would talk to me, given that the piece in the *Times* and the Rome interview both made it clear that he felt people did not understand what really happened that night or who the real Kermit Washington was. Tomjanovich, I believed, would be more difficult, and in my mind there would be no book without his cooperation. For better or worse, the two men were entwined in each other's lives forever.

With the help of Travis Rogers, Rome's radio producer, I tracked Washington down at his restaurant outside Portland, Oregon. I explained that I thought there might be a book in his and Tomjanovich's story if both would cooperate. "I'll do it," he said, "but I think you'll have a tough time with Rudy. I know he doesn't like to talk about it."

Tomjanovich had come back from the punch, after going through five surgeries, to play again in 1978–79. He had retired after the 1981 season and had been with the Rockets ever since as a scout, assistant coach, and, since 1992, the head coach. He had become a coaching star, winning back-to-back NBA titles in 1994 and 1995, and was about to coach the 2000 U.S. Olympic men's basketball team, which would win the gold medal in Sydney.

At that moment I had a contract with my publisher to do a golf book during 2001. My feeling was that I would take a shot at

Tomjanovich, and if he didn't want to do it, that would be that. I would be disappointed, because I really believed there was a good book to be done, but I would move on. I contacted Tim Frank, who was then the Rockets' public relations director.

If there is an unsung hero in this book, it is Tim Frank, if only because the one person who has put more time into seeing it reach completion is me. By the time I reached the finish line, Tim, who now works for the NBA, had taken to answering my phone calls by saying, "What'd you forget now?" Or, "Whose number did you lose this time?"

I told Tim what I was hoping to do. His answer was direct: How can I help? At that moment, all I wanted was a guarantee that the letter I was going to write to Rudy telling him why I wanted to do the book would get to him, not end up in the trash next to a secretary's desk. "Send it to me," Tim said. "I'll put it in his hands myself."

He did. The return phone call was, I thought, not surprising. "He just doesn't feel like he wants to go through it all again," Tim said when he called back. I understood. I thanked him for trying. Then Tim said one more thing: "John, I wouldn't want to lead you down the wrong road here, but I honestly believe if you ever sat him down alone, face-to-face, the answer might be different. No guarantees. I could be nuts. But he didn't just blow it off as if it was crazy."

I kept that in mind. Maybe down the road. I had a golf book to write. In January I began the research. The book, which I may go back to someday, was supposed to be about players who go through the PGA's Qualifying School and what the next year of their lives is like. I put together my group of players and went to Tucson to start the year. Something was nagging at me while I was there. I liked the guys I was working with. I love golf. But it didn't feel right. Maybe the idea was too similar to *A Good Walk Spoiled*. Maybe it was just too much travel with two little kids at home. Something wasn't working.

Two weeks later I was supposed to continue my research in San Diego. Now, San Diego in early February is not exactly a daunting assignment, especially when it is snowing and 25 degrees in Washington. San Diego is the best West Coast tournament to go to as a reporter: no pro-ams to deal with, great working conditions at the golf course, and the hotel is across the street from an excellent swimming pool. Perfect. I had plans to spend time with three of my golfers.

And I didn't want to get on the plane. My gut was telling me something. I sat back and pictured myself not doing the book. Immediately I felt better. I had been back and forth for weeks with this notion, but I decided to go with my gut feeling. I called Esther Newberg, my agent-for-life, and told her what I was feeling. I was prepared for some serious moaning and groaning. "If that's the way you feel, then don't do it," she said. "You're allowed to do this at this point in your life."

I took a deep breath, relieved. "Do you want me to call Michael?" she asked, referring to Michael Pietsch, my editor at Little, Brown. "Absolutely not," I said. This was something I felt I had to go and tell him in person.

The next day I drove to New York, which I find much easier than flying most of the time. In the car I was flipping radio stations as I crossed the Delaware Memorial Bridge, when I picked up a Philadelphia radio station. "And tomorrow," a voice was saying, "the Sixers host the Houston Rockets in the First Union Center."

My eyes widened. Coincidence? Or karma? My meeting in New York went better than I could have hoped for. Michael Pietsch is, as my mother used to say, a mensch. He could have pointed out that I had a signed contract for this book and that he had willingly gone along with my off-the-wall idea to do a book on Patriot League basketball a year earlier and that I owed him this golf book. He did none of that. "You're doing the right thing," he said. "If your heart isn't in it, you shouldn't do the book. When you've got another idea, we'll talk."

I said nothing about the outside possibility that I might have another idea in forty-eight hours. That night I tracked down Tim Frank in Philadelphia. Any chance, I asked, that Rudy would see me tomorrow? "I'll get back to you," Tim said. An hour later he did: "We're shooting in the arena from twelve to one," he said. "Rudy says you should meet us there."

Back in the car the next morning, on my way to Philly, I put together a Letterman's list of the ten reasons why Rudy should cooperate for the book. I was going to give it my best shot. I knew this was a book I wanted to do. Whenever an idea truly excites me, I get hyper and can't stop thinking about it. That was the way I felt turning into the parking lot at the First Union Center. I figured my odds were about 10-to-1 against.

Often, as a reporter, when you are meeting someone at practice, they will wait until the last possible moment to talk to you and then say something like, "Can we talk on the way to the bus?" I walked onto the court at twelve-thirty. Five minutes later Rudy walked over, put out his hand, and said, "I heard you wanted to talk to me." No stalling or rushing here. At least I would get the chance to make my pitch.

We sat down in a corner of the almost-empty building. I told him about hearing Kermit on the radio, and about Bill Buckner. I was at Shea Stadium on that October night in 1986 when Mookie Wilson's ground ball bounced under Buckner's glove. I had never forgotten being in the Red Sox clubhouse and watching Buckner deal with wave after wave of writers, never once snapping, never once saying, "I already answered that question."

Classy as he was, as good a ballplayer as he was (almost 2,800 hits), most baseball fans remember Buckner for that one moment. In fact, most people, including many who watched the game or were in the ballpark, believe that Buckner's error cost the Red Sox the Series, that if he had made the play Boston would have won. The truth is, the score was already tied when he made the error. If he had made the play, the game would have gone to the eleventh inning, tied. There is no guarantee at all that the Red Sox would have won.

But in the lore of the game, Buckner's boot cost the Red Sox the Series. When you point this out to Boston fans—Esther, for example—they turn their noses up and say something like, "Don't defend him." He lives in their minds as the goat, and they don't want anyone using facts to dissuade them from that belief.

I told Rudy that I thought he and Kermit were like Buckner in that each had accomplished so many other things and yet, when people thought of them, they thought of *this*. I wondered how he had put it behind him and gone on with his life; who had helped him do that; what he thought now, all these years later, when it still came up over and over again.

Rudy looked straight across the court at the empty seats. "Someone once told me," he said, "that hating Kermit would be like taking poison and hoping someone else died. I've always tried to remember that."

I let those words hang in the air for a moment and then prepared to move on with my list. Before I could, though, Rudy looked at me and said, "Okay, let's do it."

I was stunned. Heck, I had about eight reasons left. Later he told me that something in his gut told him this was the right thing to do, that he believed he could trust me to tell the story properly. I will be forever grateful to him for that. We talked logistics for a couple minutes, then shook hands and he went back on the court. I walked over to Tim. He had a sheepish look on his face.

"I was really upset," he said later. "I thought Rudy would give you more than ten minutes before he turned you down."

Before Tim could say anything, I said, "He said yes."

Tim's answer was direct: "He said *what*?"

And so, this book was born.

It was different from any book I've ever done because I had to track down clips, locate people, and try to piece together events that took place almost twenty-five years before. I was amazed at how different the story was from what I first perceived it to be. I had no idea how seriously Rudy was hurt that night or what he went through emotionally long after the worst of the physical pain had subsided. I could not possibly have realized how traumatic the event was for the other players on the court, for the coaches, even for the referees, and for all of basketball. There had never been anything quite like it before in the sport. Thank God there has never been anything quite like it since.

One of the first people I spoke to during my research was Jerry West, who was coaching the Lakers the night the incident took place. West candidly admitted that just talking about it again, even after all these years, was upsetting. I could tell by the quaver in his voice that he meant what he was saying.

"The worst part of it all," he said, "is that these were two very good men. In different ways, they're both victims of that night. I don't think either one of them has ever been able to find closure with this. And I'm not sure they ever will."

I have now spent hours and hours with both of them, talking about that night and their lives before and since. As a reporter, I would be lying if I didn't say I found the story fascinating, the notion that one moment, a matter of just a few seconds, can so radically change lives. As a friend, and I now consider both of them my friends, I sincerely hope that all the time they spent talking about what occurred, and now reading what follows, will give them some kind of closure.

They both deserve it.

The Punch

1

What Hit Me?

December 9, 1977

He had always worried about the scoreboards. That morning, during shootaround, Rudy Tomjanovich caught himself staring up at the scoreboard in the Los Angeles Forum, wondering if the thing was really safe.

"I always thought about it in the empty arenas," he said. "For some reason, I worried that one day one of the damn things would break and it would come crashing down on us during a game."

Now it had. At least that's what he thought when he came to, lying flat on his back, that night in the opening minute of the third quarter. The Houston Rockets and Los Angeles Lakers had been tied 55–55 at halftime, and he was having a great shooting night: 9-for-14 from the field. His jumper, one of the NBA's sweetest, felt perfect every time he released the ball. The only surprise was that he had actually missed five times.

The Rockets had gone up 57–55 to start the second half. There was a missed jump shot at the other end, and Kevin Kunnert, the Rockets' 7-foot center, grabbed the rebound. Tomjanovich began sprinting down the right side of the court, knowing that Kunnert would feed the ball to John Lucas, his team's point guard, and there would be a chance to beat the L.A. defense down the court. He was on the right wing, looking to see if Lucas was going to feed him the ball, when he heard a whistle behind the play.

He turned and saw Kunnert, who had made it to midcourt, being wrestled from behind by Kareem Abdul-Jabbar. Another Laker, Tomjanovich wasn't sure at that moment who it was, had his back to Tomjanovich and was throwing a punch at Kunnert. Tomjanovich saw Kunnert sag to one knee as the punch landed, and he started running in the direction of the fight. "All I knew," he later said, "was one of my guys was in trouble. I just ran toward the fight, not sure what I would do when I got there."

He sprinted toward the skirmish, arms down, thinking he would perhaps wrap up the Laker who had hit Kunnert and pull him away, just as Abdul-Jabbar appeared to be doing with Kunnert. That's the way most NBA fights began and ended: an elbow or a profanity thrown; a square-off; a punch, maybe two; and then cooler heads prevailing. Tomjanovich was always one of the cooler heads. Calvin Murphy, his 5-foot-10-inch roommate, was not. Murphy was also running back in the direction of the fight. Somewhere, in the deep recesses of his mind, Tomjanovich knew that if Murphy arrived before he did, it would not be as a peacemaker. He was at full speed as he approached center court.

That was when the scoreboard fell on him.

"Tricky, what happened?"

He was lying in a pool of blood, Tomjanovich knew that. He could see Dick Vandervoort, the Rockets' trainer, leaning over him, holding a towel to try to stanch the blood gushing from his nose.

"Lie still, Rudy," Vandervoort—Tricky to all the Houston players—was telling him.

Still dazed, Tomjanovich sat up just a little bit, and the first person he saw was Walter Matthau, the actor, who was sitting in a

front-row seat. He repeated his original question. "What happened, Trick, did the scoreboard fall on me?"

"Kermit hit you."

Kermit Washington was the Lakers' 6-foot-8-inch power forward. He was listed in the media guide as weighing 240 pounds, all
of it rock-hard muscle from years of weight lifting. On that night
Washington's weight was down to 222, the result of hours of tire-
less off-season rehab work he had done after undergoing knee surgery the previous season. At any weight Washington was one of the
league's strongest men, a self-made player who used strength,
intensity, and work ethic to make up for a lack of offensive skills.

Washington often joked about his shooting ability. "I would
always say to the referees, 'Hey, I'm being fouled, call a foul,'" he
said. "And they would look at me and say, 'Kermit, if we call the
foul, you're just going to miss free throws and embarrass yourself.
Keep playing.'"

So he played. Very hard. He was part of a generation of
enforcers, players whose job it was to protect their team's star.
Abdul-Jabbar was the Lakers' star. Washington was his protection.
That meant he did the dirty work defensively and on the boards,
and if any kind of skirmish broke out, it was his job to make sure
nothing happened to Abdul-Jabbar. There were limits to what he
could do. On opening night in October, Abdul-Jabbar, frustrated
by the physical play of Milwaukee Bucks rookie center Kent Benson, had hauled off and slugged Benson, breaking his hand. He
had missed 20 games and the Lakers had struggled to a 9–14 start.

It was Washington whom Tomjanovich had seen throw the
punch at Kunnert. As Kunnert's knees buckled and Abdul-Jabbar,
who had been trying to separate Kunnert from Washington, swung
him away, Washington became aware of someone approaching
from behind.

"I saw a blur of red," he said. "I grew up in the streets. You learn
there that if you're in a fight and someone is coming up from
behind you, you swing first and ask questions later."

He turned and swung, a straight right hand that landed just under Tomjanovich's nose. At the very last instant, as Washington turned and faced him, Tomjanovich sensed danger. He tried to throw his hands up to protect himself, but it was too late.

"I don't have any memory of throwing my hands up," Tomjanovich said. "The only reason I know I did is because I saw it on the tape. The last thing I remember is running toward the fight. Then I looked up and saw Tricky. There's nothing in between."

In between was a punch that landed with devastating force. It was thrown by a very strong man, pumped up on adrenaline from being in a fight, at a man running full speed right into the punch, completely unprotected. Describing what happened later, doctors likened the collision of Washington's fist and Tomjanovich's face to a collision between two locomotives traveling at full speed. The doctor who worked on Tomjanovich later that night, a specialist in head and neck trauma, said the injuries Tomjanovich suffered were not unlike those suffered by someone thrown through the windshield of a car traveling 50 miles per hour.

"I'll never forget that sound," Abdul-Jabbar said. "I had turned Kunnert away from Kermit, and suddenly I heard this *crack*, like a melon landing on concrete. It's twenty-four years ago, but I can still hear it."

The punch knocked Tomjanovich straight backward, and he landed on the back of his head, out cold within a second. Every person on the court and almost every person in the Forum that night remembers the next few minutes as if they were played out in slow motion.

Upstairs in the press box, the writers looked at each other almost as soon as the punch landed and then began heading downstairs—almost unheard of in the middle of a game.

"It was the sound," Thomas Bonk, then the Rockets' beat writer for the *Houston Post*, remembered. "No one had ever heard a punch that sounded like that. Even from where we were, all the way upstairs, the sound resonated. Punches aren't supposed to do that. It was frightening.

"We were used to fights. Back then, fights broke out in the NBA every night. When Kermit and Kunnert squared off, your first response was, 'Oh look, another stupid NBA fight, what else is new?' And then in an instant it all changed and it became terrifying."

While most of the writers used the stairs behind the seating area that would take them directly to the hallway where the team locker rooms were, Ted Green of the *Los Angeles Times* bolted out of his chair and ran directly down the center aisle of seats to get courtside.

"The first thing that was stunning was that you could actually hear the punch from where we were," he said. "None of us had ever heard a punch from where we sat. The second thing was the blood. It started spreading around Rudy's head almost as soon as he hit the floor. I'd never seen anyone shot in the head, but if I had, that's what I imagined it would look like."

Green estimates that it took him about forty-five seconds to sprint from his seat to courtside. He got to within twenty-five or thirty feet of Tomjanovich and saw him lying there, blood all over him and the court, while players milled around in shock and Vandervoort worked on him.

"He wasn't moving," Green said. "He probably didn't move for a total of two minutes, maybe three. But it felt like hours while I was standing there. I remember thinking, 'He's dead. My God, he's dead. How could this happen? How could this possibly happen?' It was completely out of context, this whole scene I was looking at, and it was absolutely horrifying all at once."

No one was more horrified than Jerry West. A Hall of Fame player in his second year as the Lakers' coach, he had seen his share of fights. But never anything like this. "I was in shock when I saw it," he said. "Absolute, complete shock. It was an awful feeling. I felt sick to my stomach."

Abdul-Jabbar felt the same sensations. "There was just so much blood," he said. "I kept thinking, 'How can there be so much blood from one punch? Something is wrong here.' The only thing that kept me from panicking completely was that his legs were moving a little. Otherwise I would have been worried that he was dead. It looked that bad."

The whistle Tomjanovich had heard had been blown by Bob Rakel, the referee trailing the play. Rakel had seen Kunnert and Washington square off, and when Washington threw the punch at Kunnert he blew his whistle, in part to call a punching foul, in part to try to get the players to back off. Ed Middleton was the other official, and he had been in full sprint trying to get to the other end of the court to pick up the completion of the Rockets' fast break. He was almost at the baseline when he heard his partner's whistle and turned to see what had happened. When he saw the melee at midcourt, he turned and followed Tomjanovich in the direction of the fight. The next thing he knew, Washington had spun around and thrown the punch and Tomjanovich was on the floor.

At that moment, everything stopped. No one on either team had any desire to fight anymore. While Rakel was telling Washington he was ejected from the game, Middleton stood behind Vandervoort, who had raced off the bench the minute Tomjanovich went down. "I remember telling someone we were going to need more towels to mop up all the blood," Middleton said. "Then I looked down and got a good look at Rudy's face. I had to go over to the scorer's table and lean over to get my breath back. I was afraid I was going to be sick."

Calvin Murphy, the little guard whom no one in the NBA wanted to fight, had raced past Washington to get to Kunnert, who was staggering in Abdul-Jabbar's arms. When he heard the punch and saw Tomjanovich go down, he left Kunnert and reached his best friend's side no more than a second or two before Vandervoort. Washington was a few feet away, being ejected by Rakel. Murphy stood rooted to the spot, staring first at his unconscious teammate, then at Washington.

"My first thought was, 'I'm going to kill the sonofabitch,'" Murphy said. "There was no question in my mind about it. I couldn't believe what I was looking at. I couldn't believe he had done that to Rudy. I saw the security people starting to take him off, and I took a step toward him, because I was going to kill him. That was absolutely my intent: kill the sonofabitch who had done that to my buddy."

But when Murphy tried to put one foot in front of the other, he found he couldn't move. His legs were rubbery. It certainly wasn't fear. Murphy was one of the league's smallest men, but he was every bit the enforcer that Washington was. He had been a Golden Gloves boxer as a teenager, and unlike most of the league's players, he actually knew *how* to fight. Unofficially he had been in seventeen full-fledged fights during eight years in the league and had never lost. The fight that people remembered most was one against Sidney Wicks, then of the Boston Celtics. Like Washington, Wicks was 6-8 and about 225. Murphy had jumped into the air, grabbed Wicks by his Afro, pulled him down to his level, and punched him into submission.

Now he stood frozen as Washington left the court. "It was an act of God," Murphy said years later. "It had to be. On any other night I would have killed him. But something happened and kept me there, right where I was. It had to be an act of God. There's no other explanation."

John Lucas had been in the lane when the whistle blew. He continued to the basket, put an uncontested layup through the hoop, and caught the ball as it came through the net. He turned and ran back to the scene with the ball still in his hands. "My first instinct was to turn and run," he said. "I saw Rudy, I looked at Kermit, and I thought, 'Oh my God, what has happened here?'" he said. "I remember I had the ball in my hands, and the first thing I thought was that I just wanted to get out of there. I just didn't want to be at that place. It was too gruesome."

Tomjanovich knew none of this when he came to. He wasn't in that much pain when Vandervoort got him into a sitting position, but he was confused. It hadn't been the scoreboard; it had been Kermit Washington. "I was dazed and woozy, and Tricky was telling me Kermit hit me. All I could think was, 'Why would he hit me? I wasn't even fighting with him.'"

It was several minutes before Tomjanovich could stand up. Nowadays, he wouldn't have been allowed to move. He would have been told to stay down and a stretcher would have been brought out for him. But this was 1977. He got up slowly, aided by Vandervoort, with a towel over his face to try to stop the blood. Getting up, he looked right at West. It was then that he understood for the first time that this was more than a bloody nose.

"He just had this look on his face," Tomjanovich said. "It was the kind of look you see when someone can't believe what they're seeing. I remember thinking I must look pretty bad. But I had no idea how bad."

Tomjanovich had no idea how fortunate he was that Vandervoort had figured out very quickly that he had a serious injury. As he left the court with Vandervoort, Tomjanovich was trailed by Dr. Clarence Shields, one of the Lakers' team doctors. Washington had already left, escorted by security and by Dr. Robert Kerlan, the Lakers' senior team doctor, who went back to the locker room with him to examine his hand.

As he walked off, Tomjanovich could hear a man directly over the tunnel leading to the dressing rooms screaming profanities at him. "He should have killed you, Tomjanovich," the man yelled. "Should have killed you."

Standing in front of the man, eyes filled with tears, was a youngster Tomjanovich recognized as someone who had come to his basketball camp years earlier. Tomjanovich wasn't sure whether the boy was crying because of what he looked like or because of what the man was yelling. Either way, he went from wobbly to furious in an instant.

"Let's get this done fast, Trick," he said. "Put some gauze in my nose or whatever and get me back out there."

Vandervoort said nothing. Once they were out of the arena and in the hallway under the stands, they had to walk past the Lakers' dressing room and around a corner to where the visitors' dressing room was located. The first person Tomjanovich saw in the hallway was Washington. By then the media was in the hallway—Bonk and George White from Houston and two of the three Lakers beat writers—Rich Levin of the *Herald-Examiner* and Mitch Chortkoff from the *Orange County Register*. Green was still on the court.

"Kermit was still wound up," Bonk said. "He was pacing up and down in the hallway, just all pumped up on adrenaline, when Rudy and Vandervoort got there."

Seeing Washington, Tomjanovich turned in his direction. "Why'd you hit me like that?" he demanded.

"What?" Washington screamed back. "What? Hit you? Ask Kevin Kunnert. Ask him what happened."

"I'm asking you, you sonofabitch," Tomjanovich yelled back, and he started toward Washington.

He didn't get far, though, because Vandervoort and the security people intervened. "Good thing," Tomjanovich said later. "If I'd gotten near him, he probably would have killed me."

In fact he almost certainly would have killed him.

Once it became apparent to Tomjanovich that he wasn't going to get to Washington, he and Vandervoort proceeded to the locker room. Dr. Shields had already gone ahead and placed a call to the pager of Dr. Paul Toffel, a thirty-four-year-old who specialized in head trauma. Toffel was at a pre-Christmas fund-raiser for the University of Southern California Medical Center at a hotel not far from the arena. When he called Shields back, Shields told him there had been a fight during the game at the Forum. "I've got a guy here who appears to have a severely broken nose and other facial injuries," he said. Toffel told him he would meet the player in the emergency room at Centinela Hospital as soon as he could get there.

"Do me a favor and tell them to get started right away on X rays," he told Shields. "That way I can see what we're dealing with as soon as I arrive."

At that moment Tomjanovich was sitting on a training table, with no intention of going to a hospital. He had a game to finish. "If my nose is broken, hook me up with a mask," he told Vandervoort. Firmly, Vandervoort told him there would be no mask and no more basketball on this night.

"There's an ambulance outside," he said.

"Ambulance?" Tomjanovich said. "What the hell is that about?"

A few minutes later he was in the ambulance. Then he was in the hospital and they were making X rays. He wondered what he must look like, because the looks he was getting from the people in the emergency room were not that different from what he had seen on the court from Jerry West. "And these were people who were used to seeing stuff," he said.

Dr. Toffel arrived a few minutes later, still in his tuxedo. When he was given the X rays, his eyes went wide. "Oh my God," Toffel said to the emergency room doctor who had given him the X rays. "This isn't a sinus injury. The posterior portion of his face is way out of alignment." (Translation: the top part of his skull was actually about an inch off line from the lower portion.)

"Who is this guy?" Toffel asked.

"Rudy Tomjanovich. Plays for the Rockets."

Toffel knew the name, knew Tomjanovich was a very good player.

Tomjanovich was wondering when he was going to get to call his wife back home in Houston when Toffel, now wearing scrubs over his tuxedo, walked in carrying X rays. He introduced himself, put a glove on one hand, and told Tomjanovich that he was going to see if he could move his upper jaw.

"It moved very easily," Toffel said later. "Which confirmed what the X rays had shown. I knew then this was a very serious situation."

Tomjanovich was still trying to figure out the quickest way to get out of the hospital. He asked Toffel if whatever he was going to do was going to take long and, more important, if he couldn't play any more basketball that night, how soon would he be back? The Rockets had a game in Phoenix the next night. Could he play there?

Toffel looked Tomjanovich in the eye. "No, Rudy, you can't play tomorrow," he said. "You aren't going to play basketball for a while. You aren't going to play any more this season."

Tomjanovich, whose eyes were already swelling shut, looked at Toffel as closely as he possibly could. Even though they were slits, his eyes told him that Toffel was completely serious. Any pain he was feeling disappeared, replaced by rage. "Not play this season?" he repeated. "Okay, look Doc, I know you gotta do what you gotta do, but give me an hour. I promise I'll come right back. I need to go back and find the guy who did this to me."

In Tomjanovich's mind at that moment, he was about to walk out of the emergency room, hail a cab, and go back to the Forum. Not play for the rest of the season? Now he really wanted to get Kermit Washington, regardless of the consequences. "I can't ever remember being angrier than I was at that moment," he said.

Toffel's face didn't change expression. His voice was very soft. "Rudy, let me ask you a question," he said. "Do you have any kind of funny taste in your mouth?"

Tomjanovich's eyes opened slightly. "Yeah, I do," he said. "It doesn't taste like blood either. It's very bitter. What is it?"

"Spinal fluid," Toffel said. "You're leaking spinal fluid from your brain. We're going to get you up to ICU in a few minutes and we're going to hope your brain capsule seals very soon. Do you know what the ICU is, Rudy?"

Tomjanovich nodded. He knew what ICU stood for: intensive care unit. The rage was gone. It had been replaced by fear.

"You're in trouble, Rudy," Toffel said. "We're going to work very hard to get you through this. But you can't be negative right now about anything or anyone. You have to work toward getting better, a little bit at a time. We don't need any anger or anything negative. Do you understand?"

Tomjanovich nodded again. By now he was in shock. Less than an hour ago, he had been a basketball player, doing what he loved and being paid a lot of money to do it. Now a doctor was telling him his life was hanging in the balance. He was twenty-nine years old, with a wife and two young children. At that moment all he wanted to do was see them again. Nothing else mattered.

While Tomjanovich was being taken to the hospital, Kermit Washington sat on a table in the empty Lakers locker room as Dr. Kerlan put stitches in his hand. A few minutes later he showered, dressed, and went home. His wife, Pat, who was almost eight months pregnant, was there with their two-year-old daughter, Dana.

He had been in fights before. In fact the previous season in Buffalo, he had decked John Shumate during a scuffle on court and then taken on most of the Braves' bench. He had fought with Dave Cowens, the Boston Celtics' star center, in another incident. But something told him this was different. Dr. Kerlan had said they were taking Tomjanovich to the hospital and that he had a badly broken nose and some facial injuries. He had seen the blood on the court, had felt the punch land. He wondered if he would be suspended by the NBA, which had passed new antifighting rules before the start of the season in response to a spate of fights in previous years.

As he walked to his car he heard someone calling his name. It was the man who patrolled the players' parking lot during games. He didn't know the man's name, but they always exchanged greetings before and after each game.

"Kermit," the man said as Washington opened his car. "I saw it. I saw what happened."

Washington nodded, not really eager to get into a conversation at that moment.

"Kermit," the man said, "you're in a lot of trouble. Big trouble."

Washington's stomach twisted into a knot. He wasn't sure why, because at that moment he didn't know how badly Tomjanovich was hurt, but something told him the man was right.

He was in a lot of trouble.

2

An Overcast Friday

As with most disasters, the day that would change the lives of Rudy Tomjanovich and Kermit Washington forever began routinely. It was an overcast Friday in Los Angeles, six weeks into the NBA season. Both the Rockets and the Lakers had gotten off to poor starts, especially given that each had arrived in training camp with high hopes.

The Lakers had finished the 1976–77 regular season with the league's best record, 53–29. But they hadn't been the same team after Washington tore up his knee in the last game prior to the All-Star break, and when they faced the Portland Trail Blazers in the Western Conference finals—a team they had beaten three straight times when Washington was healthy—they were swept in four games. The Blazers, led by Bill Walton, went on to beat the Philadelphia 76ers in six games to win their only NBA championship.

In Houston everyone connected to the Rockets firmly believed that the championship trophy sitting in Portland could easily have been in Houston instead. The Rockets had won a franchise record 49 games and had reached the conference final for the first time in team history, where they faced the 76ers. The Sixers were loaded, the overwhelming favorites to win the title. They had returning All-Stars George McGinnis and Doug Collins, the massive young center Darryl Dawkins, and had added the extraordinary Julius Erving. Erving came from the financially strapped New York Nets, who virtually gave Erving's contract away for $3 million in order to have enough cash to buy their way into the NBA along with three other teams from the now-defunct American Basketball Association.

Trailing three games to one, the Rockets had won game five in Philadelphia. Back in Houston, game six had gone to the wire. In the waning seconds, with Philadelphia leading by 2, John Lucas had weaved his way through traffic to the basket and made what appeared to be a game-tying layup. But there was contact between Lucas and Collins on the play and a whistle blew. If the foul was on Collins, the basket would count and Lucas could win the game with a free throw. But Jake O'Donnell, one of the NBA's most respected officials, called the foul on Lucas, wiping out the basket, and the 76ers hung on to win and advance.

"At worst it should have been a no-call," Tomjanovich said years later. "Doug was right under the basket. You can't call a charge when the defender is under the basket like that."

"Jake made the call," Lucas said years later. "But he could have gotten help from his partner on it." O'Donnell's partner that night was Joe Gushue. "Philly guy," Lucas said. "He was from Philly." He smiled. "Which means nothing, of course."

To a man, the Rockets were convinced that if they had forced a game seven, even playing in Philadelphia, the pressure on the 76ers would have been overwhelming. If they had won that game, they would then have faced Portland, a team they had handled throughout the regular season, winning three of four games. "It was definitely right there," Tomjanovich said. "That call was one of those you think about for a long time." He smiled. "I still think about it."

The reason for the Lakers' early-season struggle in 1977–78 was easy to pinpoint: no Kareem Abdul-Jabbar. In his ninth season in the league, Abdul-Jabbar was the most dominating offensive presence in the game. At a listed 7-foot-1 (most players insisted he was at least 7-3), he was unstoppable when he set up in the low post and unleashed his skyhook, a shot that was actually released above the rim. It couldn't be blocked, and Abdul-Jabbar had made it into an art form. But his temper tantrum in the opening game put him on the sidelines for 20 games, and without him the Lakers were a shadow of themselves.

The Rockets had had no major injuries. They just weren't playing very well. Teams had adapted to playing against their big lineup—Kunnert at 7 feet, Moses Malone at 6-10, and Tomjanovich at 6-8—and were taking advantage of their lack of quickness on defense. Coach Tom Nissalke had taken to tinkering with the lineup to try to create more favorable matchups. After a 6–12 start, Nissalke went to a starting lineup that included Malone, Tomjanovich, and rookie Robert Reid up front and Lucas and Calvin Murphy in the backcourt.

One person the tinkering did not sit well with was guard Mike Newlin. He had been a starter for most of his seven-year NBA career. He was 6-foot-5, 220 pounds, and a good enough shooter to score from outside, strong enough to get to the basket if a defender came up to deny him his jump shot. But with Nissalke going with the smaller lineup, Newlin had seen his minutes dwindle. He had spent his entire pro career in Houston. In fact he had been the first player the team had signed to a contract in 1971 after the franchise relocated from San Diego. He liked to call himself "the original Houston Rocket."

The original Rocket was not pleased with his loss of playing time. A year before, he had heard rumors throughout the season that the Rockets were trying to trade him. But he had a clause in his contract that allowed him to be traded only to certain teams, and he had made it clear to the Rockets that he didn't want to be moved. Now he had decided enough was enough. He and Nissalke clashed often.

"As much as I loved Houston and loved the guys I was playing with, I wanted out," he said. "Especially if I could be traded to a good team." After Nissalke changed the lineup Newlin asked team president and general manager Ray Patterson to see if he could make a deal for him. It was unusual for NBA general managers to go on the road with their teams, but Patterson, who had come to Houston from the Milwaukee Bucks five years earlier, was on the trip to Los Angeles because his daughter lived there.

Shortly after the team returned from its game-day shootaround at the Forum, Newlin got a call from Patterson to come up to his room. "When I got up there, Ray told me they were about to make a deal," Newlin said. "He asked me if I had a choice, would I prefer the Celtics or Lakers. I told him to let me think about it and tell him after the game. I went back to my room thinking I was probably about to play my last game as a Rocket that night."

Patterson has no recollection of that meeting, but Newlin's memory is very specific. He made no bones then—and makes no bones now—about Nissalke. Even though he had spent his entire career—six-plus years—with the Rockets, the notion of going to the Celtics or the Lakers excited him. He said nothing to his teammates, knowing that nothing was final and the deal could still fall through.

Newlin went back to his room to ponder his future. By then Tomjanovich was relaxing in his room and Washington was sitting down at his home in Palos Verdes with his wife and daughter to eat his pregame meal, which was almost always a plate of pasta.

The referees assigned to the game had arrived in Los Angeles that morning and had checked into the Hacienda Hotel, a few miles from LAX. The Hacienda always gave NBA refs favorable rates, and often, if officials were assigned more than one West

Coast game on a trip, they would leave their things at the Hacienda for several days. "In those days the [San Francisco] Warriors played in the Cow Palace, which was right near SFO," Bob Rakel said. "You could work a game up there and catch a late flight back to L.A. and not have to worry about checking out and checking into hotels. It made life simpler."

Rakel was forty-four and had been officiating in the NBA since 1968. He had grown up in Cincinnati with a refereeing pedigree—his father had been a referee, and his brother Ron was also a referee and had worked in the ABA for several years. Rakel had been a salesman for a garage door company when he got a last-minute call in the fall of 1967 to work an NBA exhibition game. The following summer he was invited to work at Kutcher's Resort outside New York City in a series of exhibition games. That fall, Dolph Schayes, the league's supervisor of officials, offered him a job.

His partner that night was Ed Middleton, who had returned to the NBA the previous season after nine years in the ABA. Middleton was ten years younger than Rakel, one of a host of NBA officials who—like Joe Gushue—had come out of the Philadelphia area.

The way officials worked in those days was entirely different from the way they work now. Today there are three officials assigned to every game, and they will usually have some kind of pregame meeting, if not in the hotel, then at the arena, to go over all the possible scenarios they may face in a given game. Then there were only two officials working; there was a lot less videotape available and a lot less communication from the league office.

"We would always read the paper going into a given city to see if there had been anything brewing between the two teams," Rakel said. "If one of us had worked a game between the teams and something had happened, we would discuss it, or if there had been a specific problem, the league might make us aware of it. But it wasn't as extensive as it is now."

The NBA in 1977 was very different from what it is today. This was two years prior to the arrival of Larry Bird and Magic Johnson and seven years before Michael Jordan joined the two of them to form the triumvirate that turned the league around. These were what Commissioner David Stern, then the league's outside counsel, called "the dark days."

"We were looked upon as a league that was too black, too violent, and too drug-involved during the late seventies," he said. "The drug problem existed, though it was probably not as bad as it was sometimes portrayed. The violence was without question a major issue, something that had to be dealt with."

The previous season the league had seen forty-one fights that had led to at least one ejection. That didn't count all the skirmishes that broke out and were stopped before someone had to be ejected. If there had been any doubt about the need for a crackdown, it had been wiped out during game two of the finals, when Darryl Dawkins and Portland's enforcer, Maurice Lucas, had gotten into a frightening fight near the end of the game.

"One thing was obvious," Stern said. "You couldn't allow men that big and that strong to go around throwing punches at each other."

Brent Musburger, who did the play-by-play on that game for CBS, remembers thinking when that fight broke out: "This is bad, very bad. Here we have the league's showcase event and we're looking at a near riot. I knew [NBA commissioner] Larry O'Brien had to be squirming watching that unfold."

The owners voted that summer to strengthen the rules governing fighting. Previously the commissioner could fine a player a maximum of $500 and suspend him for up to five days without pay for fighting. Under the new rules O'Brien had the authority to fine a player up to $10,000 and suspend him indefinitely. O'Brien had been given the opportunity to flex his new muscle right away when Abdul-Jabbar slugged Benson on opening night. The fine was

$5,000, but O'Brien opted not to suspend him since he had broken his hand and would be out for six weeks anyway.

The owners had also discussed the idea of going to three-man officiating crews. The previous season there had been some experimentation with three-man crews, and the officials had thought it worked well. As the game got faster and the players stronger, it was more and more difficult for two men to control a game. But going to three-man crews would mean hiring a new wave of officials. Money was tight for most owners. They voted the change down.

So it was Rakel and Middleton working that night in Los Angeles. The only player on either team whom either one of them had ever had trouble with was Abdul-Jabbar. Two years earlier, at the end of a frustrating loss in Boston, Abdul-Jabbar had yelled at Rakel that he was a racist as they left the court. Several writers heard the comment and wrote about it. The next time Rakel had a game in Los Angeles, Abdul-Jabbar approached him during warm-ups.

"I owe you an apology," he said. "I was out of line in Boston. I got frustrated and said something I shouldn't have said."

"Apology accepted, Kareem," Rakel said. "But I'd like you to do something for me."

"What's that?"

"Get on the PA system and repeat what you just said, so as many people will know about the apology as know about the original statement."

Abdul-Jabbar shook his head. "I can't do that, Bob."

"The strange thing is, I never had a problem with Kareem before that night in Boston or after that night," Rakel said. "I wasn't going to let it affect the way I worked his games. But obviously I remembered it."

The December 9 game was the first between the teams that season. They were scheduled to meet again the following Wednesday in Houston. The Lakers were 9–14 and had another game at home on Sunday night, against the Buffalo Braves. Then they would fly to New Orleans to play the Jazz. The Rockets had a brutal weekend ahead. From L.A. they would fly first thing Saturday morning to Phoenix to play the Suns and then fly from there to a game in Seattle on Sunday. The Rockets had won three of four since Nissalke's lineup changes but were still just 9–13.

The Lakers would have 58 games left on their regular-season schedule after the game with the Rockets. The Rockets would have 59 games left.

In 1977 the Los Angeles Forum, modestly known as the Fabulous Forum and then, when the corporate pox took over arenas, as the Great Western Forum, was one of the NBA showplaces. It had opened in December of 1967, and Jack Kent Cooke, who owned both the Lakers and the Los Angeles Kings of the National Hockey League, had come up with the idea of moving the media, which traditionally sat courtside directly across from the team benches and the scorer's table, upstairs. That allowed him to put in a row of seats that was practically inbounds. The seats were almost always occupied by celebrities and CEOs. Among the first to buy one was Doris Day.

Today every NBA arena is set up this way, and sitting in the front row is a sign of having made it in most NBA cities. Front-row tickets in the Lakers' current home, the Staples Center, now cost $1,200 a game, more during the playoffs, when people know that sitting there almost guarantees that you will be seen on national television.

Back then the NBA wasn't nearly the glitz-factory it is now. There was one national TV contract—with CBS—that called for a Sunday Game of the Week and very few other exposures. There were no national cable networks. Playoff ratings had been so low the past few seasons that CBS was on the verge of taking all playoff games—even the finals—out of prime time and airing them at 11:30 P.M. on videotape.

The best players in the league were not exactly fan-friendly. One was Abdul-Jabbar, a reticent superstar who had converted to the Muslim faith and changed his name from Lew Alcindor in 1971, after he and the Milwaukee Bucks had won the NBA title in his second season in the league. His conversion did not sit particularly well with a public that, a year later, would overwhelmingly elect Richard Nixon to a second term as president. Bill Walton's politics weren't any more popular with most NBA fans than Abdul-Jabbar's. He was considered a radical and had a number of friends, notably sports activist and counterculture figure Jack Scott, known for their left-wing positions on many issues, including the legalization of marijuana and other drugs.

Walton and the Trail Blazers had won the NBA title in 1977 and were dominating the league again early in the 1977–78 season. The once-proud Boston Celtics, who had been led to titles in 1974 and 1976 by center Dave Cowens, were struggling. John Havlicek, the last star left from the Bill Russell era, was planning to retire at the end of the season. The great New York Knicks teams of the early 1970s were long gone, leaving the 76ers and the Washington Bullets, a solid but unexciting team, as the best teams in the east.

Player salaries had escalated, but they hadn't yet exploded. Rudy Tomjanovich, a four-time All-Star, was making $300,000 a year. Kermit Washington, in the final year of a five-year contract he had signed as the number five pick in the 1973 NBA draft, was making $120,000. Most coaches in the league made less than six figures. There was talk of franchises folding, especially when the league expanded by four teams in 1976, adding the Indiana Pacers, New York Nets, San Antonio Spurs, and Denver Nuggets from the ABA in order to make the ABA go away. That meant there were twenty-two teams, too many for a league where revenues were spiraling downward.

The Lakers had come into the league as the Minneapolis Lakers—thus the name—in 1949 and had moved to Los Angeles in 1960. They had been a power in the league throughout the sixties, led by Jerry West, Elgin Baylor, and later Wilt Chamberlain. But they couldn't get over the mountain that was the Boston Celtics, losing to Bill Russell's team four times in the finals. But in 1972, the year after Baylor retired, they became the league's dominant team, winning a record 33 straight games en route to a 69–13 regular-season record. They then rolled through the playoffs, beating the Knicks in the finals in five games, avenging a wrenching seven-game defeat to New York in the 1970 finals. The Lakers made the finals again the following year, but this time the Knicks won in five games. Chamberlain, though still a dominant player, retired.

Looking for help inside, the Lakers drafted Washington, who had averaged 20 points and 20 rebounds a game during his senior year at American University. Pete Newell was the Lakers' general manager and Bill Sharman was the coach. Scouting in those days wasn't nearly as sophisticated as it is now. "You depended a lot on the college coaches to tell you the truth about someone's character," Sharman said. "I remember when we were back east going to see Kermit play at American. Two things stood out—he was a very strong rebounder, but you could figure that out looking at a stat sheet. The second thing you had to see: he was great at turning to throw the outlet pass, and when he wanted to, he could throw the ball the length of the court as if it was a baseball. That got my attention.

"Then, when we talked to the coaches about him, we heard he was a terrific youngster, good student, really good character. We knew we were going to be rebuilding. Elgin and Wilt were gone; Jerry was going to be gone soon. He seemed like a good block to put into place for a long time to come."

Newell had been a great college coach, leading the University of California to a national title in 1959 and the national championship game a year later before retiring at the age of forty-two. ("The pressure was too much," he said. "I was smoking so much I was afraid I was going to burn the building down during practice.")

He was also impressed with Washington's strength, but what he liked most was his work ethic.

"He wasn't a smooth player by any means, and he certainly wasn't a shooter," he said. "But he was clearly someone who was going to work hard and get better. We figured anyone who could leap as quickly as he could and throw the outlet pass the way he did could learn to shoot the ball. That could be taught."

The Lakers took Washington with the fifth pick in the first round, a pick they had acquired in a trade with the woeful Cleveland Cavaliers. A year later West followed Baylor and Chamberlain into retirement. His departure was something of a relief to Washington, who was terrified of him. "I was completely intimidated by him in practice," he said. "He was so competitive and so intense that I was scared to make a mistake. Since I was a rookie, I made them all the time. It was embarrassing."

After the Lakers had struggled during West's final year and been worse the next year, Sharman and Newell knew they had to make some kind of major move to improve the team. Even though the Lakers had been to the finals five times in six years from 1968 through 1973, Jack Kent Cooke was a demanding owner who wouldn't put up with mediocrity for very long. Abdul-Jabbar was unhappy in Milwaukee, and the Bucks were looking to move him—but only in return for a lot of players.

"Looking back, the deal seems like it would have been automatic from our point of view," Sharman said. "But I had doubts, almost everyone on our staff had doubts. We were giving up a lot. The one who pushed for the deal was Pete. Thank goodness we listened to him in the end."

In the end Abdul-Jabbar came to the Lakers for four good players: Junior Bridgeman, Brian Winters, David Meyers, and Elmore Smith. No one was more thrilled with the deal than Washington. "All through college the person whose picture I had on my desk was Kareem," he said. "He was my hero, the player I wanted to be like most if I could. Now I was going to get a chance to play next to him. It was literally a dream come true."

How much he would actually get to play next to Abdul-Jabbar was a different question. Adjusting to the NBA had not been easy for Washington, specifically the part about moving from center to forward. In college he had been able to camp out in the low post and overpower people. If he missed a shot, he beat people to the boards with his quickness. But in the NBA he had to play farther from the basket, and at 6-8 he couldn't just jump over people. He was a suspect shooter and teams knew that, making him an offensive liability.

As a rookie he had only played in 45 of the Lakers' 82 games, averaging less than 10 minutes per outing in the games he appeared in. It got a little better the next season: 55 games, almost 18 minutes a game. Most of his points came off offensive rebounds. The first year with Abdul-Jabbar, things got worse. He was fighting injuries, sore knees and a bad back, and played in only 36 games. He wasn't anywhere close to being the player either he or the Lakers had envisioned when he had been drafted. There were still two years left on his contract, but Washington was certain that if he didn't show marked improvement in his fourth season, he would be long gone, since the fifth year was an option year. There was no salary cap at the time, and Jack Kent Cooke had plenty of money, but he wasn't about to pay $120,000 to a player who was producing at the rate Washington had produced during his first three seasons in the league.

"I knew I had to do something," Washington said. "I was miserable. Basketball had become who I was; it was my identity and I was failing. I was willing to do anything to get better. The question was, what could I do?"

The person who came up with a potential solution was Michael Cardozo. At the time, Cardozo worked for the law firm that represented Washington: Dell, Fentress, and Craighill. Donald Dell, the one-time Davis Cup tennis team captain, who had gotten into the business of player representation a few years earlier, had been one of four agents Washington had interviewed during his senior year of college. "I wasn't crazy about any of them," he said. "But I was most comfortable with Donald."

Cardozo, who would leave the law firm a year later to become general counsel in the Carter administration, handled legal affairs for Dell's clients. When Washington told him he was at a loss to figure out how to become a better NBA player, Cardozo made a suggestion: go talk to Pete Newell. "The idea was that Pete had been a great college coach," Cardozo said. "If he was willing to work with Kermit, he could teach him fundamentals, especially on offense, where he needed help most."

Newell's role with the Lakers had changed by then. Sharman had been forced to retire as coach after the 1976 season because he was having throat problems that made it almost impossible for him to talk. Jerry West replaced him as coach, and Sharman became general manager. Newell was pushed out of the general manager's job and named a "consultant." In a sense, that was a huge break for Washington, because Newell had time on his hands. When Washington approached him, Newell was skeptical at first but agreed to work with him.

"We'll meet at seven o'clock in the morning," he told Washington, figuring if he wasn't sincere about working hard the starting time would scare him off.

"I'll pick you up," said Washington, who lived a few blocks from Newell.

They worked five mornings a week that summer in the gym at Loyola Marymount University. Newell worked on Washington's footwork and taught him how to turn, face, and shoot, drilling him over and over and over. Washington was exhausted. "It was a living nightmare," he says now, repeating one of his favorite phrases.

But by the time training camp began, Washington was a different player. West, the new coach, had made it clear during the off-season that he wanted Washington traded. It was time to admit the team had made a mistake drafting him so high, time to see what they could get for him and move on. But West was impressed by the "new" Kermit Washington. He was quicker, he could handle the ball better, and he could even hit the occasional short jump shot, which made his inside game much more effective. By the end of training camp Washington was in the playing rotation.

The first 55 games of that season were everything Washington had always hoped his NBA career would be. He was playing regularly, getting a little bit less than 30 minutes per game. He was averaging 9.7 points and 9.3 rebounds, second in rebounding on the team, behind only Abdul-Jabbar. The team was playing superbly and Washington was a key element, especially defensively and on the boards. "He was important to us for a number of reasons, not the least of which was taking inside pressure off of Kareem," West said.

Not to mention defensive pressure. More often than not, Washington would guard the other team's best inside player, since the Lakers didn't want Abdul-Jabbar risking foul trouble. That was fine with him. As long as he was playing, he was happy.

The only problem was his knees. Washington had been a remarkably durable player in college, missing just one game. But he had taken a hard fall in an exhibition game as a rookie, landing hard on his tailbone (aka, his butt). He didn't think much about it and took no time off. Eventually he began to feel back pain on a regular basis, and when he didn't get that treated, running differently because of the pain eventually led to a throbbing pain in both knees.

"As a rookie, you just didn't go in and ask for time off because you were sore," he said. "A lot of guys played with pain. I wasn't even playing that much, so I certainly wasn't going to ask for time off from practice, because that was the only time I got to play, really. Looking back it wasn't very smart, but at the time it felt like the only thing to do."

Not playing very much kept the knee problem from worsening. But when he began playing 30 minutes per night, Washington could feel the pain in his knees, especially the right knee, more and more as the season wore on. Driving to the Forum for the team's last game before the All-Star break, he said to Pat, his wife, "If I can just get through tonight and rest for the next four days, I think I'll be fine."

He didn't get through that night. Late in the second quarter, on a drive to the basket, he felt the knee go completely. "I could feel it tearing inside," he said. "I looked down, and my kneecap was hanging on the side of my leg."

They carried him off. He had surgery the next day. Then came rehab and another summer at Loyola Marymount with Newell. "I had come too far to not make it all the way back," he said. "Pete worked me even harder than the first summer. But I knew it would be worth it."

It was. Even though the team had struggled without Abdul-Jabbar, Washington had flourished. Through 23 games, he was fourth in the league in rebounding, with slightly more than 11 per game. Now Abdul-Jabbar was back and everyone expected the Lakers to make a move in the standings. Houston and Buffalo at home on a Friday and a Sunday certainly appeared to be an excellent starting point.

While Washington was fighting to establish himself as a solid NBA player, Rudy Tomjanovich had no such problems. He was in his eighth season in the league and had played in the last four All-Star games. After averaging 30 points a game during his senior year at Michigan, he had been the number two pick in the 1970 draft, taken behind St. Bonaventure center Bob Lanier but ahead of Pete Maravich, college basketball's all-time leading scorer. There were a lot of raised eyebrows in San Diego when the Rockets chose Tomjanovich ahead of Maravich, especially since the flashy Maravich would, if nothing else, put people into seats for a franchise struggling to survive.

But the general manager in San Diego liked Tomjanovich's ability to shoot from long range, his willingness to mix it up inside, his attitude, and his quickness to the boards. The general manager was Pete Newell. Two years after drafting Tomjanovich, Newell left the Rockets and joined the Lakers. A year after that, his first pick in the draft on behalf of the Lakers was Kermit Washington.

The Rockets had come into existence in 1967, part of the NBA's second expansion. In 1966 the league had made the Chicago Bulls its tenth franchise. One year later San Diego and Seattle were granted teams. Those twelve were joined the next year by Phoenix and Milwaukee. Two years later Buffalo, Portland, and Cleveland were added. That meant the league had nearly doubled in size in a five-year period.

Tomjanovich was the classic wide-eyed rookie in San Diego. Neither he nor his new wife, Sophie, had ever spent any time outside the Midwest. They drove cross-country from Michigan to San Diego after their wedding and found themselves in paradise. They lived less than a mile from the beach and waited for a winter that never came.

As much as the Tomjanoviches loved San Diego, Rudy's rookie season wasn't an easy one. For reasons he never understood completely, his playing time was sporadic. Some nights he would play for extended periods; others he played hardly at all. He learned later that Alex Hannum, the coach, was in the midst of an ongoing battle with Newell and that he had not been Hannum's choice as the team's top pick. Once the team drafted Tomjanovich, Hannum wanted to use him in a trade. Newell was firm: the kid was staying. That might have explained why Hannum, without any real explanation, kept finding ways—at least in Tomjanovich's mind—to keep him on the bench. He played less than 15 minutes a game that first season and averaged a dismal 5.3 points per game.

Tomjanovich was so disturbed by what was going on that he would often go to a local gym at night to shoot, taking Sophie with him as a rebounder. "Very romantic stuff," she said years later.

At season's end everything changed. The Rockets were sold to a group in Houston. Hannum was gone as coach, replaced by Tex Winter. Sophie and Rudy set off on another cross-country trek, this one landing them in Texas in the middle of August. They were from Michigan by way of San Diego. Houston in August was a complete shock.

"We were sick for weeks," Tomjanovich said. "You go outside, it's a hundred and five; inside it's fifty. Hearing about weather like that is one thing, living with it is another."

They adjusted gradually. One thing that helped was that Winter immediately installed Rudy as a starter. The team was worse than it had been the year before—dropping from 40 wins to 34—but Tomjanovich was playing. The Rockets were a strange franchise. To try to drum up support, they played "home" games all over Texas, including several in El Paso, which was almost as close to San Diego as it was to Houston. They played a number of games in the Astrodome, often with nearly 50,000 empty seats as witnesses.

Slowly the team and the franchise got better. Calvin Murphy had arrived the same year as Tomjanovich as the team's second-round draft choice. He and Tomjanovich were friends right from the start; as different in temperament as two people could be, but bonded by their love for the game and, it seemed, by the fact that each man felt he had a lot to prove as a basketball player. Murphy had always been overlooked because of his height—he had finished second to Maravich in national scoring each of his three seasons in college, yet wasn't selected in the first round—and he played every game with a huge chip on his shoulder. Tomjanovich always felt people didn't really believe in him. He remembered the newspaper headlines in San Diego after he had been drafted: "Rudy Who?" He was fully aware of the people in San Diego who preferred Maravich and was convinced that his coach didn't respect him and that most people looked at him as an overrated white stiff who couldn't possibly be athletic enough to adjust to the NBA.

By the end of their rookie season, Tomjanovich and Murphy were road roommates, such close friends that when the players were given the right to single rooms on the road a few years later, they continued to share a room. Their wives also became close friends.

The team made the playoffs in 1975 and won a first-round series from the aging New York Knicks. A year later Ray Patterson, who had arrived from Milwaukee in 1972 as team president and general manager, made two moves that made the Rockets into a legitimate NBA contender. First he made what looked like a solid deal, sending Joe Meriweather and Gus Bailey to the Atlanta Hawks for Dwight Jones just prior to the 1976 draft. He also persuaded the Hawks to swap first-round picks, since they were getting two players to the Rockets' one. This ended up giving them the number one pick in the draft, and the player the Rockets chose was John Lucas, a lightning-fast point guard from the University of Maryland.

A few months later, Patterson made another deal, this one a gamble: he gave up his 1977 and 1978 number one picks to Buffalo in exchange for 6-foot-10-inch wunderkind Moses Malone. In 1974 Malone had become the first high school player to skip college to turn pro when he signed with the ABA's Utah Stars. He had landed in Buffalo two years later and hadn't yet hit his stride as a pro. But he was still only twenty-one.

Patterson and the Rockets saw Malone as a work in progress. When he was added to Lucas, Tomjanovich, Murphy, and Mike Newlin, who had been the team's number two pick out of the University of Utah (behind the immortal Cliff Meely) in 1971, it was clear that this was a team on the come. The 49–33 record in 1976–77 and the near miss in the conference final against the

76ers had convinced everyone in Houston that big things were ahead. After their nomadic first seasons and the acres of empty seats in the Astrodome, the team was now in the brand-new Summit with a young team worthy of the building. Even the poor start in the fall of 1977 was looked at as a temporary setback, nothing more. They were just beginning to find themselves, having won three games in a row when they flew to San Francisco to start a four-game West Coast swing that would conclude with three straight games on the weekend, the first in Los Angeles on Friday night.

3

That Was Then . . .

The NBA in 1977 was an entirely different entity from the NBA in 2002. Not only was the salary structure light years away from where it is now, the lifestyle was completely different. There was no such thing in the league as a charter airplane. Teams traveled commercially, in coach, the players squeezing uncomfortably into their seats, usually on the first flight available the morning after the game. Anyone who traveled in those days often saw groups of very tall, very bleary-eyed men moving through airports in the predawn hours.

Coaches were genuine authority figures. Free agency existed, but only in a limited sense, because teams had to be compensated for the loss of a player. That meant if a general manager signed a free agent, he risked having his team damaged or even gutted, because it was the league that decided on the compensation to be given the player's former team. As a result, if you as a player didn't get along with your coach, chances were pretty good you were going to be stuck on the bench for a while. And if you were on the bench, you couldn't prove to another team it was worth taking a chance on signing you.

Players and coaches were far more accessible to the media. To begin with, there were far fewer media outlets. ESPN was still two years from its launch, and *USA Today* was six years away from publishing for the first time. None of the twenty-four-hour news services that now glut the airwaves existed. Writers often traveled on the same flights as the players. Their lifestyles weren't all that different. The difference in salary between most players and most writers wasn't that great. Often they ate and drank together.

The writers and coaches on teams even played basketball together at times. Rich Levin, the Lakers beat writer for the *Los Angeles Herald-Examiner,* had been a backup forward on UCLA's national championship teams in 1964 and 1965. Ted Green, the *L.A. Times* beat writer, was also a very good player. Occasionally he, Levin, and whoever else was around would engage Lakers coach Jerry West and his assistant coaches in pickup games. Legend has it that one morning Green got hot and began burying shots from all over the court. Each time he would score, West, one of the greatest guards in the history of the game, would respond by hitting a shot over Levin. Finally, exasperated by yet another West basket, Green screamed at Levin, "Geez, Rich, do I have to do *everything?* Can't you stop him *once?*"

To which Levin responded, "Ted, in case you haven't noticed, this is Jerry fucking *West* I'm trying to guard!"

"You had a job to do, they had a job to do, everyone understood that," Green said. "But it was almost collegial at times. I liked almost all the players. I genuinely liked Kermit Washington and enjoyed his company on the road."

A number of players chose to hang with the writers on the road. Mike Newlin, who, like Washington, had been an academic All-American in college, enjoyed the writers because their interests tended to be broader than those of most of his teammates. "I loved to read, anything I could get my hands on," he said. "There weren't a lot of guys in the locker room who had much interest in most of the books I was reading. The writers did."

Television played a minor role in the life of the league. Cable TV was just starting to emerge as a factor, mostly in major markets like New York and Los Angeles. Game times were rarely changed because of television, and there probably weren't more than a half-dozen players in the league who would be recognized by most people walking down the street in their hometown.

"In a lot of ways it was less stressful then than it is for the players now," Kermit Washington said. "Sure, they're making a lot more money now—a *lot* more—but their lives aren't their own. The lives most of us led in the league in those days were fairly close to normal." He smiled. "The worst part was trying to fit into those coach seats on six A.M. flights."

To Washington, and to most NBA players, that was a small price to pay given that they were doing what they loved and being well paid to do it. "I think most athletes will tell you they'd play for nothing," Washington said. "It's not quite that simple, since we all need to make a living once we become adults. But what you arc doing as a professional athlete is playing the game you *did* play for nothing as a kid because you loved it, and now you're being paid a lot of money to keep on playing. I think more of us understood how lucky we were back then, more than the athletes do today. Nowadays a lot of them feel they're owed the living they make and the lifestyle they lead."

The crowd in the Forum on the night of December 9 was a reflection of what the NBA was in those days. The attendance was 10,645, meaning the building was a little more than half-full. If the Lakers had been off to a better start, there might have been another two or three thousand in attendance, but the game certainly wouldn't have been a sellout.

Ted Green's brief advance on the game didn't even make the front page of the *L.A. Times* sports section that morning. The lead story in sports was the California Angels' trade of second baseman Jerry Remy to the Boston Red Sox for pitcher Don Aase. Jim Murray's column was about a middleweight boxer. On the front page of the newspaper, Anwar Sadat was calling his opponents in the Arab world "moronic dwarfs," and AFL-CIO president George Meany was calling for the creation of 4 million new jobs at the organization's convention, which was being held in downtown Los Angeles.

That both teams were having difficult seasons was reflected not only in their mediocre records but in the atmosphere in their locker rooms. Jerry West, in his second season as the Lakers' coach, was already beginning to have doubts about the job. Like many great players, he found it difficult to be patient with players who didn't approach the game with the intensity or the intelligence he had brought to the court—which was most players. He liked his rookie point guard, Norm Nixon, but wasn't crazy about his other guards, notably Ernie DiGregorio, a one-time rookie of the year who was struggling to find minutes with the Lakers.

The one player West had who could look him in the eye in a playing sense was Kareem Abdul-Jabbar. But coaching Abdul-Jabbar was no picnic. He was moody, often angry. There were times when Abdul-Jabbar would just leave practice if something happened that didn't make him happy. As was true in games, he didn't like any sort of physical play, and one player who always played physically was Washington. One day in practice when Washington was shoving Abdul-Jabbar around on the inside, Kareem simply picked up his things, bounded up the steps of the Forum to the level where the players parked their cars, and left.

"Never said a word to anybody," said Ted Green, who witnessed the incident. "He went from jostling with Kermit to out of the building in about forty-five seconds."

"I would always try to tell Kermit that the purpose of practice wasn't to get somebody hurt," Abdul-Jabbar said. "His answer was that if he didn't practice the way he was going to have to play, he wouldn't be ready to play. I understood that, but there were times when he crossed the line."

Washington had been a pleasant surprise to West right from the beginning of his coaching tenure. When he had taken the job he was convinced that one thing he and Bill Sharman, who had replaced Pete Newell as general manager, had to do was find a way to move Washington. But the Washington who showed up for training camp in the fall of 1976 after his summer-in-hell with Newell was a completely different player from the Washington West had wanted to trade. By the end of training camp he was either starting or coming off the bench very early in games and had become an important part of the team.

"He brought things to the table that we needed," West said. "He was especially important to Kareem because of the things he was willing to do."

Specifically, he did the things Abdul-Jabbar didn't like to do: mix it up inside; guard the other team's most physical inside player; rebound in traffic. At 7-1, Abdul-Jabbar was a very good rebounder—he averaged 11.2 rebounds per game for his career—but most of his rebounds came as a result of his size or his positioning on defense. Washington would go after the tough offensive rebound Abdul-Jabbar often had little interest in. And when scuffles broke out, as they often did, the person who was expected to step in to keep Abdul-Jabbar from getting into trouble was Washington.

"In those days every team in the NBA had an enforcer, a policeman," said Jack Ramsay, who coached the Portland Trail Blazers to the championship in 1977 with Maurice Lucas acting as the enforcer for Bill Walton. "There was so much physical play and there were so many fights, you had to have one guy the other team didn't want to mess with under any circumstances."

The role of the enforcer had become so important that *Sports Illustrated* had done a cover story on the subject early in the 1977–78 season. Most of the players selected were power forwards like Washington and Lucas. The exception was the Rockets' Calvin Murphy, all 5-10, 165 pounds of him.

"Calvin was one of the few players in the league who truly knew how to fight," Mike Newlin said. "He actually had a fighting style. Size didn't matter to him. In fact he preferred fighting big people. They were terrified of him. He just beat the crap out of people."

Everyone in the league had a story about a Calvin Murphy fight. The one in which he had destroyed 6-foot-8 inch Celtics forward Sidney Wicks was the most legendary. "I think he got in nine punches by my count," said Tom Nissalke, the Rockets' coach at the time. "Wicks never got off a punch." The replay of that fight was popular in a lot of NBA arenas, especially at the Summit in Houston, where it was often shown on the replay screen on the scoreboard prior to games.

One night when the Celtics were in town, the replay appeared once more on the big screen during warm-ups. As it did, Nissalke saw Celtics coach Tom Heinsohn walking toward him. Heinsohn was 6-foot-8 and had played at about 240 during his Hall of Fame career with the Celtics. His face was red by the time he got to Nissalke.

"That replay shows up one more time," he said, pointing a finger at Nissalke, "and the next fight they're gonna replay will be between you and me."

"Tom," Nissalke said, "I'll take care of it right away."

The replay wasn't used again—when the Celtics were in town.

Washington had balked when asked to pose for *SI*'s enforcer pictures. He understood his role and knew why the magazine wanted him to take part. But even though fighting was sometimes part of what he did on the court, he didn't think of himself as fierce or mean, certainly not cut from the same angry cloth as Murphy or Lucas. He agreed to pose for the photos but refused to produce the angry look the photographer was after.

"Just one, Kermit," the photographer said, exasperated. "Just look a little bit tough."

Washington complied. "And that was the one picture they used," he said.

A lot of stories written about Washington, especially those written during his college days at American University, included the phrase "gentle giant." Off the court he was soft-spoken and polite. The writers liked him not only because he was cooperative and friendly but because he could talk about subjects that had nothing to do with basketball.

"Kermit was a go-to guy in the locker room," Rich Levin said. "He was always good with a quote, and he was usually the guy you stood around and killed time with while you were waiting for Kareem to show up."

But he was a fierce player, strong and aggressive, and more than willing to mix it up when necessary. He never looked for a fight, but he never backed away from one either. And he understood that if Abdul-Jabbar got into a skirmish—which he often did—it was his job to intervene.

He'd been thwarted in that regard on opening night, when Abdul-Jabbar came up behind Kent Benson, slugged him, and broke his hand. Washington was having the best season of his career through the Lakers' first twenty-three games, averaging almost 12 points and more than 11 rebounds a game. There had never been a better time for him to play well. His contract was up at the end of the season, and it was becoming apparent that he would be negotiating from strength based on the way he was playing.

Kevin Kunnert was also in his contract walk year. He had come into the league the same year as Washington—1973—chosen in the first round of the draft by the Chicago Bulls but traded to the Buffalo Braves without ever playing a game, because the Bulls didn't want to pay a number one pick more money than their veteran stars Jerry Sloan and Norm Van Lier were making. He had grown up in Dubuque, Iowa, and had played at the University of Iowa, becoming the school's all-time leading rebounder in his senior year.

Because he was from a small town, a lot of NBA people thought of him as a cornpone. The phrase "big ole farm boy" was used to describe him almost as often as "gentle giant" was used on Washington. Kunnert was certainly big, 7 feet tall and 230 pounds, but he was a surprisingly effective player away from the basket. He had a funky-looking shot that made him appear to be falling backward when he released the ball, but he had a soft touch.

Midway through his rookie season he was part of a four-player trade that landed him in Houston, where he became a solid, consistent player, starting frequently while playing about 30 minutes most nights. He consistently averaged about 11 points and 9 rebounds a game. He wasn't quick, but he was strong enough to push people out of the low post and he played without fear and with an understanding of the game and his role.

He was popular with his teammates because he had a dry sense of humor and was willing to do whatever he was asked to do to win. "He was never a 'me' guy," Tomjanovich said. "If you needed him to rebound, he'd rebound; guard, he'd guard; shoot, he'd shoot. You liked having him on your side."

"There's only one basketball," Kunnert said, remembering his days with the Rockets. "We had Rudy, Calvin, Moses, Luke—all guys who liked to shoot the ball. I was happy to rebound, play defense, and win games. Which we did."

Kunnert and Washington had met two years earlier when they played on an NBA team that had gone to Mexico during the summer. The team had been put together by ProServ—formerly Dell, Fentress, and Craighill—which represented both of them. They had spent some time with each other, occasionally having breakfast together. They hadn't become close friends by any means, but there was mutual respect. Each played a similar role for his team— one at center, the other at forward—asked to do the dirty work inside to protect the stars from foul trouble, from injury, and, if need be, from fights.

"In those days you didn't get friendly with too many guys on other teams," Kunnert said. "You had a job to do, and that sometimes meant getting physical. But Kermit was someone I would say hi to when we played, because we'd spent some time together and he seemed like a perfectly nice guy."

Like Washington, Kunnert was easygoing and easy to like off the court. But he wasn't gentle on the court. "He was the nicest guy you'll ever meet," Newlin said. "But on the court, he didn't take any crap. He had a temper, and if you pushed too hard he'd push back."

"He had an edge," said Jack Ramsay, who coached him later in his career. "You wouldn't guess it talking to him, but he didn't take any crap once the game started."

Kunnert was coming off the bench for the Rockets when they came to Los Angeles, backing up Moses Malone at center but also spending some time at power forward when Nissalke wanted to rest Tomjanovich or Robert Reid. Malone, Tomjanovich, and Reid started that night along with Lucas and Murphy. Up front for the Lakers it was Abdul-Jabbar, Washington, and Tom Abernethy, a second-year player from Indiana whom West liked because of his ability to guard small forwards. He was in the lineup because of an injury to Jamaal Wilkes, and it was his first NBA start. The rookie Norm Nixon and veteran Earl Tatum started at the guard spots.

It was a normal NBA night throughout the first half. West put Washington on Malone to keep Abdul-Jabbar out of foul trouble. At the other end, Abdul-Jabbar was making Malone look like the twenty-two-year-old kid he still was, scoring over him with his skyhook and getting him into foul trouble. Midway through the second quarter, Malone had four fouls and had to come out for Kunnert. The game stayed close for one reason: the Lakers couldn't guard Tomjanovich. No matter who West put on him, Tomjanovich scored. Abernethy knew how to play defense because he had played under Bob Knight at Indiana. But he wasn't about to stop

Tomjanovich on a night when Rudy T's shot was finding the net as if the ball were equipped with radar. By halftime he had hit 9 of 14 shots and had 19 points. If the 3-point line had existed in those days he probably would have had 4 or 5 more points, since at least half his shots came from way outside.

At the break the score was tied, 55–55. Over the course of an eighty-two-game NBA season, coaches rarely rolled out fire-and-brimstone speeches at halftime. Players usually didn't want to hear them, and every coach knew he could only go to the well so many times with emotional talks. Most saved them for the playoffs, crucial games at the end of the season, or, occasionally, for nights when the team was being completely outplayed. Even on some of those nights, the coach might not bother, knowing his team was tired from a long road trip or playing back-to-back or just the grind of the long season.

Neither West nor Nissalke had much to say during the break. West decided Abernethy was still his best bet defensively on Tomjanovich because, at the very least, he would be willing to chase the constantly moving Tomjanovich around the court. Nissalke, not wanting Malone to pick up his fifth foul quickly in the third quarter, decided to start Kunnert at center.

The second half began routinely. Murphy hit a shot to give the Rockets a 57–55 lead. Nixon missed a shot for the Lakers. Underneath, Abdul-Jabbar and Kunnert went after the long rebound and got tangled. Kunnert came down with the ball and managed to quickly outlet it to Lucas. While most of the players sprinted the other way, Abdul-Jabbar and Kunnert pushed and shoved at each other.

There was history between the two men. Like most centers, Kunnert found Abdul-Jabbar almost impossible to guard. His best chance was to be physical with him, push him out of the low post if he could, frustrate him if possible, and hope to get him out of his rhythm. Abdul-Jabbar knew what Kunnert was trying to do. Intellectually he understood it. Emotionally it annoyed him.

"He wasn't a skilled player," he said of Kunnert. "So he would push and shove, throw elbows, sometimes try talking to me. He had a mouth on him. We'd had our share of verbal exchanges in the past, and I knew he wanted me to throw an elbow back or square off. I dealt with that from people my whole career."

"Of course I pushed and shoved, that's what you did with Jabbar," Kunnert said. "The coaches would always tell me, 'Don't let him set up in the post.' So I would try to beat him to the spot and keep him from getting position."

Abdul-Jabbar had nailed Kunnert with an elbow the previous year, on the opening possession of a game, catching him right above the eye and sending him flying. Kunnert landed on his tailbone and ended up in the locker room getting stitches.

"When I came back out, Kareem apologized," Kunnert said. "He said he didn't know I was there. I didn't really believe him, but I figured, okay, fine, that'll be the end of it."

Now the two centers were pushing and shoving again. Bob Rakel, the trail referee, watched closely, debating whether he needed to whistle a double foul but not wanting to stop play unless he absolutely had to. "Houston had a break, so I didn't want to stop the flow of play," he said. "And I was hoping the two of them would just get clear of each other and keep playing."

Up in the press box, Ted Green noticed the Abdul-Jabbar–Kunnert skirmish and rolled his eyes. "Kareem was always getting into these little flare-ups with players he considered to be beneath him," he said. "The notion of a Kevin Kunnert pushing him was personally insulting. Almost always, when these things happened, it was with a white guy. I don't think I ever saw Kareem fight with a black player. Kunnert was just the kind of player he didn't respect. He wasn't graceful, he wasn't an All-Star, he was just sort of a solid plodder, but someone who was competitive enough to get into Kareem's face. Kareem didn't like that."

Seeing the contact between Abdul-Jabbar and Kunnert, Washington lingered in the backcourt, knowing if it escalated it was his job to step in and finish whatever Abdul-Jabbar or Kunnert might have started. Before things got that serious, though, Kunnert got away from Abdul-Jabbar and started up the court. The Rockets already had a numbers advantage with Lucas, Murphy, Reid, and Tomjanovich filling the lanes. Only Abernethy, Nixon, and Tatum were in position to get back. Tomjanovich ran toward the right corner, looking for a shot.

"I was doing the thing I loved to do most," he said with a smile. "Running the break, getting open, and waiting for Luke to get me the ball. My shot felt so good that night. I didn't think I was ever going to miss."

Lucas with the ball on the break was as good as it got for the Rockets. He had such a great feel for the game that the other players were always convinced he would deliver the ball to the right spot. "I always felt like I could *hear* the other guys when we were going down the court," Lucas said. "Rudy had those big old clunky feet. So if I heard 'clomp, clomp, clomp,' I knew it was him. Moses would come running down mumbling something like, 'Middle, I'm middle.' You heard the words, didn't understand them, so you knew it was Moses. Murph was always screaming in that high-pitched voice of his, 'Luke, me, me, me!' So when I heard soprano, it was Murph. And if I heard someone yelling words I couldn't understand because I needed to look them up in the dictionary, I knew that was Newlin."

The four Rockets were in full flight when Kunnert got free of Abdul-Jabbar. As he tried to burst upcourt to trail the break, Washington tried to hold him up. "Routine move," he said. "A guy has a step on you, especially if his team has a break, you grab his shorts, hold him up, and push past him. It's a foul, but you rarely got caught, because the trail referee had to be focused by then on catching up to the play because the ball was already moving down the court."

Trailing the play by a couple steps, Abdul-Jabbar saw Washington grab Kunnert's shorts and thought little of it. "That was a routine move in those days," he said. "At that point my focus was to try and catch up with the play," he said.

Until the moment when Washington grabbed Kunnert's shorts, there is no dispute about what took place. The next few seconds are in dispute. According to Washington, Kunnert responded to his grabbing his shorts by turning around and elbowing him in the head.

"I was going by him and he elbowed me in the head," he said. "My first reaction was, 'It's an accident, forget it.' I knew Kevin Kunnert from the summer trip. I also knew I'd fouled him, so if he did take a shot, okay, we're even, let's get on with it. Then he did it a second time, right above the eye. That's when I stopped and turned on him."

Kunnert says the elbow he threw was aimed at Washington's arm and was designed to do nothing more than get himself free from Washington's grip. "When he grabbed my shorts, I reacted the way any player would react," he said. "I reached down with my right arm, pushed his hand off of me, and said, 'Get the fuck off of me,'" he said. "My momentum kind of spun me backwards, so I ended up facing him. I wasn't looking for a fight, but I was ready for one. Before I could even think to get my hands up to protect myself, he threw a quick right that missed. When that happened, I thought, 'Okay, we're going to fight.' I started to bring my hands up to cover for the next punch, when Kareem came up from behind and pinned my arms."

Abdul-Jabbar agrees that Kunnert's elbow hit Washington below the shoulder. "But then, as he spun to face Kermit, he threw a punch at him. That's when Kermit threw his first punch, and I jumped in to grab Kevin and try to get him out of there. I didn't want a fight, and I didn't want Kermit getting ejected for getting in a fight. Unfortunately, when I grabbed Kevin, I pinned his arms. That wasn't my intent, but when I did he couldn't protect himself from the next punch Kermit threw."

Kunnert denies throwing the punch Abdul-Jabbar says he saw. But he doesn't blame him for grabbing him from behind. "He was doing the right thing," he said. "In an NBA fight, if you're a bystander, the best thing you can do is try and get the guys apart. I know that's what Kareem was trying to do. When it was all over he said he was sorry he had pinned my arms, and I told him I knew that wasn't his intent. I know what he was trying to do; he was trying to grab me and get me out of there to break the thing up. But what he ended up doing was pinning my arms so I was defenseless when Kermit threw the next punch. He nailed me pretty good with it right above my eye. I remember being stunned and starting to drop to one knee as Kareem was swinging me out of the way. I was woozy for a few seconds, down on a knee. I started to get up and I was thinking to myself, 'Where's Tricky?' Usually in a situation like that he'd be on the court in seconds. The whistle had already blown to stop the play, so there was no reason for him not to come out. Then I stood up and saw him on his knees with a towel on Rudy's face. I had no idea what had happened. Then I saw the blood."

The combination of Washington's strength and Tomjanovich's momentum produced an awful result. Washington knew how to throw a punch. Unlike Murphy, he had never formally trained to box, but he loved the sport and had studied great fighters. He had even told his close friend Josh Rosenfeld, who had been a manager at American University during Washington's career there, that he fantasized about someday fighting Muhammad Ali. When he worked out, his favorite song was the theme from *Rocky*. Often he would shadowbox in the locker room before games to let off steam. When he saw the blur of red coming from behind, he turned and threw a right hand that started from behind his ear and landed just under Tomjanovich's nose with extraordinary force.

Only at the last second did Tomjanovich see the punch coming. That was when he threw up his hands—too late, never getting them above his shoulders. To this day he has no memory of seeing

Washington turn toward him or of the punch itself. He remembers thinking that Kunnert was in trouble and running back downcourt to help break up the fight. And then he remembers lying in a pool of blood asking Vandervoort about the scoreboard.

In the press box Chick Hearn, who has done play-by-play for the Lakers on radio since 1961, said on the air what everyone in the building was thinking: "Oh my God!"

Hearn, who is still the voice of the Lakers at the age of eighty-five, remembers finding it difficult to believe that Washington would be the person delivering such a punch. "Kermit played an aggressive game and at times he had to be our enforcer," Hearn said. "But I always saw him as a gentle soul. There were plenty of players in the league who I could see throwing a punch like that one. Kermit Washington wasn't one of them."

The force from Washington's right hand catapulted Tomjanovich backward. He landed squarely on his back, his head bouncing off the floor of the Forum, and then as he lost consciousness rolled over into a fetal position. Instantaneously, what had been just another skirmish on another NBA night had become, to use Washington's oft-used phrase, a living nightmare.

The building went quiet. "It was," said Mike Newlin, "the loudest silence you have ever heard."

The first person to react to what had happened was Vandervoort, the Rockets' trainer. He reached Tomjanovich in a matter of seconds, while other players were milling around in shock. He gently rolled him onto his back so he could get a towel on his face and try to stanch the blood gushing from Tomjanovich's nose and mouth. The sound had terrified everyone; the sight of the blood spewing from Tomjanovich's nose like a geyser made it worse. Years later, Ed Middleton, the referee, would remember that he called for more towels to mop up the blood. What he didn't remember, according to Ted Green, was that he was *screaming* for the towels.

"I had this awful sense of dread in my stomach," Middleton said. "The sound of it, then the sight of it, actually made me feel physically ill."

Rakel, who had seen Washington throw the punch from behind, stepped in front of him to tell him he was ejected from the game and pointed him in the direction of the locker rooms. Washington didn't argue or debate with Rakel. He was also in shock at that moment. Today he can't remember anything anyone said to him on the court after the punch landed. He doesn't even remember Rakel telling him he was ejected.

Jerry West didn't say anything to Washington. He stood rooted to the spot, staring at Tomjanovich. As Vandervoort got Tomjanovich into a sitting position, a towel covering his face, Tomjanovich found himself looking right at West. It was at that moment that it first occurred to Tomjanovich that something awful had happened.

"Funny thing is, I got that look a lot in the next few days," Tomjanovich said. "It was as if he'd seen a ghost or something. I remember wondering, 'Why is Jerry looking at me like that?'"

4

Did You Hear
About Rudy and Kermit?

They all remember the towel.

As Vandervoort got Tomjanovich slowly to his feet, he had pressed a towel against his nose to try to stanch the bleeding.

"By the time Rudy stood up, the towel was completely red," Kareem Abdul-Jabbar said. "It was as if someone had pressed a button and changed the color."

As frightening as the scene was, no one on court could possibly know how seriously Tomjanovich was hurt. Tomjanovich had no idea what was going on. "All I knew was I was shooting the hell out of the ball that night and we had a chance to win in that place for the first time in years," he said. "I was still dazed when Tricky got me up, trying to figure out what had happened still. It wasn't the scoreboard, he said, it was Kermit. But why? Why would Kermit hit me? Why did Jerry West have that strange look on his face? And most important, how quickly could Tricky get some gauze in my nose or whatever so I could get back out and finish the game?"

These days Tomjanovich never would have been allowed to walk off the court. An EMS unit would have come on court, his head and neck would have been immobilized, and he would have been taken off on a stretcher. He would not have been allowed to move at all, much less stand up.

But this was 1977. On the Lakers bench, Dr. Clarence Shields, who worked with longtime team physician Robert Kerlan, could see that Tomjanovich was going to need to be looked at by a doctor in the locker room, so he followed Tomjanovich and Vandervoort as they left the court. Ball boys were still trying to mop the blood off the floor.

"It was all so out of context," Mike Newlin said. "The whole scene. One minute we're playing a basketball game, the next he's lying in this pool of blood. We'd all been in fights, seen fights, seen blood. But nothing like this."

No one had been in more fights or seen more blood than Calvin Murphy. He was completely beside himself as Tomjanovich left the court. He and Abdul-Jabbar were longtime friends, dating back to their eastern roots (Abdul-Jabbar, New York; Murphy, Connecticut). Tears in his eyes, he turned on Jabbar. "How could you let that happen, Kareem?" he screamed. "Why didn't you grab Kermit? Why didn't you stop him? How could this have happened? How?"

Abdul-Jabbar knew Murphy was angry and upset and there was no sense explaining to him that he'd had his hands (literally) full trying to get Kunnert out of Washington's way and had never even seen the punch.

When he later looked at the tape, Murphy refused to buy Washington's explanation that he reacted on pure instinct. "Your first instinct is to protect," he said. "You hear someone coming from behind, you turn and get your hands up. Then, if you need to throw a punch, you throw it. Kermit turned, saw Rudy clearly, and threw the punch. He was angry. He wanted to hurt somebody. Not the way he did, I know that. But this wasn't an act of self-defense. If it had been, he would have just been covering up."

Kunnert, who had shaken his wooziness during the stoppage in play, had a dull pain above his eye but was able to stay in the game.

"I didn't want to, though," he said. "All the emotion of the basket-ball game was gone. I didn't want to be out there. I was just too upset by what had happened. I'm not sure if I did it consciously, but I fouled out of the game. . . . I got three quick ones the next few minutes. I just didn't want to play."

Neither did Abdul-Jabbar. "I couldn't even begin to tell you if we won the game that night," he said. "And I can remember the outcome of most games I played in. It was as if we were all in the middle of a bad dream."

The Rockets won the game. While most of the players floated through the rest of the night like zombies, Murphy was a man pos-sessed. He took it upon himself to win the game for his roommate. "I was so angry, unbelievably angry," he said. "I just kept telling myself there was no way I was going to have to tell Rudy we lost when I talked to him, because I knew he'd never forgive me for that."

Lucas remembers being scared to get anywhere near Murphy. "He was so wound up that whenever he scored, he would run down the court and try to slap your hand so hard he hurt you," he said. "He sprained both my thumbs because he hit my hands so hard. I finally ran away from him whenever I saw him coming. I thought I was going to get seriously hurt. He had a look in his eye that no one wanted to mess with."

Tomjanovich had more to worry about than the outcome of the game at that point. The first time he actually saw Washington was when he got into the hallway under the stands. Washington was outside the Lakers' dressing room, adrenaline still pumping from the fight. The writers who had come downstairs remember him pacing up and down, still wound up, when Tomjanovich came into view. Seeing Washington, Tomjanovich pulled the towel—a second one, the first already blood-soaked—off his face for a moment. That was when he demanded to know why Washington had hit him.

When Washington screamed something at him about Kevin Kunnert, Tomjanovich was infuriated. Fortunately there were enough security people in the hallway to keep them apart.

In his autobiography, *A Rocket at Heart,* Tomjanovich says that it's a good thing the security people separated him from Washington, because "he [Washington] certainly would have won the fight because he had better boxing technique than me—since I had none."

Losing the fight would have been the least of Tomjanovich's troubles if Washington had delivered another punch. No one had any idea how fragile Tomjanovich was at that moment. "With good medical care, administered quickly, patients in his condition will usually pull through," Paul Toffel, the doctor who later performed multiple surgeries on Tomjanovich, said. "Anything less and you lose them."

Another punch and Tomjanovich probably would not have made it.

Once he and Washington were kept apart, Tomjanovich went up the hallway and around the corner with Vandervoort and Dr. Shields. NBA locker rooms aren't open to the media during a game, so the writers, who had witnessed the exchange in the hallway, couldn't talk to either player—not that Tomjanovich was in any condition to converse.

"Let's get this done quick," he told Vandervoort.

Vandervoort nodded, turned him over to Shields, and went to call Sophie Tomjanovich in Houston, figuring she would be listening to the game on the radio and would be terrified, wondering exactly what had happened to her husband.

Sophie Tomjanovich wasn't listening to the game. She had listened to the first half while getting the children, four-year-old Nichole and one-year-old Melissa, ready for bed. The game had started at nine-thirty Houston time. With the girls in bed by halftime, Sophie did what any young mother left alone with two children would do: she dove into bed.

"I remember Rudy was having a great shooting night the first half," she said. "I also remember I was exhausted. I couldn't stay awake another minute."

It was sometime shortly after eleven o'clock when the phone rang, waking her from a sound sleep. As soon as Sophie heard Vandervoort's voice she knew something was wrong—a lot more wrong than he was implying.

"Rudy got hurt in the game, I didn't know if you were listening," he said. "But he's okay."

"What happened?"

"It's probably a broken nose. That's it, a broken nose."

"A broken nose. That's all?"

"Probably. The doctor is looking at him now. We'll probably send him to the hospital for X rays. But he's okay."

Sophie Tomjanovich knew it wasn't all that simple, and her gut told her it wasn't just a broken nose. "Dick sounded too tired, too drained for it to just be a broken nose. I kept saying over and over, 'It's just a broken nose?' But he wouldn't tell me anything more. He said he would call again when he knew more."

While Vandervoort was on the phone, Tomjanovich was lying on his back on a training table as Shields examined him. Shields asked him to open his mouth. He couldn't. His back teeth were stuck together. "Oh damn, the caps on my back teeth must have come loose," he said, through what he was now aware were clenched teeth.

Then it hit him: he didn't *have* any caps on his back teeth.

"That freaked me out," he said. "I mean, what was going on with that?"

There was also the matter of the bitter taste in his mouth. Shields told him an ambulance was going to take him to the hospital. He had already paged Toffel and told him he needed him to get to the emergency room at Centinela as soon as he possibly could.

Tomjanovich was still someplace between fear and rage. The look on Jerry West's face, the taste in his mouth, his teeth sticking together, were all clues that something was seriously wrong. But there was also the notion inside him that you don't go to the hospital in an ambulance just because someone decks you with a punch, even someone as strong as Kermit Washington. He was still waiting for Vandervoort to come back and tell him he could stanch the bleeding with some gauze and get him back on the court.

But that wasn't happening. Instead he was being led out of the building to the ambulance Shields had talked about. Tomjanovich kept thinking the same thing over and over: "This is crazy. I've got a game to play. This can't be real."

In 1977 most people got the bulk of their sports news out of the morning newspaper. Most local late-evening news shows gave their sports anchors between two and three minutes to recap the day's events. Taped highlights from that night's games were rare. The sportscasters read as many scores as they could, perhaps threw in a quick taped interview with a local athlete, and tossed it back to the news desk. There was no taking highlights off a satellite, no such thing as the Internet. If you lived on the East Coast, your paper probably didn't print West Coast box scores until two days after the game was played. The outcome of a Rockets-Lakers game played in L.A. on a Friday night would not be known to most on the East Coast until Sunday morning.

News traveled much more slowly. The notion that the highlights of a regular-season basketball game, especially one played on the West Coast, might show up in any market other than the two whose teams were playing was pretty much out of the question.

Back at the arena, the writers were told that Tomjanovich had been taken to the hospital for precautionary X rays and he appeared to have a broken nose. All the writers were on deadline, especially tight ones since the game had been delayed by the incident, so their stories the following morning didn't hint in any way that Tomjanovich's condition might be more serious than that. The subheadline on George White's story in the *Houston Chronicle* said "Tomjanovich's nose broken in fight." Ted Green's story in the *Los Angeles Times* described the fight and the scene on the floor when Tomjanovich went down, but he could not say anything more than White could in his story.

Once he was finished writing, knowing he would be expected to follow up on Tomjanovich's condition for Sunday's paper, Green drove to Centinela Hospital. "The funny thing was, in those days the notion of a sportswriter going to a hospital to check on an athlete's condition was kind of foreign," Green said. "Imagine if something like that happened today. There would have been ten camera crews outside the hospital, reporters all over, PR people handing out releases, and some hospital spokesman coming out to brief the media every thirty minutes or so. That night I just walked into the emergency room, found a nurse, and asked if I could find out how Rudy was doing."

What the nurse told Green stunned him: "He's in intensive care."

Intensive care? With a broken nose? Green asked for more details. Could he talk to a doctor? No, none was available to talk to him, the nurse said. Green asked the nurse if she had seen Tomjanovich when he came in. She nodded.

"What did he look like?" he asked.

"It was as if his face was inverted," she answered quietly. "It really did not look good."

Tomjanovich's entire head was swollen by the time he reached the hospital, and he felt as if his eyes were starting to swell shut. He was still going from rage to confusion to fear when Toffel walked in, introduced himself, and began to examine him. That was when he asked the question about playing the next night in Phoenix.

Toffel knew he had to answer the question directly and gently. He had dealt with patients who had been through similar trauma to what he was seeing at that moment, but they had been car accident victims or people who had been hit over the head with baseball bats. The instant he looked at the X rays, he knew he was going to be dealing with a patient who had just suffered a life-changing injury. The fact that the victim was a professional athlete, someone who wasn't used to being unable to do things physically, made the situation that much more delicate.

Toffel was acutely aware of just how emotionally painful insensitivity could be in a hospital setting. In 1965, during his first year of medical school, his father had gone in one morning to open his shoe store in south-central Los Angeles in the aftermath of the Watts riots. The neighborhood was still under curfew, but Mike Toffel opened the store every morning, ready to work. Only on this morning he was held up at gunpoint by two robbers. Paul Toffel, working a summer job outside town, got a phone call from the people who ran the business next door to his dad's.

"They told me he'd been shot and taken to the hospital," he said. "I thought he had probably been shot in the arm or something. My dad was such a tough guy. He'd had throat cancer a few years earlier, lost his voice box, and just kept on going. I didn't think anything could really hurt him. I got to the hospital, went to the front desk, and said I was there to see Mike Toffel. The guy looked at his list and said, 'Oh yeah, Toffel, that's the DOA in room six.' He'd been shot right through the heart. I never forgot how that felt."

Now Toffel had to explain as gently as he could to a basketball player that the least of his concerns at that moment should be when he was going to play basketball again.

"Rudy," he said, "you aren't going to play in Phoenix tomorrow night. You aren't going to play for a while." He paused, knowing what he said next would hurt. "You aren't going to play again this season."

If Tomjanovich's eyes could have opened, they would have been as wide as can be. His emotions, which were bouncing off the walls of the examining room, bounced back to anger. He was raging again, wanting a piece of Kermit Washington, regardless of his condition, regardless of his ability (or inability) to actually hurt him. In the instant that Toffel said he wouldn't play again for the rest of the season, all he wanted to do was lash out at Washington.

Toffel understood all this. When Tomjanovich told him he needed an hour to go track Washington down, it was clear that his mind wasn't in a logical or reasonable place at that moment. "The natural thing, especially for someone that competitive," Toffel said, "is to think revenge, getting even. But there was no getting even. The only thing I could help him with was getting better. I had to get him away from those angry thoughts to thoughts about his condition, on how he was going to start getting better."

Toffel was reading Tomjanovich's mind. All he was thinking about at that moment was what Washington had just taken away from him—for no reason. This was supposed to be The Year for the Rockets. They were going to move up a notch from where they had been a year before—one or two plays from the finals, perhaps a championship. Now this young doctor was looking at him with great concern and telling him as calmly as he could, no more basketball this season. What the hell could possibly be so wrong? A broken nose doesn't put you out for the season. What in the world was going on?

Toffel had to get Tomjanovich to focus on what was ahead, not what had already happened. He knew that for Rudy, as it was for anyone dealing with major physical problems, his mental health was going to be important.

So he asked about the bitter taste he knew Tomjanovich had to be experiencing in his mouth. Yes, Tomjanovich answered, what the heck was that?

"Spinal fluid," Toffel said. "You're leaking spinal fluid from your brain, Rudy." He then explained how serious his condition was.

He could see by the look on Tomjanovich's face that he had his attention now, so he plowed on. When he said "ICU," he knew Tomjanovich was no longer thinking about Kermit Washington. "We've got to get you neurologically stable," he said. "In other words, we've got to see to it that we get your brain capsule to seal. Then we'll start working to get your face fixed."

The rage bounced out of Tomjanovich, replaced again by fear. "Are you saying I could . . ." His voice trailed off. He couldn't say the word "die." Knowing he had made his point, Toffel turned encouraging.

"We're going to get you through this, Rudy, but it's going to take a while. You can't waste any energy on negative thoughts. Small victories, one at a time, that's what we're going to go for. I want you to appreciate every good thing that's going to happen and not even think about what's already happened. It accomplishes nothing. Celebrate victories, okay, Rudy?"

He understood. He had to flush the rage, but that wasn't easy. The fear helped put the rage aside, but it didn't remove it completely. Before they sent him to ICU, they got him a telephone. It would be the middle of the night in Houston by now, but he had to talk to Sophie. He knew Vandervoort had been calling her, but she would need to hear his voice for reassurance.

When Sophie answered the phone—wide awake, waiting for the call—his rage came out again. "Real anger," she remembered. "Lots of cursing, lots of how could this happen, lots of can you —— believe this? He wasn't even making a lot of sense he was so angry and, I assume, because he had some painkillers in him by then. But the anger was almost good for me to hear, because if he had sounded scared, I would have been scared."

Once he finished talking to Sophie, Tomjanovich knew he had to make one more phone call before he went upstairs. Calvin Murphy was pacing in his hotel room, unable to sleep; sick with fear; sickened by the sight he had seen; wanting to lash out at someone because he hadn't lashed out at Washington when he had the chance.

"I had gotten to the point where when something went wrong in my life, with basketball, with my family, whatever it was, the person I talked to was Rudy," he said. "I needed to talk to Rudy that night about how angry I was, but he wasn't there. I was losing it."

And then the phone rang and Rudy was there. He was trying to tell Calvin he was okay, he was hurt, the doctor said he was out for the season, but he would be back. He didn't say anything about spinal fluid or the ICU. Now it was Murphy who was raging. He was screaming into the phone that this wasn't fair, that Kermit Washington had to be thrown out of basketball, that he would get him and he was going to get anybody else who even touched one of his teammates, breathed on one of his teammates.

"No," Tomjanovich said firmly. "Murph, you got to make me a promise that you won't start anything tomorrow or the next night or with any of the Lakers next week."

"But Rudy, look at what he did . . ."

"I know, but getting you suspended for fighting isn't going to make me better. I got enough on my mind right now without having to worry about you getting in a fight over this. You have to promise me you won't fight."

"But Rudy . . ."

"Promise, Murph, promise."

Years later, as he retold the story of that night, tears rolled down Murphy's cheeks. "Think about it," he said. "The man is in the hospital, he's in terrible shape, he has no idea what's going to happen to him, and he's worried about me. Everyplace we went the next few weeks, I couldn't get that out of my mind. And then I would think, 'I may never play with him again, he may never come back.' And I'd break down and cry every time."

No one on either team had any clue about how badly Tomjanovich had been hurt. Even so, the rest of the game was played in a fog— by everyone except Murphy. Fueled by anger and fear, he scored

20 points in the second half and 28 for the game. Led by Murphy's performance, the Rockets won the game, 116–105, their first victory in the Forum in four years.

"I have almost no memory of the second half of that game," Mike Newlin said. "I remember Calvin, because he took over the game. But I think we were all just wondering what was up with Rudy. We knew he had gone to the hospital, but that was it."

Abdul-Jabbar remembers even less. "Who won the game?" he asked. "After what happened, it didn't seem to matter. I can remember a few days later, sitting in a hotel room reading the *New York Times*, and I realized that I had been sitting there for forty-five minutes without reading a word. Now, there aren't many things in the world I enjoyed more than sitting by myself in the morning and reading the entire *Times*. But I can remember that day I couldn't focus on the paper at all because I kept hearing that punch and seeing Rudy on the floor and all the blood around his head. Even now, talking about it, it all comes back again."

The Lakers were stunned; the Rockets stunned and angry. When the media came into the locker room after the game, Mike Newlin minced no words. "If I had a gun," he said, "I would gladly shoot the guy."

Newlin's comment earned him a letter of reprimand from the NBA.

Driving home from the arena, Kermit Washington had a sinking feeling that his life had changed every bit as much as Tomjanovich's. It wasn't just what the parking lot attendant had said or even the sight of Tomjanovich on the floor. He had been in fights before, but nothing like this. When he walked in the door, Pat Washington knew right away that something had gone terribly wrong. Almost eight months pregnant, with a two-year-old to take care of, she hadn't been listening to the game. Shortly after she had put Dana to bed, her phone had rung. It had been Jessica Smith, the wife of Elmore Smith, one of the four players traded to Milwaukee two years earlier in the Abdul-Jabbar trade. The two women had been close friends when Smith played in Los Angeles, and Jessica Smith was calling to see how Pat was feeling, remembering that Dana had arrived early and her due date was now six weeks away. They were in midconversation when the operator broke in to say she had an emergency phone call.

The call was from Jackie Chaney, whose husband, Don, was on the Lakers' injured list but had been at the game anyway. Sitting in the stands, Don Chaney was as frightened as everyone else when he saw the punch. "Seeing what I saw and knowing how strong Kermit was, I knew it was very, very serious," he said. "I told Jackie she better call Pat and warn her. When the game ended, I drove to the hospital to see what I could find out. They just told me Rudy was in intensive care. The whole thing was impossible to believe."

Jackie Chaney got to a phone, called the Washington house, and got a busy signal. That was when she asked the operator to break in. "Kermit is okay," she said immediately, knowing that the emergency call would make Pat wonder if something had happened to her husband. "But be prepared. He was in a fight and he hurt someone badly. He's probably going to be scared when he gets home."

Jackie Chaney's prediction was accurate. As soon as Kermit walked in the door, Pat knew her friend hadn't been exaggerating. "He was scared and upset," she said. "He was worried about Rudy. He said he had tried to call the hospital but they wouldn't tell him anything. He was crying when he talked to me about it. He kept saying, 'I never meant to hurt him that way. I saw him coming from behind and I thought he was going to jump on me like in Buffalo.'

"I felt awful for him, because I knew he would never hurt anyone on purpose that way. I didn't know what to say. There was nothing I could say to comfort him. I couldn't tell him, 'Rudy will be fine,' because I didn't know that. I couldn't say, 'I'm sure the league won't be too tough on you,' because I certainly didn't know that. So I just listened. It was a long night."

Kermit and Pat had talked in the past about Kermit's penchant for fighting. Pat worried not so much about punishment as she did about his getting hurt. The previous year's fight in Buffalo had frightened her. "It seemed as if he was taking on the whole team," she said.

That fight had started with some pushing and shoving under the basket between Washington and John Shumate, another hard-nosed 6-8 power forward. When Shumate had challenged him, Washington decked him with one punch. At that point Fred Foster, another of the Braves, had run at him from behind and jumped on his back. Washington had shed him with what Abdul-Jabbar described as "a shrug that sent him flying."

"The whole thing happened right in front of their bench," Abdul-Jabbar said. "It started with Shumate, then came Foster. By the time he sent Foster flying, you could see the circle around him growing. No one wanted to go near him. They were afraid."

There were other fights and near fights in Washington's career. There had been a fight with Dave Cowens in Boston that had led to a bench-clearing brawl between the two teams, and there had been other skirmishes that had involved pushing and shoving and glaring but no one landing any punches.

"Nowadays I probably would have been ejected a lot, because it doesn't take much to get ejected," Washington said. "Back then, though, you really had to do something to get ejected. I had only been ejected twice [Shumate and Cowens] before the Rudy fight. My job was to protect Kareem and step in when necessary. I was supposed to be an intimidator."

All well and good to be intimidating, but Pat Washington lectured her husband about knowing when to stop, where to draw the line. Later in the 1976–77 season, he was thrown out of practice one day for slugging backup center C. J. Kupec. Josh Rosenfeld, who had known both Kermit and Pat since their college days, was living in Los Angeles at the time and was a regular dinner visitor. While Pat was fixing dinner, Josh and Kermit sat in the living room.

"I asked him how practice had gone that day," Rosenfeld said. "He looked around the room and then said very softly, 'Not well. I got into a fight. I got thrown out.' I don't know how Pat heard him, but she came flying out of the kitchen, screaming, 'Did you get into a fight again? When are you going to learn?'"

Pat Washington wasn't screaming now. There was no point. She could see the hurt in her husband's eyes and hear the pain in his voice. This was no time for a lecture. "Maybe it will turn out Rudy isn't hurt so badly," she said, searching for a positive spin. "Maybe it won't be as bad as you think."

Kermit said nothing in response. He got into bed and tried to sleep. It was no use.

Rudy Tomjanovich wasn't sleeping either. His eyes had swollen shut, which might have been a blessing, because it kept him from even thinking about trying to look in a mirror. Lying in his bed, all he could think about was his family. He had decided that if he could never leave his house again because he looked like the Elephant Man, he would be okay with that as long as he could be with Sophie and the girls.

The hospital chaplain had come into the room to ask if he wanted to pray. No, Tomjanovich said, thanking him. He told him he felt he had a relationship with God that would allow him to feel close to him throughout the night. In his autobiography, Tomjanovich would write that during those first couple of nights he was talking often to God and he felt his presence through the entire ordeal. "It was all quite real," he wrote.

Only it wasn't.

Tomjanovich remembered going to church with his parents twice when he was a child—on the same day. "I never understood it," he said. "We'd never gone, then one morning we went, and later that day we went back. I never quite figured out what it was about."

He had never been a churchgoer and hadn't given much thought until that point in his life to spirituality. He had turned down the chaplain's offer not because he didn't need him but because he didn't believe he was worthy. "My thinking was, I had never prayed before, I had never gone to church, so here I was in this crisis and now I was going to pray? It didn't seem right. My thinking was, if I was God and all of a sudden here I was praying, my attitude would be, 'Oh sure, now you want to talk.' I just couldn't bring myself to pray for myself. It felt wrong."

Lying in bed, Tomjanovich could hear sounds coming from the other side of the curtain in the ICU. He could hear someone talking very softly, saying, "Come on, sweetheart, wake up, you have to wake up. I know you can wake up. Please wake up."

He asked a nurse who was in the next bed. He was told it was a little girl who had been in an automobile accident. She was in a coma, fighting for her life. After the nurse left, Tomjanovich finally prayed—for the little girl. "She was worthy," he said. "I asked God to let her live, to let her wake up."

Several days later Tomjanovich learned the little girl had died. He was devastated. God hadn't even listened to his prayer for someone else. It reconfirmed his notion about being unworthy.

He dozed very briefly in fits and starts throughout that first night, unable to see a clock, unable to see much of anything. It felt as if a week had passed when the sun began to come up. Toffel was in to see him shortly after he woke up. The leakage from the brain capsule appeared to have stopped. He wasn't out of the woods yet, but it was a major step in the right direction.

For the first time since he had turned and seen Kevin Kunnert engaged with Washington and Abdul-Jabbar, a moment that now seemed to be a lifetime ago, Rudy Tomjanovich smiled. At least he thought he smiled. Given the condition of his face, he couldn't be certain.

"This is a victory, Rudy," Toffel said.

Tomjanovich tried to smile again. "So Doc," he said, "how do we celebrate?"

"You just did," Toffel told him.

5

Who Hit Whom?

During Kermit Washington's last three years in college, one of his closest friends had been Josh Rosenfeld, one of the basketball team's managers. Rosenfeld had worked briefly in Philadelphia after graduating and then moved to California in 1976. He had rented an apartment near the Washingtons' home in Palos Verdes and at Washington's urging began working out with him in the weight room to build up his 5-foot-8-inch, 130-pound body.

Prior to the start of the 1977–78 season, Rosenfeld had moved back east, taking a job with the Dorf Features Service, an outfit that supplied high school sports coverage to several newspapers, most notably the *Newark Star-Ledger.* Each night during the NBA season, the sports staff at the *Ledger* ran an NBA pool. The staffers took turns running the pool throughout the season. Whenever Rosenfeld's turn to run the pool came up, everyone knew that the tiebreaker for that night would have something to do with Kermit Washington.

On December 9, Rosenfeld ran the pool. His tiebreaker was, "How many rebounds will Kermit Washington get tonight against Houston?"

The next day when Rosenfeld arrived for work, he found that there had been a tie in the pool. In those days, the wire services rarely moved a full box score—minutes, field goals made/missed, free throws made/missed, rebounds, assists, steals, fouls committed—on regular-season NBA games across the wire. Instead they moved what was called a short box, which consisted only of field goals made/missed, free throws made/missed, and total points. That morning's *Star-Ledger* didn't have a story on the game since it had ended well after midnight East Coast time, missing the paper's late deadlines.

"Hey, Rosenfeld, we need to find out how many rebounds your buddy Kermit got," someone shouted at Rosenfeld when he got to his desk.

Rosenfeld puffed his chest out a little bit. "No problem," he said. "I'll just call and ask him."

Knowing it would be midmorning in Los Angeles, he picked up the phone and dialed his friend's number. Pat answered the phone.

"I could tell by her 'hello' that something was wrong," Rosenfeld said. "I said, 'Pat, is everything okay?' She just said, 'I'll let Kermit tell you.'"

When he heard his friend's voice on the phone, a jolt of horror ran through Rosenfeld. Either something had happened to two-year-old Dana or something had gone wrong with Pat's pregnancy. It had to be one of those two things.

"His voice was a monotone, like he was in some kind of shock," Rosenfeld said. "I remember it like it was yesterday. I said, 'I know something's wrong, do you want to talk about it?'"

"Not really," Washington answered.

"Is Dana okay?"

"She's fine."

"Pat?"

"Fine."

"The baby?"

"Fine."

"Kermit, how'd the game go last night?"

There was a long pause, then Washington said, "I got thrown out."

Rosenfeld immediately guessed—at least in part—what had happened.

"A fight?"

"Yes."

"Do you want to tell me about it?"

"No."

Rosenfeld didn't push it. He had never heard Washington like this, so he knew it hadn't been just an ordinary NBA fight. He hung up and went and found the late wire story on the game. It described the fight and said Washington had been ejected after breaking Rudy Tomjanovich's nose. That didn't seem so bad. The next morning a friend of his living in L.A., another AU grad, called him.

"Did you hear about Kermit?" he said. "He almost killed Rudy T."

Then he read him the story in that morning's *Los Angeles Times,* which said that Tomjanovich was in the intensive care unit in guarded condition.

"Oh my God," Rosenfeld said, stunned. Now he understood Washington's tone. It hadn't been just another NBA fight. He knew, just as the man in the parking lot had known, that Washington was in serious trouble.

Whenever there was a fight or an ejection in the NBA, it was standard procedure for the lead official to write a report on the incident and send it by telegram to NBA officiating supervisor Norm Drucker. Both officials, Bob Rakel and Ed Middleton, understood that this was not an ordinary fight or an ordinary ejection. In fact Rakel took the unusual step of allowing the media into the officials' locker room after the game, even though he limited his comments to explaining what the rules were that caused Washington to be ejected.

Rakel and Middleton agreed that the proper thing for them to do, given what they had seen, was to each write a report for Drucker. Each had seen the punch from a different vantage point and had a different view of how the fight had unfolded, since they were at opposite ends of the court. They knew that Washington would undoubtedly face both a fine and a suspension, so getting as much detail as they could into the hands of the league as soon as possible was important.

They decided to write their reports that night, before going to bed, so that it would be fresh in their minds. "Ordinarily you might do a report like that the next morning on the plane going to the next city," Rakel said. "But you knew when people saw this there was going to be tremendous reaction. We wanted to make sure we got the league the information fast and that we got it right."

Both men were torn by the events of the evening. Each liked and respected Washington and Tomjanovich. "Kermit is a good guy," Middleton said. "He was the kind of player you respected as a referee because he worked hard, he never gave you a hard time about a call, and everything he did was out front. There was nothing sneaky about him. What happened that night was as much bad luck as anything else. He had no idea he could hurt Rudy that badly, and there isn't any doubt in my mind that he had no intent to hurt him that badly."

"But he did."

Rakel felt the same way. He liked Washington, respected his game, and felt awful that what had started out as a skirmish between Kunnert and Abdul-Jabbar had somehow escalated in a matter of seconds into a bloodbath. "There were times when I would think back on that game and wonder if there was anything I could have done differently," he said. "Should I have jumped in on Jabbar and Kunnert? Could I have gotten to Kunnert or Kermit before the punches began? In the end, the answer was no. Jabbar and Kunnert got untangled, there was no reason to stop the game. Kunnert and Washington started so quickly there was no time to do anything except maybe step in between and get knocked flat myself. But I wondered about it more than once."

If anyone was to be second-guessed after the incident, it was the team owners, who had voted against adding a third official for that season. If there had been a third official, Washington might not have grabbed Kunnert's shorts. A year later, in large part because of the Washington-Tomjanovich fight, the NBA added a third official. Soon after, that move all but disappeared from the game because the trail official was in position to see it happen. With two officials, the trail had to get upcourt much quicker and didn't have the time or the positioning to focus on that move.

That night, though, it was just Rakel and Middleton, and their job once the game ended was to tell the league what had happened. They had to put aside any feelings they had for Washington and put in writing what they had witnessed. Rakel's report would be more significant, in part because he was the lead official, but more important because he saw the entire thing unfold. Middleton had been running downcourt with his back turned when Abdul-Jabbar and Kunnert had started flailing at each other. Both men had a clear view of Washington's haymaker punch. Like everyone else, they were stunned by what they saw and by the result.

Rakel's telegram, which he sent as soon as he returned to his hotel room, read as follows:

> Relative to game Friday evening, Houston at Los Angeles. In third quarter a scuffle broke out at mid court between Kevin Kunnert and Kermit Washington resulting in a punch thrown by Kermit Washington at which time play was stopped and Kermit Washington was ejected and charged with a punching foul. Immediately after this scuffle was broken up, he pivoted and contacted a most vicious blow into the face of Rudy

Tomjanovich. In 10 years of refereeing basketball, I have never witnessed a more vicious act. I strongly recommend severe punishment.

Middleton's telegram, sent a few minutes later, wasn't much different:

Game, Houston at Los Angeles, December 9th. With approximately 11 minutes remaining in the 3d period, a scuffle broke out at mid court area between Kevin Kunnert and Kermit Washington. Kermit Washington punched Kevin Kunnert. It was broken up by fellow referee Bob Rakel. I got to the area and as I got there Kermit Washington turned and punched Rudy Tomjanovich in the face. This was a most severe act by this player and should be treated accordingly. A punching foul was called against Kermit Washington and Kermit Washington was ejected from the game.

From Washington's point of view, the most damaging part of the two reports—other than the description of the punch itself—was Rakel's recounting of the Washington-Kunnert skirmish. There was no denying the severity of the punch or the damage it did. But Rakel made it clear that—in his view—*only* Washington had thrown a punch prior to Tomjanovich's arrival on the scene. Rakel liked Washington and wasn't crazy about Kunnert. "He was kind of an agitator," he said years later. "He was the kind of guy who would set a screen in the post and if he thought you weren't looking an elbow might come up. He could be sneaky. He wasn't a problem or anything, but at times he was an agitator."

And yet there was no mention in Rakel's report of Kunnert throwing an elbow. He said only that a scuffle broke out between Kunnert and Washington and Washington threw a punch at Kunnert, resulting in his ejection. In other words, Washington was going to be ejected even before Tomjanovich came into the picture. It is certainly possible that Rakel didn't see Kunnert's elbow or elbows, but the fact that he was the official following the play and didn't see Kunnert do anything that merited either a foul call or mention in his report did not help Washington then and, perhaps more important, does not help him now.

"I still remember most of it very well," said Rakel, who retired from officiating in 1984 and lives now in Albuquerque, New Mexico. "What I questioned myself most on was the scuffle between Kunnert and Jabbar. They were tangled up. If I had blown the whistle then, maybe the whole awful thing wouldn't have happened. But as a referee you don't want to stop play at one end of the court when the ball's at the other end. And the two of them *did* get clear of each other, so in that sense I did the right thing. You try not to use the whistle unless you have to. Then Washington and Kunnert got tangled, and it all happened so fast. Jabbar came in to get Kunnert away, but Kermit got in that punch.

"As a referee, you always tried to get in between two players if they looked like they were going to throw punches before a punch is thrown. You've got to use your instincts. In this case, I didn't have a chance. One minute it looks like they're running downcourt, the next they're squared off and Kermit throws the punch. Then, when I tried to move in between them, here comes Rudy. . . ."

Rakel's voice trailed off at that point. "I think it changed the way I officiated. I was always a little more cautious after that when a skirmish broke out. I think I decided, maybe subconsciously, that if I was going to make a mistake, it was going to be on the side of caution, break them up when they didn't need it rather than not break them up and wish later that I had.

"What we all saw that night isn't something you ever forget," he said. "The whole thing is still pretty clear in my mind." His voice was very soft. "I just hope," he said, "that I never witness anything like that again in my life."

Middleton was also affected by the incident. "I always thought I had a pretty good instinct for trouble coming," he said. "After that, if I saw a player nail another player, I would say to the player who had been nailed, 'Do *not* retaliate. If you do, you are going to be in trouble, no matter what the other guy did.' I tried to cut trouble off before it started whenever I could."

After receiving the reports from the two officials, Norm Drucker followed up with a phone call to Rakel. Drucker passed his handwritten notes on the conversation on to Jack Joyce, a former FBI agent, who was then the NBA's director of security. Rakel's oral report, as recorded in Drucker's notes, was almost identical to his written report:

> In the 3d quarter, I was trailing the play when I noticed Washington and Kunnert scuffle at mid-court. Washington then punched Kunnert in the eye. Jabbar and I acted as peacemakers. At this point, Tomjanovich, who was in the game, came back from front court. At this point Washington pivoted and Tomjanovich, coming toward him at a trot, was punched by Washington. It was the most despicable act I've ever seen in a pro game. On TV I saw a clip of this punching act. In my estimation, Washington decided to punch any Houston player and hit Tomjanovich as he was the closest.

The TV tape was now beginning to make the rounds. It was crude, almost blurry, but there was no missing the ferocity of the blow or what it did to Tomjanovich. It was also incomplete in that it showed none of the events that led to the moment when Washington turned and punched Tomjanovich. All it showed was Kunnert being swung away from Washington by Abdul-Jabbar and Washington turning as Tomjanovich approached. At the last second, Tomjanovich's hands came up as he saw the punch coming, but it was too late. The punch connected, Tomjanovich's head snapped back, and his whole body flew through the air before he landed on the back of his head a few feet away, crumpling into almost a fetal position.

No one had ever seen a punch like this one in a basketball game. By Saturday night, the tape was showing up on TV around the country and reports were beginning to filter out of Los Angeles that Tomjanovich was in intensive care in Centinela Hospital because of the severity of the blow. In New York, Brent Musburger, who was then the play-by-play man for CBS's NBA network broadcasts, saw the tape and couldn't believe it.

"There were guys in the league I believed capable of doing something like that," he said, echoing Chick Hearn and many others. "Kermit Washington was absolutely not one of them."

Musburger was the host at the time of CBS's football pregame show. There was almost no reason to ever show an NBA highlight on the show, especially in December. He knew the minute he saw the tape that this would be an exception to the rule.

"When you as a network have a contract with a league to do their games, you are in a very real sense a PR arm of the league," Musburger said. "I mean, let's be honest. If the public likes the league, the network gets better ratings and then everyone is happy. So you tried to put the best face on things that you could without crossing the line to being a total shill. There was no way to put a good face on this. You had to show the tape and let people judge for themselves. I hated doing it, I really did, because I liked Kermit so much and knew how damaging it was going to be for him. But there really wasn't any choice."

That was pretty much where everyone found themselves that weekend: without a choice. Neither Bob Rakel nor Ed Middleton had any desire to condemn Kermit Washington. Brent Musburger didn't want to hurt him or the NBA. But none of them felt they had a choice. Events had clearly overtaken them all.

The other person who had a clear view of what had happened between Kunnert and Washington was Abdul-Jabbar. Once he and Kunnert untangled, Kunnert raced upcourt with Washington a step behind and Abdul-Jabbar about three steps back.

"Kermit did reach out and grab him by the trunks to try to push past him and get upcourt," Abdul-Jabbar said. "Kunnert's first response was understandable. He slapped his hand away and hit him just below the shoulder with an elbow. But then he turned around and threw a punch to the right side of Kermit's face. That's what really started it, no two ways about it.

"But at that point I really didn't care who started it. I didn't want it to go any further. Kermit, away from the court, is one of the kindest, most decent people I've ever met. I think he actually made a point of *not* intimidating people with his size. But on the court he had some bully in him, especially when he was provoked. I saw that he had been provoked, and I tried to get there and get Kunnert out of the way before anything more could happen. I was being selfish. I didn't want a fight because I didn't want Kermit to get thrown out of the game."

As Abdul-Jabbar came up behind Kunnert, intending to get him out of Washington's reach, Washington threw a punch at Kunnert that missed. Abdul-Jabbar regrets what happened next. "I grabbed Kevin's arms so I could swing him away. But I wasn't fast enough. I ended up pinning his arms so he couldn't defend himself, and before I could get him out of the way, Kermit nailed him right in the eye. At that point I was able to swing Kevin out of there while Kermit tried to get in a couple more punches. I got him turned away, and that's when I heard that sound."

Kunnert's version of the seconds leading to the punch is identical to Abdul-Jabbar's except for the assertion that he threw a punch at Washington's face. "That's just not true," he said. "Kareem says I threw a punch. Kermit says I threw an elbow. The only elbow I threw was the one to Kermit's shoulder. I did that just to get him off me. If I had wanted to elbow him in the face, I could have. But I didn't."

The bottom line, even twenty-five years later, is that it wasn't absolutely clear then what happened between Kunnert and Washington and it isn't clear now. Four men were in position to see what happened. Abdul-Jabbar remembers Kunnert giving Washington an elbow to the shoulder and throwing a punch at his face; Washington remembers taking two elbows in the face; Kunnert remembers slapping Washington on the hand, uttering a profanity, and then elbowing him in the shoulder. The only man who clearly has no ax to grind among the four is Rakel, and all he saw was "a scuffle," followed by Washington punching Kunnert.

All of that led to the moment not in dispute: The Punch. From the time the incident occurred, beginning with the scene in the hallway when the bloodied Tomjanovich demanded to know why he had hit him, Washington has asserted that Kunnert is as culpable as he is because the two elbows he alleges Kunnert threw led to the fight and The Punch.

"It's never been about Kevin Kunnert and me, it's always been about me," Washington said. "I know I have to take responsibility for what happened to Rudy, and I've certainly paid a price for that. But what about Kevin Kunnert? He's the one that started the fight. Kareem testified to that in the trial, but no one believed him. Why not? I'll tell you why not, because it was the word of two black men against a white man, and most of the people in our society will believe the white man, not the black men. That's just a fact.

"The same with the NBA. Who buys the tickets to the game—white people or black people? The answer is white people. So they were going to come down on me, the big black guy who beat up the two white guys. It only made sense. That's why I knew I was in trouble that night. If I had hit a black guy that way, it wouldn't have been nearly as bad. And if I had been the white guy and Rudy had been the black guy, I might have been fined fifty dollars. There are people out there who would have made me into a hero for it. But that's not the way it happened. The NBA was going to get me."

The NBA *was* going to get him. And there's no doubt that, especially in 1977, there were plenty of white people more than willing to make a black man into a villain in a heartbeat. John Lucas, who is black, doesn't think race had anything to do with what happened. "It didn't matter what color you were when you saw what happened or watched that tape," he said. "An awful thing occurred. It doesn't mean Kermit is a bad guy, because he's not, he's a good guy. But he did a bad thing that night. It wasn't about the NBA being out to get him or anyone else. It was about him doing something he should not have done. Period."

6

Sixty Days
and Ten Thousand Dollars

By Sunday morning most of the country knew that something extraordinary had taken place in Los Angeles on Friday night. The tape was being played and replayed, not just on sports shows, but on news shows—including the network news shows—because it was so shocking in nature. The *Los Angeles Times* had confirmed that Tomjanovich was in intensive care.

And both teams had games to play—the Lakers at home against the Buffalo Braves, the Rockets on the road against the Seattle SuperSonics. The Rockets had played in Phoenix on Saturday night and been routed 110–93 by the Suns.

"We were all still in a daze," Tom Nissalke said. "We still didn't know exactly what was going on with Rudy. But we knew it wasn't good, because Murph had talked to him and he had told him he was done for the season according to the doctor. That pretty much floored us all."

Kermit Washington was in the starting lineup that Sunday night. He had received a phone call on Saturday from Jack Joyce, the league's security chief, asking for his version of events. Washington says now he didn't spend much time talking to Joyce because he was convinced the league had already made up its mind about who was right and who was wrong in the incident. He had also received a call from Donald Dell, his agent, who had been informed by the Lakers that his client was in trouble.

"I told him to keep his mouth shut, not talk to the media, and let me handle whatever came next," Dell said. "I hadn't seen the tape yet, but I'd been told the punch was devastating. I told Kermit to be patient, to let me deal with [NBA commissioner] Larry O'Brien, and we'd do whatever we had to do. I knew he was facing something severe, because Larry had made it clear before the incident he wasn't going to tolerate any more fighting. But I knew Larry pretty well, and I was convinced he would be fair—*if* Kermit didn't go around publicly rocking the boat."

Dell was, in fact, a friend of O'Brien's. In 1968, when O'Brien had been running Bobby Kennedy's presidential campaign in the Midwest, one of his advance men was Donald Dell. O'Brien had gone on to become the chairman of the Democratic Party, and it was his office in the Watergate office building that had been burglarized on the infamous night of June 17, 1972. Three years later O'Brien had gotten out of politics to become commissioner of the NBA. To date it had not been a smooth ride. It was about to get rougher.

Washington also got a call from Lakers owner Jack Kent Cooke. According to Washington, Cooke said essentially the same thing to him that Dell had said: Stay quiet, lie low, and we'll work things out. Dell remembers getting a similar call from Cooke. Both men say that Cooke, who died in 1997, never called again.

"I really thought at first that Mr. Cooke would stand by me," Washington said. "He liked me. I remember once he called the locker room at halftime of a game against the Celtics. Cowens was just killing us, and he asked to talk to me. He said, 'Kermit, we cannot allow this to happen. You must play that Cowens fellow more physically.' I think he wanted me to go out there and hit him, but I wasn't going to do that. I just told him we would all try to do a better job."

Washington's memories of that weekend are a blur. Since he hadn't heard anything from the NBA other than Joyce's phone call, he showed up at the Forum on Sunday for the game against Buffalo. Before the game he ran into Ted Green. He had read Green's story in the *L.A. Times* that morning describing Tomjanovich's condition and speculating on his future.

Green's lead was direct and to the point: "Rudy Tomjanovich is in intensive care and Kermit Washington is in extensive trouble."

The story went on to say that Washington was almost certain to be fined and suspended once the NBA had gathered all the facts, especially given O'Brien's vow to crack down on fighting. It pointed out that Abdul-Jabbar had been fined $5,000 for giving Kent Benson a black eye and that O'Brien had said then that he would have suspended Abdul-Jabbar if he hadn't broken his hand in the fight and sidelined himself for 20 games. Green also raised the specter of a lawsuit. No NBA player had ever sued another player or a team, but the Rockets were already talking about the possibility the day after the fight.

"Once we heard that Rudy was going to be out for the season, the thought of a lawsuit started to come up," Nissalke said. "The feeling we all had was that Rudy certainly had a lawsuit and so did the team. Clearly we had both been damaged."

Like everyone else at the game, Nissalke had no idea how badly Tomjanovich was hurt after he walked off the court. The blood had scared him, but when Tomjanovich got up and walked off under his own power, Nissalke breathed a sigh of relief. "I figured worst-case scenario he'd be waiting for us in the locker room when the game was over," he said. "Knowing how tough Rudy was, if he'd come back to the bench before it was over, I wouldn't have been surprised."

He was more than surprised—stunned—when Jerry West came looking for him after the game. West had talked to Dr. Shields, who had said he was convinced Tomjanovich's injuries went well beyond a broken nose. When West told Nissalke that Tomjanovich had gone to the hospital in an ambulance and that Shields was very concerned about his condition, Nissalke felt sick to his stomach.

"The guy should be suspended for the rest of the season, especially if Rudy can't play again," Nissalke angrily told the media that night. "The guy is an idiot."

No one was more shocked or upset by what had happened than Pete Newell. He had been working Friday night doing color commentary on the University of Southern California radio network. Driving home from the Los Angeles Sports Arena, Newell flipped on his car radio to find out who had won the Lakers-Rockets game.

"I'll never forget it," Newell said. "The first thing I heard was Chick Hearn saying that there was no further word on Rudy Tomjanovich's condition, that he had been taken to Centinela Hospital. I thought, 'My God, what in the world happened to Rudy?' This was one of my favorite guys, after all, someone I had taken with the second pick in the draft even though a lot of people thought I was crazy to do it. So I was very concerned about Rudy. I kept listening to hear if they had any more information. A little while later, just before I got home, they said something about how devastating the punch Kermit Washington had thrown had been. Oh, what an awful feeling that was. There wasn't anyone in the league I was closer to than Kermit. Now I'm hearing that he's the reason Rudy's hurt so badly."

Newell pulled into his driveway a few minutes later. His wife, Nell, was waiting for him at the door. She had watched the game, had seen the punch. Her description was harrowing. Later Newell saw the tape. When he did, he was convinced that he knew exactly what happened.

"All those summer mornings, Kermit and I spent a lot of time in the car going to and from our workouts," he said. "He talked a lot about growing up in Washington, what it was like, how scared he was all the time. He told me a story about being in a fight in the schoolyard one time and someone came up from behind and pinned his arms and he ended up getting beaten up. He was just a skinny kid back then. Now he had this great physique that he had built up through the years. Then he got jumped from the back in Buffalo. He said that reminded him of when he was a kid. I remember him saying to me, 'Pete, one thing I guarantee you, no one will ever get me from behind again.'

"When I saw that tape, I knew what had happened. Rudy came from behind. He wasn't going to hit him or try to hurt him, I know that. Kermit knew it too—*later*. But not then. At that moment he was back in the schoolyard, and he was going to be sure that no one was going to pin his arms again. He reacted."

Washington went to practice on Saturday after making one more attempt to call Tomjanovich in the hospital. He was told, as he had been told Friday, that Tomjanovich was in intensive care and not taking phone calls. At practice that day, he asked Ted Green what he thought might happen to him. Green had been making phone calls the entire morning, asking just that question. The NBA was still fact finding and waiting for the tape to arrive from the West Coast, but Green had a pretty good sense that Washington was going to be treated very severely.

"All you had to do was look at the track record that year," Green said. "O'Brien made it clear he would have suspended Kareem, and he had suspended Adrian Dantley a week earlier for a fight that never really got started. I told Kermit I thought he'd get the maximum fine and a lengthy suspension."

What, Washington wondered, did lengthy mean? Could it be the whole season, which was what Nissalke was lobbying for?

There was no way to know. West told Washington to just play hard and play well—and stay out of trouble until they heard something from the league. The Lakers beat Buffalo the following night in overtime. Washington started and had 11 points and

8 rebounds. He spoke to the media after the game and kept his comments low-key: He was very sorry Rudy had been hurt. He had tried to call him in the hospital. He had no idea what the NBA would do. He had never intended to hurt Rudy.

He was scared that night, as scared as he had ever been in his life.

"I had worked so hard to get to where I was," he said. "It's not as if I had all this great talent. I'd put in all that time with Pete in the summer. The first year I had torn up my knee, now I was facing a long suspension. And I knew it was going to be long. I was convinced Larry O'Brien had his mind made up about me, and he had never met me. I just felt so helpless. People were acting as if I had just turned around and punched Rudy for no reason. It wasn't that simple a story, but no one wanted to hear it."

The following morning Washington flew with the team to New Orleans. The Lakers were scheduled to play the Jazz on Tuesday, then fly to Houston and play the Rockets on Wednesday. There was little doubt in anyone's mind that the suspension would be handed down before the Lakers got to Houston. There was no way O'Brien or the league wanted Washington in uniform in Houston with Tomjanovich still in the hospital in Los Angeles.

By Monday morning, the league had all the information it felt it needed. Jack Joyce had spoken to the players involved—except for Tomjanovich. The referees' reports were in hand and so was the tape. The only real question was how hard O'Brien would come down on Washington.

"You have to remember what was going on in the league back then," David Stern said. "Everyone—the owners, Larry, the players too—was concerned about fighting. I've heard Kermit say through the years he didn't intend to hurt Rudy the way he did and that the punch was a by-product of a fight that had already started. I believe every word of what he says. But in the end, when Larry had to make his decision, what mattered was the result—which was devastating. If he had seen it as an act of self-defense, that he would have been hurt had he not acted, it might have been a little different. But I don't think he saw it that way."

Russ Granik, who is now Stern's number two man in the league office, was working as a lawyer in the office at the time. He goes a step further than Stern when discussing what the league did and why. "I would say most of the rules we have today governing violence and fights really grew out of that incident," he said. "We were aware before then that we had a problem, but this incident made it crystal clear the potential dangers of letting men this size take full swings at one another. There are times we get criticized for being *too* hard on those who are on the periphery of a fight, but remember, Rudy wasn't in the fight that broke out. The more people who get involved, the more dangerous a fight becomes. We had to take steps to keep these sorts of things from happening again."

Granik paused. "Try to imagine the result if Shaquille O'Neal landed a clean blow on someone. That's not to say Shaquille would do something like that. But there are too many players with tremendous strength in this league to take any chances at all."

Several months after Granik made his comment, an enraged Shaquille O'Neal took a wild swing at Chicago's Brad Miller. The punch didn't land cleanly, but the incident reminded people again why the NBA tries so hard to keep brawls from breaking out. Basketball fights aren't like hockey fights, because it is difficult to get leverage on ice skates. And they aren't like football fights, where the players are wearing helmets. In the aftermath of the O'Neal incident, trying to explain what the worst-case scenario might have been, almost everyone brought up the same thing: Kermit Washington and Rudy Tomjanovich. Even now it remains the benchmark for how horribly wrong a fight can go.

"Sometimes we have to suspend people in situations where it hurts us competitively," Stern said. "[Like] the Miami-Knicks playoff fight a few years ago, when Patrick Ewing wandered onto the court and never threw a punch and we had to suspend him because that's what the rules said we had to do. Was it good for us to suspend all those people that night? No. But Kermit and Rudy was far worse. We can't ever let that happen again."

And so it was no surprise when the word from New York reached New Orleans on Tuesday morning. Washington was coming out of the locker room after the morning shootaround when he ran into Ted Green.

"Did you hear?" Green asked.

Washington knew exactly what Green was talking about as soon as the words were out of his mouth.

"What is it?" he asked.

"The fine's ten thousand dollars," Green said. "The suspension is at least sixty days. You can apply for reinstatement then."

The $10,000 was no surprise. The sixty days was crushing. It would be mid-February before he could play again. The season would be almost over. And it was sixty days without pay. Washington lived comfortably, but he wasn't so wealthy that losing more than one-third of his annual salary was something he could simply brush off.

He wondered if he would ever play in the NBA again.

Those same thoughts, for very different reasons, had entered Rudy Tomjanovich's mind often in the three days that had passed since the fight. The leakage from his brain capsule had stopped by Sunday night, and on Monday he had been moved out of intensive care. That was the good news. The bad news was, he had gotten a look at himself in the mirror.

"I really did look like the Elephant Man," he said. "My face was swollen like a melon, about twice its normal size."

He had almost laughed when a hospital worker came into his room and asked him if a truck had hit him. No, he answered, he had been hurt in a basketball game.

"Basketball game?" the man had answered. "What happened, the scoreboard fall on you?"

Back in Houston, Sophie Tomjanovich was trying to organize her life so she could fly to Los Angeles to be with her husband. She had called her mother in Detroit on Saturday to see if she could fly down to take care of the girls. Her mother was able to get a flight on Sunday, so Sophie made plans to fly to L.A. on Monday. Some of the other wives came by the house to see how she was doing, which was not very well.

"I was doing the brave thing when people were around," she remembered. "But I was really quite scared. I had no idea how badly Rudy was hurt or what was going to be involved in getting him better. He had said they were telling him he couldn't play the rest of the year, but I wondered if that was just softening him up to tell him he'd never play again. I felt like there was no way for me to have an understanding of what was going on until I got out there."

Just before Sophie left for the airport on Monday, Calvin Murphy came by the house. The team had flown home from Seattle on a red-eye, and Murphy came to the house with Rudy's travel bags. "It was almost as if he had died," Murphy remembered. "I told myself the whole way over there I had to be strong for Sophie, tell her everything was okay. So I got about two steps inside the door and lost it completely."

Seeing Murphy was comforting for Sophie. It made her feel less alone, knowing that she wasn't the only one shedding tears and not sleeping at all. She promised to call the Murphys and give them a full report as soon as she got to Los Angeles and had a chance to see Rudy. "I was girding myself," she said.

All the way to Los Angeles she prepared herself. She checked in at her hotel, changed clothes, and took a cab to the hospital. "I wanted to look like I was doing okay even if I didn't feel like I was doing okay," she said. "I let myself cry one more time at the hotel and then said, 'Okay, enough. He can't see how scared I am, because it will scare him.'"

She took a cab to the hospital and found Paul Toffel waiting for her. As soon as Toffel saw her coming down the hall, he knew who she was without ever having met her.

"For one thing, she was tall [5-8], someone you would think would be married to a basketball player," he said. "But she also carried herself in such a confident, poised way, I just knew she was Rudy's wife right away. When we shook hands, you would have thought she was there to pick her husband up after a routine physical. She was a picture of calmness."

"Yeah, right." Sophie laughed. "Calm outside, collapsing inside. Thank goodness he was there to talk to me before I went in to see Rudy."

Toffel gave Sophie a short pep talk to let her know what she would be facing once she walked into the room. He started with the good news: Rudy's condition had improved greatly since Friday. He was going to need surgery, probably several times, but none of it was likely to be life-threatening. That time, he was convinced, had passed. But what she was going to see wasn't going to be pretty. What's more, it was *absolutely* imperative that she not recoil in horror or shriek or run from the room or, most important, break down and cry.

"You would be entitled to do any or all of those things," Toffel told her. "But you just can't."

Sophie understood. She told herself she had done all her crying in the hotel and in the cab. She walked into the room and there was Rudy, who had gotten out of bed in anticipation of her arrival. She embraced him gently, then pulled back to take a look. Rudy's swollen, battered face was filled with concern.

"You know something, Rudy," she said. "I think this is an improvement. Really."

Rudy tried to smile. Then he groaned. "My God," he said. "Everyone around here is a comedian."

The day before, when Toffel had started to explain to Tomjanovich what sorts of surgery would be necessary to repair his face, he had said, "You know, I've seen pictures from before this happened, Rudy. This is no great loss."

Tomjanovich understood exactly what his wife and his doctor were doing. Just as he understood when Sophie sided with a gruff nurse who insisted on poking and prodding him constantly. "Good," Sophie said when he complained. "There are enough people running around here spoiling you half to death."

The joking was medicine for Tomjanovich, a different form of painkiller. Toffel had told him that he would need surgery to fix his jaw and to realign his skull. He would also need plastic surgery for the shattered bones in his face. "I want to be home for Christmas," he told Toffel. "I want to be with my girls."

Toffel said it would depend on how he came through surgery but he would certainly try.

While Tomjanovich was in the hospital dealing with great physical pain, Kermit and Pat Washington were dealing with pain of a different kind.

It first hit Pat a couple of days after the punch when she went into the grocery store. As she was checking out, she noticed two other women whispering to each other and pointing at her.

"Are you talking about me?" she asked. "If you are, why don't you say what you have to say so I can hear."

The two women said nothing, but the looks on their faces convinced Pat that her instinct had been correct.

That was difficult. So were the threatening phone calls—"To this day I don't know how so many people got our phone number," she said—and the hate mail that began to pile up. Not surprisingly, a good deal of it was racial. "Lots of N-words," she said. The mail got to be so bad that several neighbors volunteered to go through it to separate the hate mail from the real mail. They would throw the hate mail away, then bring the rest to Pat.

But nothing prepared her for her next trip to the obstetrician. Her due date was a little more than a month away. When she arrived for her appointment, she was surprised when an associate of her doctor came into the examining room to see her. "I'm really sorry, Pat," he said. "My partner doesn't want to deliver your baby because of what happened with your husband. I tried to tell him that you don't let anything affect your relationship with a patient, but he didn't want to hear it. I'll take care of you from now on, and I'll deliver your baby for you. I'm truly sorry."

Pat wondered how anyone could be so cruel.

Kermit became a virtual shut-in. He hated going out in public, because he was convinced everyone was pointing at him and whispering about him. "There weren't a lot of six-eight black men wandering around in the Palos Verdes area," he said. "It wasn't like I could go out and not be recognized, especially since my picture was in the paper every day and the tape was on TV every night. I would wake up early, because I couldn't sleep, sit around and worry all day, and then go to bed at five o'clock. I was exhausted from doing nothing."

The low moment came eight days after the fight. Kermit and Pat were home watching television. Kermit was still awake, in large part because he wanted to stay up to watch his favorite show, *Saturday Night Live*. The phone rang. It was Kermit's brother, Chris, calling from St. Louis.

"Well, you're really famous now," Chris said, trying to sound cheerful.

Kermit knew better. "Why?" he asked.

"You're on *Saturday Night Live*."

Sure enough he was. During the Weekend Update segment, Garrett Morris had come on to do the sports. His lead story was on the fact that once again a black man was being unfairly depicted as overly aggressive. As Morris railed on, the tape of Washington throwing the punch at Tomjanovich was run over and over and over again. Each time, Rudy appeared to fall backward a little bit farther and land a little bit harder.

"Look at that, look at that," Morris said at one point as Washington's fist crashed into Tomjanovich. "The brother barely touched him." Pause. "Maybe we need a different angle."

"A living nightmare," Washington said. "That's what my life had become, a living nightmare. I felt as if Pat and I were out on an island all by ourselves. A few friends called, but not many. What could they say? I never heard from the Lakers except for the first call from Jack Kent Cooke telling me not to worry about a thing, that he would take care of everything. Kareem called. Ernie DiGregorio called and came by the house. So did Don Chaney. They were great. That was it. I just felt as if my whole life had turned upside down, and I had no idea how to turn it around again."

Pete Newell called, counseling patience. He was convinced the Lakers would do the right thing and stand by him. "For one thing, Kermit, they need you," he said. "Without you they have no one to protect Kareem inside."

In fact both teams were struggling. The Rockets had lost five straight in the aftermath of the game in Los Angeles, including a loss at home to the Lakers. That game was one of two the Lakers had won in their next six after the fight.

"We were like zombies," Tom Nissalke remembered. "To start with, we'd lost our best player. Beyond that, we were an emotional shell. After Calvin went off the rest of the game in L.A., he just wasn't there the next few games. Everyone on the team felt close to Rudy. Knowing he was still in the hospital made it very tough for anyone to focus on basketball."

In Los Angeles the Lakers felt as if they had a terrible public relations problem on their hands. Clearly Washington was going to be a pariah around the league for a good long while. The tape had now been seen everywhere. The *Saturday Night Live* incident had ensured that non–basketball fans would be as aware of what had happened as basketball fans. (Remember, this was late 1977, when *SNL* was still a national phenomenon, with John Belushi, Dan Aykroyd, Bill Murray, Gilda Radner, Jane Curtin, Laraine Newman, and Morris heading up the cast.)

The question Lakers management was dealing with was simple: should they bring Washington back when his suspension was over? West wanted him back. He felt time would heal the wounds brought on by the punch and that the team needed Washington in the lineup. It certainly wasn't playing very well without him.

"Beyond that, I thought we owed it to Kermit to stand by him," West said. "What happened was horrible. There was no excuse for it. But that moment wasn't who Kermit Washington was. He made a terrible mistake and paid a price for it. But I didn't think we needed to desert him because of it."

Bill Sharman, now the general manager, was on the fence. He had been talking to teams about trading Washington *before* the punch took place. The Lakers were guard-starved, and if the right deal could bring a quality guard to the team, Washington was one chip that might be dealt. He was a solid player with a definite role on the team, but rebounders are more easily replaced most of the time than scorers. When the punch occurred, there were questions about whether trading Washington was still viable, but Sharman was still looking to move him if he could find the right fit.

Exactly where Jack Kent Cooke stood on the issue wasn't clear to anyone at first. But one thing *is* clear: if Cooke had wanted Washington to stay in Los Angeles he would have stayed. Washington had been one of Cooke's favorite players. He liked his aggressiveness. The phone call he received from Cooke right after the fight comforted Washington. But then nothing.

"The month of December," he said, "was one of deafening silence in my life."

It would get louder soon enough.

7

Red to the Rescue

Like everyone else in the league, Red Auerbach was horrified when he heard—and saw—what had happened in Los Angeles. Auerbach was the most famous coach in the history of the NBA, having coached the Boston Celtics to nine championships. In his heyday, Auerbach would announce that a game was won by lighting a cigar on the bench—thus the term victory cigar—an act that would get a coach thrown out of the building these days.

"I'd'a had to go outside to light up nowadays," said Auerbach, who, at eighty-five, still keeps a cigar lit throughout most of the day.

In 1966, after winning his ninth title, Auerbach retired from coaching, turning the team over to his best player, Bill Russell, elevating him to player-coach while he, Auerbach, remained with the team as general manager. By promoting Russell, Auerbach was making a statement: Russell was the first African American hired as a coach or a general manager in one of the four major team sports. Auerbach, who is Jewish, had been born in Brooklyn in 1917 and knew a little bit about prejudice and bigotry. He was the first coach in the NBA to start five blacks and had a reputation among black players for being completely color-blind.

"Red treated everyone the same," said Sam Jones, another of Auerbach's Hall of Fame players. "Awful."

Which is why the players loved him. Only one color mattered to Auerbach: green, as in Celtics green. If you could make his team better, you could be from Mars and he would find a uniform for you. When he decided to stop coaching, Auerbach wanted Russell to be the coach because he thought Russell was best qualified for the job. "When I announced that I was going to step down at the end of that season, Russell came to see me," he said. "He had tried to talk me out of [retiring], even called my wife to try and get her to talk me out of it. But that wasn't going to happen. I needed to quit. I wasn't eating, I wasn't sleeping, I was a mess. I looked at a picture of myself that year and I looked like death warmed over. If I hadn't stopped coaching, it would have killed me.

"I explained this to Russell. He says to me, 'Okay, if you really won't coach, let me coach. Because I don't want to play for anyone else.' I thought about it and then told him okay—as long as he kept it a secret until I was ready to make the announcement. He agreed. At the time, it hadn't even occurred to me that he would be the first black coach. Which was probably good. Because if I had announced that I was giving Russell the job and he would be the first black coach, he probably wouldn't have taken it. That's the way he was."

Auerbach intended to wait until the end of the season to announce Russell as the coach. But in the NBA finals that year, the Los Angeles Lakers, coached by one of Auerbach's more heated rivals, Fred Schaus, came into Boston Garden and won the first game in overtime. There were no interview rooms in 1966. The press would crowd into one corner of the locker room to talk to the coaches. Auerbach was peppered with questions about what had gone wrong, what special strategy had Schaus unveiled to steal game one on the famed parquet of Boston Garden?

"Nothing went wrong," Auerbach said. "They just kicked our butt. Oh, by the way, we're having a press conference tomorrow morning to introduce our new coach. You see that guy over there?" He pointed at Russell a few feet away. "He's going to be coach of the Celtics next year. Any more questions?"

Thirty-five years later, Auerbach still smiles retelling the story. "The next day in the papers it was almost as if the game didn't happen," he said. "Poor Fred. His big moment and no one wrote a word about it. We went out and won game two easily after that."

The margin was 20, and when the game was over, Schaus was still complaining about Auerbach stealing the Lakers' thunder after game one. The Celtics went on to win the series in seven games—the third time in five years they had beaten the Lakers in a seven-game final series.

The new team of Auerbach and Russell proved successful. It certainly didn't hurt coach Russell to have player Russell in uniform. The team did not win the championship in 1967, losing in the division finals to the record-breaking Philadelphia 76ers team led by Wilt Chamberlain, but came back to win the title again in 1968 and 1969, beating the Lakers—now led by Chamberlain—in game seven for the title in 1969. Russell retired from both coaching and playing after that championship, his eleventh as a player. Auerbach was left to rebuild. His first big step in that direction came in 1970 when he drafted Dave Cowens out of Florida State. At 6-foot-9, Cowens was too small to play center in the NBA. Only he was so tough and so competitive that he turned the Celtics around, leading them to championships in 1974 and 1976.

Throughout his career with the Celtics, Auerbach's family had lived in Washington, D.C. Auerbach had gone to college there at George Washington University. His first professional coaching job had been with the old Washington Capitols. He had gone from there to Duke University, staying only half a year before being hired late in 1949 to coach Ben Kerner's Tri-Cities team. By the end of that season, he and Kerner were at odds over who would make personnel decisions. When Walter Brown, the owner of the fledgling Boston team, approached Auerbach about coaching the Celtics, Kerner willingly let him out of the final year of his contract. Auerbach took over the Celtics that summer. He has held a title in the Celtics organization—coach, general manager, president, general chairman—ever since.

His oldest daughter, Nancy, had a serious asthma problem. Living in Durham, near all the tobacco factories and in a house with a yard outside, had made the condition worse. When Auerbach accepted the job in Boston, he and Nancy's doctor both thought it would be best for the family to stay in Washington, where the weather was warmer, where they could live in the city, and where Auerbach's father-in-law, a pediatrician, would be nearby at all times.

"Probably the best decision I ever made," he said. "Living with a coach in-season is hard, especially me, because I took everything so seriously. I got home when I could, and they were glad to see me when I came home. If they'd been living with me, they all would have hated me."

Auerbach *was* intense. One night, after a Celtics victory over the Cincinnati Royals in the old Cincinnati Gardens, an outraged fan began screaming profanities in Auerbach's face as he left the court. "In those days there was no security around you going on and off the court," Auerbach said. "This guy is screaming at me, so I turned around and just popped him in the nose. He went down like he'd been shot."

The man got up soon enough and filed a lawsuit against Auerbach. When Auerbach heard he was being sued, he turned to John Havlicek and said, "Hey, John, you remember how that guy kicked me before I hit him?"

"Well, Coach, no, I don't remember that," Havlicek answered.

"Let me rephrase the question, John," Auerbach said. "Do you remember how that guy kicked me, the guy who signs your paycheck, before I hit him?"

"Oh, yeah, *now* I remember," Havlicek said.

In the end, Havlicek's testimony wasn't needed. There were so many witnesses around who thought Auerbach was entitled to slug the fan that the suit was dropped.

Auerbach continued his commute between Washington and Boston after he stopped coaching. Nancy enrolled at the University of Rhode Island, but her asthma again caused her serious problems. She came home and enrolled at American University, which was only a few blocks away from the apartment where her parents lived on Massachusetts Avenue. One of her best friends was Marty Levy, the daughter of one of Auerbach's close friends.

Shortly after Nancy Auerbach arrived at AU, Marty Levy introduced her to a friend from her dorm: Pat Carter. Pat's boyfriend was Kermit Washington. One night, after a party on campus, Kermit and Pat gave Nancy a ride home. Kermit walked into the living room, looked at the pictures and plaques, and went slack-jawed.

"Are you related to Red Auerbach?" he asked.

"Pat had no idea who the man was," Kermit said, laughing, years later. "Then a few minutes later, he came downstairs. Nancy introduced us, and he sat down and started telling stories. I was completely awed."

Auerbach wasn't awed, but he was impressed. "He was the kind of kid you liked right away," he said. "Polite, friendly, and very serious. You could tell he was going to do well in life, whatever he ended up doing."

Pat and Kermit remained friendly with Nancy Auerbach, and Kermit worked at Red Auerbach's camp for two summers. Naturally, when Kermit made it to the NBA, Auerbach kept tabs on him. "He really struggled those first couple of years," Auerbach said. "But then [the fourth year] he really improved. He had become a good NBA player, the kind of guy you really wanted on your team. If you had a guy like Jabbar, you wanted someone like Kermit there to do the dirty work. And Kermit was willing to do the dirty work."

When Auerbach heard about the incident in Los Angeles, he made a point of watching the tape. "What happened to Rudy was obviously bad, very bad," he said. "But I knew then and I know now, that wasn't Kermit's intent. For one thing, I'm convinced the kid didn't know how strong he was. But the other thing is, he didn't sneak up on him. Rudy was running right at him. I know he was going in as a peacemaker, but Kermit didn't know that. I've seen [former Pistons center Bill] Laimbeer do things that were worse dozens of times. Other guys too. It wasn't a sucker punch. It was just a horribly damaging punch."

Shortly after the incident Auerbach began hearing on the NBA grapevine that Jack Kent Cooke wanted to trade Washington, that he felt the public relations fallout from the incident was so bad that he couldn't bring Washington back in a Lakers uniform. Like the Lakers, the Celtics were struggling. They were overloaded at the guard spot, and coach Tom Heinsohn desperately wanted to get power forward Sidney Wicks out of town.

Auerbach sensed an opportunity to make a move that would help his team, even if Washington was going to be suspended for two months. "I was thinking long term," he said. "Kermit was just a kid, twenty-six, twenty-seven [actually twenty-six] years old." Auerbach had already made a call to Larry O'Brien on Washington's behalf, even before he heard he might be available. "Larry was a Boston guy, so I knew him pretty well," Auerbach said. "I just called him up and said, 'I know the incident was awful, but this isn't a bad kid. Keep that in mind.'"

Now, hearing that Cooke was looking to move Washington, Auerbach wanted to make a deal. He didn't want Cooke's basketball people, Bill Sharman or Jerry West, to get involved, because he was certain they would try to talk Cooke out of the trade. But he also knew he couldn't call Cooke directly, because Cooke wouldn't take his call.

"I'd tried to deal with him in the past," he said. "He said to me, 'My dear Red, I won't make any deals with you ever, because you know much more about basketball than I do and I'll get the short end.' I thought maybe he was kidding until I saw him quoted as saying it in the newspaper. So I knew he was serious."

Auerbach came up with an idea. He called Celtics owner Irv Levin and told him he wanted to get Kermit Washington. Cooke was living in Las Vegas at the time, staying out of California because he was in the middle of an ugly divorce. Auerbach convinced Levin to fly to Vegas and call Cooke, saying he was on vacation, and suggest dinner.

"I told him once they'd had a couple of pops to tell Cooke that he was sick and tired of Auerbach making all the trades and taking all the credit for everything the Celtics did. Then I said he should tell him, 'Jack, I want to make a deal, just you and me. None of these general managers or coaches. I know you need to get rid of Kermit Washington, and we can't get Jo Jo White and Charlie Scott to play together. You give me Washington, I'll give you Scott. You get rid of your headache, I get rid of mine. Then I can go back and tell Red, "I made a deal without consulting with you and the hell with you." '"

Whether Levin delivered his speech in those words—both Cooke and Levin are now dead—is impossible to know. But Cooke apparently agreed to the deal, because on December 27 Washington was traded to Boston (along with Don Chaney, a player Auerbach had lost in free agency but wanted back) for Charlie Scott, who had been an All-Star and a key member of the Celtics' 1976 championship team. The notion that Cooke made the deal unilaterally fits with the fact that both Sharman and West say they had no idea the trade was coming.

"I didn't even know about it until I got a call saying it was done," West said. "I was very upset. In part I was upset because we needed Kermit. He was important to the way we were trying to play. Kareem, in particular, needed him on the court. But beyond that, I felt as if we needed to be more supportive of Kermit than we were. We left him hanging out to dry after the incident. He deserved better than he got from us."

Sharman was also surprised. "I think Mr. Cooke felt we needed to make changes," he said diplomatically.

On the day the trade was made, Washington was at home, still in purgatory, counting the days until his suspension could be lifted. The phone rang and Washington answered—by then he had gotten a new phone number, so the threatening calls and the crank calls had, for the most part, stopped. It was Chick Hearn, the Lakers' play-by-play man, who by then carried an assistant general manager title with the team.

"Kermit, I just wanted to tell you how much I enjoyed working with you," Hearn began. "I'm truly sorry for what happened, and I know you are too. I really believe this is the best thing for you, though, I really do."

"What's the best thing for me?" Washington asked.

"Why, the trade," Hearn answered.

"The trade?"

It was at that moment that Hearn realized no one in the Lakers' brain trust—Cooke, Sharman, or West—had called Washington to tell him he was traded. "I was horrified," Hearn later said. "It certainly wasn't my place to deliver news like that to a player, especially under those circumstances. I was just calling to wish him luck, because I genuinely liked him. When I realized what was going on, I think I just said something like, 'Kermit, you need to call the front office.'"

Washington was too upset to call the front office. Instead he called Dell and asked him to do it. Dell called him back and told him he had been traded to the Celtics.

"Part of me was furious," Washington said. "I mean, how could someone not call me to tell me? Nothing against Chick Hearn, but he was not the person I should have heard that news from. I know his intentions were good, but it was wrong. But then when I thought about the trade, it didn't seem so bad. I mean, it was the Celtics. And it was Mr. Auerbach, who I liked so much. I realized it took a lot of courage for him to make that trade at that time, when people were trying to cast me as the devil. I'll always be grateful to him for doing what he did."

Auerbach wasn't looking for any bouquets, he was looking for a rebounder. Two important factors allowed him to make the trade: First, he was Red Auerbach. Another NBA general manager might not have been secure enough to trade for Washington while he was still under league suspension and with no guarantee that it would be lifted after two months. Second, he knew Washington and believed the incident did not represent who he was as a person.

"I had a lot of faith in the kid," Auerbach said. "I wouldn't have done it if I wasn't convinced he could help us. But I've always had a soft spot for the underdog. At that point in time, no one was a bigger underdog than Kermit Washington."

Rudy Tomjanovich was back in Houston on the day Kermit Washington became a Celtic. He had asked Dr. Toffel to do everything he could to get him home in time for Christmas, and Toffel had come through. The two of them had flown from Los Angeles to Houston on Christmas Eve on an almost empty plane. Toffel accompanied his patient because he had wired his jaw shut after setting it, and if anything happened on the flight, Toffel needed to be there to cut the wires so Tomjanovich would be able to breathe.

"For example, if something had caused him to become sick in flight," Toffel said. "With his mouth wired shut, he could suffocate in a situation like that."

Toffel had only known Tomjanovich for fifteen days as they flew east, but he felt close to him, having watched him deal with what had happened. He knew that what was to come wasn't going to be easy either. Rudy would need at least one more round of surgery—

to fix a blocked tear duct—and there would be a lot of pain ahead. Then would come rehab, because Tomjanovich had made it clear that he fully intended to play basketball again.

"Rudy, I honestly believe that something good is going to come out of this chapter in your life," Toffel said on the plane. "I know that may be tough to believe right now, but I really think it's true. You're going to be a different person because of this—you have to be. And I think you're the kind of person who can take adversity and use it to make you stronger."

Tomjanovich appreciated what Toffel was saying, and he understood the message in his words. He had made a point of not thinking about Kermit Washington since the moment when Toffel had told him that negative energy of any kind was wasted energy and he was going to need every last bit of energy he had in order to recover. He had read of Washington's suspension in the papers and moved on from there.

"The anger had really gone out of me after that first night," he said. "For one thing, I was too terrified to feel angry at anyone for the first couple of days. Then, when I started to feel a little better, there were so many other things to think about and so many things I had to do that there wasn't time to think about Kermit or even to think about how I felt about Kermit.

"He just wasn't important to me. What was important to me was getting home to see my girls, being with Sophie, and getting better. I just wanted to get better."

He knew the process would be slow, because Toffel had explained that to him. He knew his return home would be joyful, but not easy for his family. He wondered how Nichole and Melissa would feel about the way their dad looked. Sophie was going to have to learn how to work the wire cutters so she could cut the wires open if something went wrong.

But at least he was home. Jim Foley, the Rockets' public relations director, met them at the plane with a sheepish look on his face. Tomjanovich's return was supposed to be a secret, but somehow a local TV station had gotten word and sent a crew. Foley apologized. Tomjanovich really didn't care. It was Christmas Eve and he was home. A TV crew filming his arrival wasn't about to ruin that.

When he walked through the door and hugged his daughters, they both looked at him wide-eyed. Nichole, who was four, kept asking, "Daddy, why did the man do that to your face?"

"I didn't have an answer for that one," he said.

Trey Washington was born in Los Angeles on January 26, 1978. He was named for a former football player whom Kermit had become friends with while working out in the weight room at American. By then there were a little more than two weeks left before Kermit would be eligible to come off the suspended list. The league had called to say that Commissioner O'Brien wanted to hold a hearing in his office on January 30 before deciding whether to lift the suspension.

"Tell them I'm not coming," Washington told Donald Dell on the phone. "They've already taken all this money from me, why should I pay to fly cross-country when they've already made up their minds about me?"

Dell didn't know whether to laugh or cry. He had been back and forth with O'Brien and with David Stern, the league's outside legal counsel, ever since the suspension. He knew nothing was cast in stone, but he was convinced that the hearing was nothing more than a formality so that O'Brien could look Washington in the eye, make it clear that he better not ever be involved in anything resembling this again, and then reinstate him.

"Kermit, if you want to play again, you have to come to New York," Dell said. "It's as simple as that."

"Fine," Washington said. "I won't play. I can get a teaching job."

He was only half-kidding. He had already looked into the possibility of getting work as a teacher if he wasn't reinstated. Money was starting to run short. He had paid the league $10,000 and he hadn't been paid since mid-December. By the time the two months was up, he would have lost more than $53,000 in salary in addition to paying the fine.

"Kermit, you love to play," Dell said. "I know it, you know it. Come to New York and you'll play again. I'm almost certain of it."

Washington didn't like the "almost" part. He wanted a guarantee, but he knew Dell couldn't give him one. He also knew that no teaching job was going to pay him anything close to what basketball paid. He would be a free agent at the end of the season. He needed to show teams he could still play in the wake of the incident so someone would sign him. Finally, Dell was right. He did love to play. He loved preparing to play. For the first time since college, he had gotten out of his workout regimen. He wanted to have games to prepare for again. He agreed—at last—to fly to New York.

He was still grumbling about the $500 he had paid in airfare when Dell met him at his hotel for breakfast on the morning of the hearing. Dell had spoken with O'Brien once more in the interim, and O'Brien's parting words to him were, he thought, important: "Donald," he had said, "you know I'll be fair."

"I thought that was a tipoff," Dell said. "Larry O'Brien *was* a fair guy, and I was convinced he had done his homework and knew Kermit wasn't a bad guy. My sense was that unless Kermit came in and really acted like a jerk, he was going to reinstate him."

O'Brien had done his homework. In addition to the referees' reports and the report he had received from security chief Jack Joyce, he had checked on Washington's reputation around the league. He had also received a number of letters and phone calls from people telling him that this was a good guy. Auerbach had called him; Pete Newell had written to him. Josh Rosenfeld, Washington's college friend, had also written to him.

"After the suspension happened, I was so upset, I thought I should write O'Brien a note just so he could know some things about Kermit that he probably didn't know," Rosenfeld said. "I was in the city, so I decided to go by the NBA offices and deliver the letter personally so it would get to him that much faster. As I was about to get off the elevator, who is getting on? Larry O'Brien.

"So I rode down with him, introduced myself, and handed him the letter. He must have stood and talked to me in the lobby for twenty minutes. I remember him saying to me, 'You aren't the first person to come forward on Kermit's behalf. I have the sense that he's a pretty special guy.' That made me feel much better about the whole thing."

David Stern remembers being fairly sure that O'Brien intended to reinstate Washington. "There had been a lot of communication with Donald," he said. "I always respected Donald. He was a very aggressive advocate for his clients at all times, and he would play every angle he could play. But he was smart enough to understand that in a different circumstance, he might be arguing the other side with just as much passion. To me, that always made him a worthy adversary."

On the morning of the hearing, Dell's most dangerous adversary appeared to be his client. Washington walked into breakfast wearing one of those western string ties and a large frown.

"Kermit, what's with the tie?" Dell said. "We're trying to make a good impression here. We want O'Brien to understand that you're one of the good guys in the sport, not one of the bad guys."

"And he'll think I'm one of the bad guys because of this tie?" Washington asked.

"No, no," Dell answered. "But it's part of the whole package."

"Okay, Donald, what do you want me to do when we get in there?" Washington said.

"I want you not to say anything until I ask you a question or O'Brien asks you a question," Dell said. "Answer every question honestly and look him right in the eye when you're talking to him."

Washington nodded. "Would you also like me to order up some fried chicken and watermelon and then maybe jump on his desk and do a tap dance? Maybe that would make all of you happy."

Dell sighed. It was going to be a long day.

When they reached 645 Fifth Avenue, they took the elevator up to the NBA offices. Walking in, Dell tried to remind Washington one more time to stay calm regardless of what was said or what he was asked. "Got you, Donald," Washington answered. "Fried chicken and watermelon. Keep everybody happy. I should smile a lot too, right?"

Dell rolled his eyes.

"I was hostile, you bet I was," Washington later said. "I didn't see why I had to fly all the way across the country so Larry O'Brien could tell me what a bad guy I was. I already knew how he felt. The suspension was proof of that."

Washington and Dell were ushered into O'Brien's office, where O'Brien and Stern were waiting. There was no stenographer and no one took any formal notes.

"I think that was due in part to Larry's legal training," said Stern. "I'm the same way. I've never kept a diary or a journal, and I don't think Larry ever did either. Plus, he was an informal guy to begin with. What took place was a hearing, but not in the sense that you would normally envision a hearing."

Washington says now that O'Brien lectured him that day. "He said to me, 'We don't need your kind in our league,'" he said. "I told him, 'Oh really? You don't know me at all. You don't know who I am. I don't drink, I don't smoke, I don't do drugs, I work in my community. Is that the kind of person you don't need in the league?'"

Dell confirms that there was an angry exchange between O'Brien and Washington, but has no memory of O'Brien saying what Washington vividly remembers. "He may very well have said, 'We don't need incidents like this in our league,' or, 'We can't have incidents like this,' but I don't remember him saying anything like that to Kermit. I think if he had, I would remember it, because it would be so unlike Larry. And I think, I would certainly hope, if he said something like that, I would have jumped in."

Stern is more adamant. "I don't remember that meeting very well," he said. "But Larry O'Brien just wouldn't talk like that. Was he concerned about the incident and the fighting in the league and our image? Absolutely. But a comment like that just wasn't Larry O'Brien."

O'Brien died in 1990, and the NBA has no written record of what was said in the hearing.

Washington remains bitter about what he believes was said. Even so, he did do what Dell had counseled him to do. He told O'Brien he had made a mistake and he was sorry about what had happened to Tomjanovich. He also told O'Brien that he wanted to play basketball again but if he couldn't, he'd be just fine. He had his college degree. He would go teach someplace. He didn't talk about the scuffle with Kevin Kunnert, because he and Dell both knew O'Brien didn't really care what had started the fight, he cared about how it had ended. When the hearing was over, O'Brien told Dell he would consult with Stern and be in touch with him as soon as he reached a decision.

The four men shook hands. Washington and Dell left, Washington still smoldering. "He's not going to lift the suspension," Washington said. "I flew all this way for nothing. He has already made up his mind."

Dell, who was just glad to be out of there without any references to fried chicken or watermelon, was too tired to argue further. "I think you're wrong about Larry, Kermit. I've known him a long time," he said. "But we'll see."

·   ·   ·

O'Brien called Dell the next morning. "I'm reinstating Kermit Washington as of February twelfth," he said. "But you better warn him. His next fight in the NBA will be his last."

Dell breathed a huge sigh of relief and called Washington. "Start getting back in shape," he said. "You're back in the NBA."

A Celtics uniform would be waiting for him in San Francisco. So would the rest of his life.

8

Too Soon to Dream

Kermit Alan Washington was born September 17, 1951, in Washington, D.C., the second son of Alexander and Barbara Washington. His brother, Eric Christopher—always called Chris—was eighteen months older than he was.

Very few of Kermit's early memories are happy ones. His mother had been a brilliant student in college, getting one B in four years at Miner's Teachers College in Washington, D.C. (which later became part of Howard University). His father had also grown up in Washington, and spent much of his adult life working at D.C. General Hospital as an X-ray technician.

Barbara Washington was a manic-depressive. She was treated often at St. Elizabeth's, the D.C. hospital for the mentally disturbed. Kermit lived with his parents until he was four years old. Then one night there was a fight involving his mother and father and his mother's brother. Kermit remembers screaming and yelling and blood. No one died, but soon after, Chris and Kermit were sent to live with their paternal great-grandmother.

This was not exactly an ideal living situation for two little boys. They wondered where their mother had gone and why they only saw their father on occasion. Their great-grandmother was extremely strict. The boys were kept on a very short leash all the time. "It was," Kermit remembered, "a miserable existence. Our great-grandmother loved us, but she had no idea how to deal with two little boys. We thought she was very mean."

One day when Chris and Kermit were playing outside, their mother came to see them. They were thrilled. She told them they were going on a trip together. The next thing the boys knew, they were on a bus leaving Washington with her. Kermit doesn't remember exactly how long they traveled—he estimates it was about two weeks—but he remembers being hungry all the time. "Sometimes my mother would get a job for a day or two and then we'd be able to eat," he said. "Other times we would try to get food at the Salvation Army or anyplace we could. We loved being back with our mother, but we were confused and scared and hungry."

Eventually, Alexander Washington figured out where his wife and sons were and brought the boys back to D.C. and their great-grandmother's house. Barbara Washington ended up back at St. Elizabeth's. Four years later Alexander came to the house one day with an announcement: he was remarrying and the boys would be moving back in with him and his new wife, who was also named Barbara. Hallelujah, thought the boys, free at last, free at last.

"It was the happiest day of our lives," Kermit said years later. "We thought our great-grandmother was the devil. She would hit us whenever we misbehaved at all. Most of the time she was mean to us. About the only time she wasn't mean was when she watched television. I remember she loved Perry Mason and wrestling.

"When dad said he was marrying Barbara and we were going to move in with them, Chris and I thought it was our dream come true. All our lives we had seen nice families on TV. Real ones. Now we were going to be a real family. That was the first time in my life I learned the hard lesson: be careful what you wish for."

The newly minted family moved into 237 Farragut Street N.W., in an area of Washington that, back then, was gang-ridden. Two gangs dominated the area, the Riggs Park gang and the Decatur Street gang. Kermit recalled, "If one gang didn't come up and take your lunch money, the other one did. Sometimes, if one gang took your money and then the other gang came after you, they'd beat you up for not having any money. Every day of your life, you would leave your house scared because you knew someone was going to come after you. It was an awful way to live."

According to Kermit, his stepmother wasn't at all pleased to find that her new marriage included two lively boys. By then Chris had established himself as a gifted student. Every time the boys took a standardized test of any kind, Chris was off the charts. Kermit was the slogger. He did okay in school, never got in serious trouble, but barely kept his head above water academically.

One thing their great-grandmother had given both boys was manners. She had insisted they respect their elders, call them sir and ma'am, and always be polite. It was a lesson that Kermit never forgot.

Life with their father and stepmother was no happier for Chris and Kermit than life had been with their great-grandmother. Worse, in fact. "At least our great-grandmother loved us," Kermit said. "Barbara couldn't stand us."

There were constant fights. Kermit remembers a time he and Chris were shoveling snow off their walk. Neither had a pair of gloves. When Chris wanted to go inside to warm his hands up, Barbara wouldn't let him in. "She said we couldn't come in until we finished the job," Kermit said. "I was too timid to say anything, but Chris wasn't. They fought all the time."

Throughout their boyhood, Chris was Kermit's protector. Chris was bigger, stronger, smarter, tougher—at least as far as his little brother was concerned. Chris was the one who stood up to Barbara, the one who made good grades in school whenever he wanted to. "Sometimes I'd have a homework assignment I had no chance to get done," Kermit said. "He'd say, 'What will you give me to do that for you?' I couldn't offer him money because we never had any. So I'd tell him I would clean up after all the animals at our grandmother's house, because he hated doing that. He'd take the paper and do it in about two minutes. It was so easy for him, I told him he should feel guilty about taking anything from me for doing it."

But even though he didn't really understand it then, Kermit could see that his older brother was troubled. He had a bedwetting problem that lasted until he was in the ninth grade. "Barbara always told him she was going to hang his sheets out the window so people could see them," Kermit said. "That was about the only time I remember seeing Chris scared."

Chris stopped working in school, although he was still in programs for the gifted. He was accepted at McKinley Tech High School based on his standardized testing. Kermit wasn't in Chris's league when it came to testing. He was scheduled to go to Roosevelt High School. The last thing in the world he wanted to do was go to Roosevelt. "It was smack in the middle of the two gangs," he said. "No matter what route you took to get to school or get home, you had to go through the gangs. I was tired of getting beat up and tired of never having my lunch money. So I lied about where I lived when I filled out the forms to be assigned a high school. I wanted to go to Coolidge, because it was safe at Coolidge. No gangs. No one checked on my address. I got sent to Coolidge."

Washington believes that the lie he told about where he lived may have saved his life. A lot of the kids he went to junior high with died before they ever got out of high school or shortly thereafter. Some joined the gangs; some didn't. Kermit never joined a gang.

"I can still see a lot of those kids I grew up with in my mind's eye," he said. "I remember playing ball with them, being in school with them. They all started out as nice little kids, innocent kids. I could name you a dozen or more who never made it to twenty-one. Killed in gang fights, killed by drugs, killed by police. I was one of the lucky ones."

By the time he got to high school, he was beginning to have some success as an athlete. He was a string bean, over 6 feet tall but weighing less than 140 pounds. He actually played some tennis, in part because his father liked to play, in part because there was so little competition in the D.C. public schools that he could be a star just by getting the ball over the net. "Then at the end of the year we'd be in a tournament with the kids from the suburban schools and I'd get killed," he said.

Chris was emerging as a football star at McKinley Tech, and Kermit played football too. He was a wide receiver and made the Coolidge varsity as a junior. By that point he had grown to 6-4 and was playing some junior varsity basketball, although he didn't start very often. He stuck with basketball for one reason: one of his best friends in school was Glenn Price, the team's best player. Playing basketball gave Kermit the chance to hang out with Price—and it meant he got a ride home every night after practice.

"I wasn't any good at all," he said. "The one thing I could do was jump a little. But I couldn't shoot, I was skinny, I was weak. Occasionally I'd get a rebound or a basket off a rebound because of my jumping, but that was about it."

He continued to struggle in school but was, if nothing else, a determined student. Every summer he would go to summer school, retaking courses to get his grades up. A lot of D's during the year became B's and C's in the summer. In a twisted way, Kermit credits his stepmother with inspiring him to do better in school.

"She was always telling Chris and me that we were worthless," he said. "She would say we would never become anything, that our mother was crazy and stupid. She made Chris angry, very angry. But she made me determined. I was going to prove her wrong. I was going to show her that I wasn't worthless, I wasn't a fool, and I was going to become something."

Like most boys, Chris and Kermit dreamed of becoming star athletes. Their father subscribed to Sports Illustrated, and every week the boys would read the magazine cover to cover, then tear the front cover off and put it on the wall of their room. Every wall in the room and the ceiling were eventually plastered with *Sports Illustrated* covers. "It was wonderful to wake up in that room every morning," Kermit said. "In that room, Chris and I were happy. We'd talk all the time about the day when we would be in that magazine. I came from a world where there were no heroes. The people in that magazine became my heroes."

During Kermit's junior year Chris emerged as a star quarterback at McKinley Tech. He still wasn't doing a lot of schoolwork, but he scored 1150 on the SATs, a remarkable score for an athlete coming out of a D.C. public school. That score got him recruited by a number of schools, and he decided finally to enroll at Texas Western. Both Kermit and Chris were familiar with the school because two years earlier Texas Western had played in the Final Four at the University of Maryland.

With five blacks in the starting lineup, the Miners had stunned all-white Kentucky in the national championship game. That game is regarded by most as the *Brown v. Board of Education* of college basketball. Within two years Kentucky's Adolph Rupp had signed his first black player, and it wasn't long before all the major colleges in the once segregated South were signing black players. The Washington brothers had pulled hard for Texas Western in that championship game, and when Chris had the chance to go there he jumped at it.

Kermit was also starting to do better in school. He had been encouraged and inspired by a biology teacher, Barbara Thomas. Early in the semester during his junior year, Kermit turned in a sloppy assignment, figuring that if he worked hard he might turn his usual D into a D-plus or a C-minus. Miss Thomas was having none of it. She told him that she knew he had it in him to do better if he would just be a little more patient and believe in himself. Kermit began taking more time on assignments, not only in Miss

Thomas's class, but in his other classes too. His grades jumped. Not to A's, not even all B's, but mostly B's with a sprinkling of C's.

When Chris got into college, Kermit decided that was what he wanted to do too. "Since Barbara had told both of us to turn in our house keys as soon as we were out of high school, I certainly had to find something to do," he said. "The problem was, I wasn't as good a student as Chris, I didn't test as well, and I wasn't as good a football player."

He wasn't a bad football player, alternating between wide receiver and quarterback as a senior. Whenever Coolidge needed to throw the ball downfield, he would move to quarterback because of his strong arm. The team was 8–2 that fall and made the D.C. city playoffs. But there were no offers of scholarships from any football schools. There were no offers of any kind.

Things got worse during basketball season. After beginning the year as a starter and getting 16 rebounds in a game, Kermit went backward. He produced less and less as the season wore on and played less and less. By season's end he wasn't playing at all. "And I didn't deserve to be playing either," he said. "I was awful. I had no confidence and no game at all. All I did the last few games was sit on the bench. I was a senior and I couldn't get in a game. My best friend [Price] was being recruited by all these schools and I wasn't even one of the seven or eight best players in my own high school. I was embarrassed."

As soon as the season was over, Kermit headed to the local schoolyards—to play basketball. "I was just so embarrassed by the way I played that I had to do something to try to get better," he said. "It had nothing to do with thinking about my future or anything else like that. I just wanted to get better so I wouldn't make a fool of myself playing ball in the schoolyard."

Onc of the people he encountered in his schoolyard forays was James Brown, who had been the best player in the city that winter. Brown, now a TV star on Fox's NFL pregame show, had gone to junior high school with Washington before attending DeMatha Catholic High School in nearby Hyattsville, Maryland, to play for the legendary Morgan Wootten. Brown had everything going for him that Washington did not: he was graduating from DeMatha, *the* high school program in the area, if not the country. His grades were so good that he had turned down several top basketball schools— including the University of North Carolina—to accept an academic scholarship at Harvard. Washington was awed by everything his old schoolmate had become. When he noticed that Brown skipped rope before and after playing, he asked him about it.

"It's the main reason I can run up and down the court forever," Brown told him. "Jump rope and you'll always have all the stamina you need."

Washington went out and bought a jump rope that day. He began jumping rope every afternoon. His stamina grew and grew. Playing every afternoon on the playground against good players, his game improved. For the first time in his life, he was obsessed with a sport.

"I was better," he said. "But I still wasn't any good. I had so far to go to get good that by improving I just became mediocre as opposed to awful."

Even so, when he heard about citywide tryouts for a D.C. all-star team that would travel to Allentown, Pennsylvania, in the spring to play in an all-star tournament, he decided to go. "To this day I can't tell you why I went," he said. "I knew I couldn't make the team, I wasn't at that level. But they had to let me try out. The rule was, any senior in the city who had played high school basketball was eligible to try out for the team. I just wanted to go and find out how far behind the real players I was."

The tryouts were at St. John's High School in upper Northwest. Washington hitched a ride there for the first day, arriving just in time. The coaches were Wootten and Joe Gallagher. There were a number of college coaches in the stands. Some were just there so that players who had already committed to them would see them there. Some were there because many of the stars were still uncommitted since, in those days, most players didn't make a college decision until late in the spring. And a few were there just hoping to find the proverbial diamond in the rough, the kid who had gone unnoticed and might help a struggling program.

No one was looking harder for an unknown that day than Tom Young and Tom Davis. Young had just become the head coach at American University, a small private school in northwest Washington that wasn't very far from St. John's. He had left the University of Maryland, where he had been an assistant to Frank Fellows, to take the AU job and had brought Tom Davis, Maryland's freshman coach, with him as his number one assistant. American was coming off a 4–19 season, so Young and Davis knew they were starting with a bare cupboard.

Since St. John's was close to AU, Young and Davis decided to go to the tryouts on the off chance that there was a player who hadn't chosen a school yet and wasn't being recruited by the big-name schools. "We weren't expecting very much," Davis said. "It was more about our need to check out anything we could and not having anyplace else to go that day than anything else."

Sitting on the bleachers with the other coaches and a few fans who had drifted in to watch the tryouts, Young and Davis noticed one kid who kept diving on the floor after loose balls. It didn't matter where the ball was or who else was going after it or if he had any reasonable chance to get the ball, the kid would just run and dive, run and dive. He had floor burns all over him.

"He had no idea, I mean absolutely no idea how to play," Young said. "But he could really run and he could really jump. And he was the most eager kid out there."

"He was wearing a white T-shirt, white tennis shorts, white socks, and white tennis shoes," Davis remembered, laughing. "He absolutely looked out of place, in part because of his clothes, in part because he really didn't have any idea what he was supposed to do."

He also seemed to have a small fan club sitting a few rows up from where Young and Davis were sitting, some kids who would get very excited whenever the skinny lunatic would throw his body through the air in pursuit of a ball. Davis moved up a few rows to sit with the skinny kid's friends.

"Who's your friend down there?" he asked.

"You mean Bird?" one of them asked.

Washington's nickname in the neighborhood was Bird because of his long, skinny legs. He had grown to 6-4 by then but still weighed 160 pounds dripping wet.

"Yeah, Bird," Davis said. "Where'd he play this year?"

The kids laughed and told Davis it would be more accurate to say he *hadn't* played at Coolidge High School. The only reason Davis knew anything about Coolidge was because it was where Glenn Price went to school. Price was being recruited by most of the top programs in the East. He went back and told Young they might be on to something, that maybe they had discovered a player no one knew about.

Of course Young and Davis weren't the only ones who had noticed Washington's athleticism. One coach, who told Washington he was from Western New England College, gave him a card after the workout was over and told him if he didn't come back to the second day of tryouts, he would guarantee him a scholarship. Washington was stunned. A scholarship to college—me? To play basketball? Maybe they had him confused with his buddy Price.

No, that wasn't the case. Washington was also approached by Joe Harrington, who was now an assistant coach at Maryland on new coach Lefty Driesell's staff. We might be interested in you, Harrington told him. What's your SAT score? Washington told him 780. "Take it again, get it to 800, and we can offer you a scholarship," Harrington said.

Young and Davis weren't in a position to offer anything. They needed more information. American wasn't governed by the Atlantic Coast Conference's 800 rule, which required any athlete receiving a scholarship to have scored 800 on the SATs. But it was a good academic school, and getting someone with 780 on his boards past admissions would not be easy. But after watching Washington at the second day of tryouts, they were convinced he was worth the risk.

When Wootten and Gallagher selected the team for Allentown that day, Washington didn't make it. "Which was the right thing to do," Washington said. "I couldn't play with those guys. They were better than me."

Young laughs now at the notion of Washington not making that team. "Morgan and Joe have spent the last thirty years arguing about who decided to cut him," Young said. "But he really was *so* raw. You could see potential, but Morgan and Joe weren't choosing a team for a couple years down the road, they were choosing a team for next week."

Young and Davis decided to do whatever they could to get Washington into school. "We weren't going to be very good the next year, we knew that," Young said. "Players were not knocking our doors down to come and play. Remember, in those days everyone had to play freshman ball, so we knew he'd have a year to learn to play before he had to play with the varsity. Was it a risk? Sure. But when we talked to him, it was so apparent that this was a quality kid. He looked you in the eye when he talked. He was confident, clearly smart."

"A lot of times high school kids, especially ballplayers who have been spoiled, have trouble giving up more than two or three words to people," Davis said. "Kermit was just the opposite. He was positively loquacious."

Still, Young and Davis needed to get his transcript. What they saw was encouraging: the SATs were low, but the grades were pretty good—mostly B's and C's. "Not spectacular," Young said. "But worth a shot."

Washington is convinced that if all the D's he had made as a freshman and sophomore had been on his record, he never would have gotten into AU. "Those summer school classes I took to get my grades up probably saved me," he said.

His father was pushing him to reconsider Maryland's offer, take the SATs again, and try to get 800. Maryland was a name he was familiar with; American University was not, even though it was not that far away from where the Washingtons lived. "Not that far, but a million miles," Washington said. "It was on the other side of Rock Creek Park. That was our version of the railroad tracks. I had never been on the other side of the park in my life."

Except for those two days when he had hitched to St. John's. Urged by his father, Washington went out to College Park to meet Driesell. He liked the tall, bald, blustery coach, who had arrived at Maryland vowing to make the school "the UCLA of the East." Driesell was honest with Washington: they had a couple of extra scholarships and they needed to fill out the roster of the freshman team. He might have a chance to play on the varsity as a junior or a senior, but he would have to improve a lot, because Driesell was planning to recruit the best high school players in the country.

"I didn't feel needed at Maryland," he said. "Lefty was very honest, and I appreciated that. But Coach Young and Coach Davis made me feel needed."

The admissions office at AU was far from certain that the school needed a student with Washington's transcript—especially on a full ride. Young and Davis didn't have the advantage of having been at the school long enough to have developed relationships with the admissions people. "We ended up basically saying, 'Look, you have to trust us, we've talked to the kid and we think he can make it here,'" Young said. "At one point, Tom and I walked out of a meeting and I said to him, 'Do you realize we're in there begging for a kid who averaged four points a game and didn't even start as a senior in high school?' But something told both of us it was the right thing to do."

Admissions finally relented and told Young and Davis that Washington would be accepted. They were elated. Joe Boylan, the newly hired freshman coach who would be Washington's coach in the fall, was dispatched to Farragut Street to bring Washington to campus, show him around, help him find a dorm, and buy him dinner. "Coach Boylan took me to a restaurant for dinner and told me to order anything I wanted," Washington said. "I ordered a steak. I think that was the first time in my life I'd had a steak in a restaurant."

Very few of his friends had any idea what American was, but Washington didn't care. He was going to college and he had a scholarship. In that sense at least he had matched Chris, who was completing his freshman year at Texas Western and had already been told he was no longer a quarterback but a defensive back. Even at the school that had started five black basketball players in the national championship game in 1966, there was no call, three years later, for a black quarterback.

Washington felt as if he had been given a new life. He would be out of the house, away from Barbara and all the talk about what a loser he was. He had gotten away from the gangs and he had lived through the schoolyard beatings and the threats. He had seen others knifed to death and shot to death. Now he was leaving. He was going to the other side of the park, where there were no gangs, no shootings, and no Barbara. He would eat steak in restaurants and he would play basketball and go to college.

"When I played, or didn't play, my last high school basketball game, if you had told me I'd be getting a scholarship to play basketball in college a couple of months later, I would have told you that you were crazy," he said. "It really was like a dream. All those nights when Chris and I would sit in our room and tell each other we were going to get out, that the way out was going to be sports and we were going to be in *Sports Illustrated* someday.

"It was all fantasy stuff, kids talking because the actual reality of our lives was so depressing. But now, all of a sudden, here it was. College, a scholarship, the whole deal. Every morning I woke up and said to myself, 'Is this really happening to you?'"

9

Welfare Memories

When Rudy Tomjanovich coached the Houston Rockets to their first NBA title, in 1994, most of the profiles written about him described "the shoemaker's son."

They were not inaccurate. Rudolph Tomjanovich Sr. was a shoemaker early in Rudolph Tomjanovich Jr.'s life, and the son still has memories of watching his father work on people's shoes in the small store he had a few blocks from the house where the family lived in Hamtramck, Michigan, a decidedly blue-collar area of Detroit. "Blue-collar" is white for "inner city."

Rudy Tomjanovich Sr. came to Detroit from Calumet, a small town in Michigan's northern peninsula, as a young man and got a job in an automobile factory. Since he was of Croatian descent, his pals decided to set him up with Catherine Modich, a young woman who worked on the other side of the factory and whose family background was also Croatian. They were married soon after they met.

Born November 24, 1948, Rudy Jr. was the first child of Rudy and Catherine Tomjanovich, eighteen months older than his sister, Frances. He has almost no early memories of his father, because his parents were separated for long stretches shortly after he was born. "I still have this memory from a morning when I was about four years old," he said. "I went into my mother's room and there was a man sleeping in her bed. I really wasn't sure at first who it was. Then she told me it was my dad. After that, he stayed for a long time, and I can remember being very, very happy about it."

Money was very tight in the Tomjanovich home at all times. Rudy Sr. worked as a shoemaker for a while, but there were also times when he was unemployed. Health problems, specifically problems with his back, often caused him to spend stretches of time in the VA hospital. At other times he picked up garbage for the city. Often he wasn't home at night. It wasn't until he was much older that Rudy figured out why.

"My father drank," he said. "Back then, you never labeled someone an alcoholic. You never talked about rehab or anything like that. In Hamtramck there were four bars on every block. It was a tough life there day-to-day, and people went into the bars and drank. I first started going into the bars and drinking when I was fifteen. No one was going to turn you down, because if they did you'd just go to the next place. They needed the business."

Hamtramck was every bit as tough a place to grow up as the inner city of Washington, D.C. There weren't any gangs, but there was plenty of drinking and fighting, and street violence wasn't uncommon. "I remember Rudy telling me recruiters didn't want to come into his neighborhood to see him because they were afraid the windows of their cars would get smashed," Calvin Murphy said. "He never talked about it much, but I know it wasn't an easy way of life. It's just not like him to make a big deal about it."

In fact, in his autobiography Tomjanovich talks lovingly about both his parents; about his mother's warmth and his father's generosity. He says more than once that "I wouldn't have traded my childhood for the world." Only later would he come to understand how deeply his childhood had affected him.

At times, when his father was unemployed, the Tomjanovich family went on welfare. His father had bought a small TV set—"I think it may have been hot, which is why he could afford it," Tomjanovich said—and the family always kept the TV on a counter in the kitchen behind some curtains. The reason for the curtains was simple: if you were on welfare, you weren't supposed to have a TV. The curtains were there in case a welfare inspector came to the house. One afternoon when Rudy was home alone watching TV, there was a knock on the door.

"Come on in, it's open," Rudy shouted.

The door opened and a welfare inspector was standing there. Whoops.

"I guess the guy didn't want me to get in trouble with my parents or something," Rudy said. "Because he didn't turn us in. I kept the front door locked after that if I was watching TV."

In his autobiography Tomjanovich writes about how embarrassed he would feel when he and his father would have to go across town to pick up the food provided to families on welfare. They would put the packages of food on a trolley and cart it back to their house. Pushing the trolley through the streets, Tomjanovich felt as if all eyes were on them, knowing where the generic packages came from.

"It was very embarrassing," he said. "I always felt like people were labeling us as failures because we were on welfare. The only thing that made it bearable was the fact that the food was better than anything else we ever ate."

There weren't a lot of kids Rudy's age in his neighborhood, so he often walked a couple of blocks over to DeQuindre Street, where there were plenty of kids to play with. Most of them were black, including his three best friends. It never occurred to Rudy that he was doing anything unusual until one afternoon when he and his pals were playing stickball in front of his house. A neighbor was walking by, and when Rudy waved in her direction, she looked away from him and thrust her nose upward as if to say, "I'm not going to talk to you when you're playing with *them.*"

The memory stayed with Tomjanovich for years. "There just wasn't any question that she was looking down on me because I was playing with black kids," he said. "I felt so humiliated at the time, as if something was wrong with *me.* Of course later I understood that the problem was hers, not mine. But being a young kid at the time with no understanding of things like that, it all sort of fell on me.

"The funny thing, looking back, is that I can't be *certain* that's what she was doing. Maybe she didn't even see me. Maybe she was looking up at the sky to see if it was raining. But standing there in the street that day, there was no doubt in my mind that she was sticking her nose in the air at me because I was playing with three black kids."

Now Tomjanovich understands the incident was part of a pattern that shaped him. He understood that his family was poor: the welfare food, sharing a house with his grandparents, his father changing jobs or not having a job. When he was a little older, he heard whispers around the neighborhood about his father's drinking. He knew his father wasn't the only person in Hamtramck with a drinking problem, not by a long shot, but nonetheless the whispers hurt. He vowed then that no one would ever whisper about him that way.

Always he felt put down, as if the world was collectively looking down its nose at him the way the woman in the street had that day. He would prove them all wrong. He would prove that he had—his word—*value.* He wasn't going to be just another poor kid whose parents had met in the factories of Detroit who grew up and went to work in a factory too.

And so he became the most driven kid in his school. Often driven kids are the product of driven parents. They have to succeed because no matter how much they succeed, it isn't enough to please their parents. But Rudy and Cathie Tomjanovich weren't like that at all. As long as their children stayed out of trouble, they were happy. "My guess is they would have been perfectly happy if I had just grown up and gone to work in a factory," Rudy said. "I think in some ways they worried about me moving away, going out into a world they didn't know anything about."

Rudy's drive came from within. It came from the looks he and his father got wheeling the welfare food through the streets. Or from the looks he *thought* they got. It came from the woman with the turned-up nose. It came from the whispers about his dad.

"I had to make A's in school," he said. "That was the way I proved my worth. Later, sports came into it, but at first it was just school."

Every single week in school was a new challenge, another opportunity to fail if he didn't make A's. Sunday nights, before going to bed, Rudy and his family would watch *The Ed Sullivan Show* and then *What's My Line?* As *What's My Line?* moved into its final minutes, Rudy could feel his stomach twisting into a knot. The end of the show meant it was time to go to bed. When he woke up it would be Monday morning. The start of another week in school. He *had* to do well that week, he couldn't fail. He wouldn't have anyone looking at him and thinking he wasn't a good student, thinking that he had no value. Every Sunday night was the same: *Ed Sullivan; What's My Line?;* stomachache.

"The worst part was, there wasn't really anybody I could talk to about it," Tomjanovich said. "My parents didn't understand. All they knew was I was making good grades in school and they were happy about that. My friends didn't understand, they just wanted to get out of school every day and go play. So it all just sat inside me all the time."

As he grew older, sports became his other outlet, the other venue where he could prove his worth. He played baseball first. He had a cousin, Mark Modich, who was two years older than he was who played on a team that won the Little League World Series when Rudy was ten. One of the coaches of that team was Mark's father, Joe Modich, Rudy's uncle. It was Uncle Joe who coached Rudy, bought him equipment, and encouraged him. It was also Uncle Joe who saw sports as a way out of Hamtramck for Rudy. "You've got good grades," he would tell his nephew. "If you keep them up and you excel at a sport, you can go to college on a scholarship."

The only problem, at least in Rudy's mind, was that he wasn't that good a baseball player. He was okay, good enough to make all-star teams as a twelve-year-old. But there were certain players—his cousin included—who were clearly on a different level. In all probability, he would have become a very good baseball player if he had continued to play. He hadn't hit his big growth spurt and wouldn't until he was a junior in high school. He was a talented athlete with a great work ethic. But something told him baseball wasn't what he wanted to do, that it wasn't his sport. The toughest problem was telling his uncle Joe, who had worked so hard to help make him a baseball player.

"Rudy, I really think you need a sport," his uncle said when Rudy finally worked up the courage to talk to him about not playing baseball anymore.

"I know," Rudy answered. "I've got one. Basketball."

He had never played the game in any organized fashion, but the bug had bitten him. He liked the fact that he could play alone if he wanted to, that he didn't need any equipment other than a ball and a net to play. In many ways the solitude of going off on your own with no one watching, no one grading you or judging you, to just work on your shot or your game had great appeal to him. Something inside told him this was the right sport for him.

"Of course the funny thing about it was, I wasn't any good at the time," he said. "But I wanted to play. I really wanted to play."

And he wanted to get good. He had been good at baseball, but not good enough. He felt he had seen his ceiling and it wasn't high enough. In basketball he had no idea how high the ceiling was, because he had never really worked at the game, never been coached the way he had been in baseball.

He began spending all his free time hanging out at The Courts. The Courts were located in the schoolyard at Copernicus Junior High School. As with all local basketball meccas, no one knew exactly why they had become *the* place for basketball players to gather. "It was smack in the middle of a white neighborhood," Tomjanovich remembered. "But guys from all over the city, most of them black, always came to play there. Maybe it was because you knew you were safe coming in and out of the area. I never did figure it out."

Like all places where multiple games are being played throughout the day and night, The Courts had a pecking order. There were two L-shaped basket supports that were reserved for the high-end games. Adjacent were three rims with straight-pole supports. The quality of play was best at the first of the L-support hoops, and it moved down to beginners at the far end of the yard. Everyone knew which court he belonged on. If you began to stand out on one court, it was time to try your luck at the next court. There you had to prove yourself again.

Tomjanovich began to move up in the pecking order. He was soon playing with older kids and fitting in as his game matured. When he wasn't at The Courts, he would find a rim near his house and work on his own. It was as if he had never played baseball.

He had a setback in his freshman year at Hamtramck High School when he didn't make the cut for the freshman team. He was stunned, hurt, disbelieving. In a now-famous story that has been told and retold in every profile ever written about him, Tomjanovich challenged the freshman basketball coach to a game of one-on-one, the deal being if he won the game, he would get a spot on the team.

He lost the game. And made the team. "He saw how much it meant to me," Tomjanovich has always said in retelling the story.

There are many stories about great athletes dealing with failure at an early age. The one told most often has Michael Jordan being cut from his high school team as a sophomore. Jordan was actually sent down to the junior varsity, but the point of the story is how he dealt with the notion of failure. The best athletes have an extra gear of drive that seems to kick in when they are challenged or, more specifically, when they are told they aren't good enough. Tomjanovich believed he had been considered not good enough his entire life. Many teenagers, after working as hard at a sport as Tomjanovich had at basketball, would have been crushed if they had been told they weren't good enough to play freshman ball. It had the opposite effect on Tomjanovich: it made him want to work even harder.

Making the freshman team as an act of charity wasn't enough for Rudy. He felt as if he was back in the streets being looked down upon either for carting welfare food with his dad or for playing with his black friends. That same knot started crawling into his stomach before practice, the one he had felt watching *What's My Line?* He had to prove himself, he had to show the coach and the other players that he had value. He just had to.

The growth spurt from his freshman year to his junior year made a difference. He went from 6-1 to 6-6 without any noticeable loss of coordination. His jump shot, which he had worked on so hard for so many hours, improved steadily. More important, he was growing into his body. He was still skinny, but he was becoming an excellent leaper, someone who could not only jump high but could jump quickly. He became a starter on the junior varsity as a sophomore and began to show signs of becoming a real player.

At the end of that season, he made some switches in his schedule so he could be in a gym class with the varsity players. One afternoon John Radwinski, the varsity coach, asked him why he was in the class. When Tomjanovich explained he was hoping to hone his skills playing against better, more experienced players, Radwinski told him he was in the wrong place at the wrong time.

"If you're thinking of coming out for the varsity next season, don't bother," he said. "You'd just be wasting your time."

Radwinski was one of those tough-guy, old-school, tough-love coaches. Tomjanovich would come to understand that later. At that moment, though, he was rocked. Again he was being told he wasn't any good, he had no value. It made him work even harder, to the point of obsession, at the game. The next fall he not only made the team but became a starter and a star. Radwinski never mentioned the gym-class comment. No doubt he thought he had done a great job motivating the insecure kid to become a better player. Whether Tomjanovich needed any extra motivation was questionable, but Radwinski had certainly supplied it.

By this time Rudy had become one of the star players at The Courts. There are always schoolyard stories that people tell and retell through the years. Tomjanovich's involved Reggie Harding, a local legend who was playing for the Detroit Pistons while Rudy was in high school. One afternoon, as the story goes, Harding and his pals showed up at The Courts looking to play. As luck would have it, Tomjanovich and two of his friends had winners on court one when Harding and company arrived.

Harding was clowning and preening throughout most of the game, which, as with most half-court games, was played to 11. Tomjanovich's team hung close until Harding started to use his size (almost 7 feet) and bulk (about 250 to Tomjanovich's 175) to control the game. But near the end of the game, Harding grabbed a defensive rebound and held the ball up with one hand, his back to Tomjanovich. Before he knew what had happened, Tomjanovich had come in from behind, snatched the ball from Harding's hand, and in one motion dunked it.

"The place went nuts," Tomjanovich said, smiling at the memory thirty-five years later. "People were screaming and clapping. I loved it. Reggie didn't. He immediately claimed that he had actually tipped it in, that it was his basket."

The argument wasn't going very well, as Tomjanovich tells the story, until one of the older men watching from the stands walked onto the court, pointed a finger in Harding's face, and said, "It can't be your basket. You never brought the ball back out [beyond the foul line] after the missed shot. The boy dunked on you. Admit it."

Harding gave in. Then he backed Tomjanovich in the next three possessions and dunked on him to end the game. Still, Tomjanovich had had his moment. "He couldn't take that away," he said, "no matter how many times he dunked on me."

Basketball moments were becoming more and more frequent for Tomjanovich by then. Even though he had become a star on his high school team, he still didn't see himself that way. He didn't get a lot of feedback from his parents, because they weren't basketball fans. In fact the first time his father came to a game, he walked in during the junior varsity game. Spotting a seat on the other side of the gym that looked good to him, he just wandered across the court while play was going on. Apparently, since he didn't see his son playing he didn't think the real game had started yet.

What's more, unlike today's athlete, who is coddled and told how wonderful he is from the moment he shows any skill, Tomjanovich wasn't receiving a lot of kudos. He wasn't drowning in recruiting letters or being flown around the country courtesy of various shoe companies.

If this had been the twenty-first century instead of the late 1960s, he would have been going to all-star summer camps, playing AAU ball around the country, and getting recruiting pitches from all the big-time college programs. But this was a different time. Recruiting was far more regional. Occasionally a superstar might go from one coast to the other, the way Lew Alcindor did in 1965, when he left New York City to enroll at UCLA. But that was rare. Most players stayed close to home, because there were no national camps to be seen in, no recruiting newsletters, and very few budgets that allowed coaches to travel more than a couple of hundred miles from their campus.

These days players start getting letters from colleges in eighth or ninth grade. Most have narrowed their choice of schools to a short list by the start of their junior year. Many announce their college decision as juniors or, at the very latest, early in their senior year.

That wasn't the way it was when Tomjanovich finished his junior year at Hamtramck in the spring of 1965. He had played well as a junior, and he would grow to 6-8 by the start of his senior year. But it wouldn't be until midway through his senior season that he would begin to think about colleges or they would begin to think seriously about him. He was pretty certain at this point that he would get a scholarship to go to school someplace. But he had no idea where that would be.

As it turned out he could have gone just about anyplace he wanted. As a senior he averaged 34 points a game—by then Radwinski didn't seem to think he was wasting his time—and being 6-8 with a jump shot to twenty feet and a 3.5 grade point average, he was every college coach's dream recruit. "The letters started coming in from everywhere," he said. "I had never thought of myself as that kind of player."

He narrowed his list to four schools in the Midwest: Michigan, Michigan State, Detroit, and Toledo. The reason Toledo made the list was that Tomjanovich's high school teammate and friend John Brisker (who would later play in the NBA) was there. Detroit, which was a basketball power in the 1960s, would mean staying at home.

The national schools showed genuine interest, notably coach Guy V. Lewis at Houston, who already had Elvin Hayes in his starting lineup. But for a kid who had never traveled anywhere, the idea of going far from home was pretty much out of the question. He ended up choosing between the two in-state Big Ten schools:

Michigan State and Michigan. He liked them both. He liked both coaches, Dave Strack at Michigan and John Bennington at Michigan State.

He actually felt more comfortable on campus at Michigan State. The students, it seemed to him, were more like the kids he had grown up with in Hamtramck, middle-class, blue-collar city kids like him. Michigan had more rich kids, more kids from out of state, and, this being the sixties, a noticeable hippie population. Tomjanovich had heard about hippies, but he had never seen one before.

"I was sort of fascinated by them," he said. "They were just so different from me. It seemed as if they were from another world."

In the end, Michigan won out for two reasons: it was closer to Hamtramck and it was, after all, the University of Michigan. Like most kids growing up in Michigan, Tomjanovich had fantasized about wearing the famous maize-and-blue uniform. Michigan was a national power in the midsixties, having gone to the Final Four in 1965 led by the great Cazzie Russell. The Wolverines had beaten the famous Bill Bradley–led Princeton team in the semifinals before losing to UCLA in the championship game. Tomjanovich wanted to be a part of that tradition. Michigan became an obvious choice.

But it wasn't an easy choice. The easy choice would have been Michigan State, which didn't have the tradition to live up to that Michigan did. Tomjanovich wasn't completely convinced he was good enough to be a star at Michigan, but he knew he had to go there and find out. He had come a long way, from being cut from the freshman team to being recruited by all the national powers.

Now, though, he was starting over. He would be just another freshman at Michigan with gaudy high school numbers. He would be in a new place, back on square one, an unknown in a school with thousands and thousands of students. He would have to prove himself to everyone: teachers, classmates, teammates.

Again.

10

Dreams Can Come True

It is a very good bet that there was no freshman on the campus of American University in the fall of 1969 who was happier to be there than Kermit Washington. He was only a few miles from the house on Farragut Street N.W., but he might as well have been on another planet.

"It was the first time in my entire life that I felt wanted," he said. "It was the first time I didn't dread going home at night. I can remember hearing myself laugh at night, talking to people in the dorm and thinking, 'What's that sound?' It was me, laughing, having fun."

He was understandably nervous about how he would fit in at AU. His SAT scores were about 350 points lower than those of the average freshman at the school, and his grades were also considerably lower than most. That was only a small concern, though; he believed that if he worked hard at his classes, he would do just fine. It was the cultural gap that concerned him more. Most AU kids were from upper middle-class to upper-class backgrounds. They had traveled, been places in their lives. Washington's only real memory of travel was the trip he and Chris had made with their mother as little boys.

The coaches were also concerned with how he would fit in. They knew he was an academic risk and admissions would be watching very closely to see how he did. They were convinced he would fit in socially, because he was bright and articulate. Classwork worried them.

It was Tom Davis who came up with the idea of getting Washington to enroll in a weight-training class. "I did it for two reasons," he said. "One, I knew it would help his basketball a lot to put a little muscle on his body. Two, I figured he could use a relatively easy course, since the school didn't have a lot of them."

Little did Davis know that he had opened a door that would change Washington's life forever. He was still at a stage where he was growing into his body as a freshman, and getting in the weight room accelerated the process. He became friends with a Ph.D. candidate named Trey Coleman, who had played football at Nebraska. Coleman—Big Trey to all his friends—took Washington under his wing, teaching him how to work with weights, how to push himself beyond what he thought were his limits, and how to work hard consistently rather than in spurts.

"He was a very serious guy," Washington said. "He would come to the games and say to me things like, 'Young man, I want you to go out there and work hard tonight for all forty minutes.' I can remember not wanting to disappoint him."

Since freshmen couldn't play varsity ball back then (the rule allowing freshmen to play was enacted in 1972), Washington played on the freshman team, coached by Joe Boylan. It was quickly apparent to Boylan, as it had been to Tom Young and Tom Davis, that Washington was as talented as he was unpolished. "He would make great plays and awful plays," Boylan remembered. "Sometimes at the same time. I remember in one game, he made spectacular steals and dunks on two plays in a couple of minutes. There was just one problem: he dunked on *our* basket."

All three coaches learned another thing quickly: Washington was not a player who responded well to yelling and screaming. He would not, for example, have done very well playing for John Radwinski, Rudy Tomjanovich's high school coach.

"When I got on guys, it was to motivate them, to try to get them to work harder," Young said. "I figured out almost right away that you didn't do that with Kermit, for two reasons. First, he was going to work hard no matter what you did. Second, if you did yell at him, he was going to take it personally and sulk and play worse. I remember one day after practice he came to me and said, 'Coach, you don't have to yell at me. Just tell me what you want me to do and I'll do it.' He wasn't kidding."

As raw as he was as a player, Washington improved with astonishing speed. He was still growing: by the end of his freshman year he was up to 6-7 and his weight was at 200 pounds and climbing. He became the best player on the freshman team, giving Young and his coaches hope for the future after the varsity finished the season 11–12. That was certainly an improvement on 4–19, but not what Young ultimately had in mind.

As well as he did in basketball as a freshman, Washington did even better off the court. His theory that hard work would pay off in the classroom proved correct. By the end of first semester, he had a regimen: classes in the morning; weight room after lunch; practice; dinner; study; jump rope; bed. "If you knew what time it was, you knew where I was on any given day," he said. "I would go out on the weekends sometimes, but on weekdays and weeknights it was the same routine every single day."

His obsession with weights reached a point that Young left orders that he wasn't to be allowed in the weight room on game days. Washington didn't want to miss a single day; Young wanted him rested when there was a game to play. "I got around him, though," Washington said. "I had a key made and went in there before anyone was in there. It would have bothered me all day if I missed, even on a game day."

Socially, Washington fit in from the start, but things got much better when he met Pat Carter, a petite, striking freshman from

Long Island. Pat Carter's grades were good enough to get her into almost any college she wanted. Her older sister was at Barnard and would go on from there to Harvard Medical School. Pat's dream was to become a U.S. senator. Since AU had one of the best government schools in the country and she thought Washington, D.C., would be a nice place to go to school, she chose AU.

The story of how she ended up meeting Kermit is a complicated one. It happened because of a friend of a friend who had once dated someone who knew another friend of Kermit's—or something like that. In any event, they were eventually set up to meet at the concession stands at halftime of a varsity basketball game after Kermit had played in the freshman game. Pat, who was as loquacious as Kermit was quiet, took one look at Kermit and said the first thing that came into her head: "My, you certainly are skinny."

That was pretty much the end of Dream Date I. "He sulked the rest of the night," she said. "He thought I had insulted him. I didn't mean it as an insult, he was just *very* skinny. I felt bad about it because I had hurt his feelings. The next day I saw him reading a book and I tried to talk to him. He wasn't having any of it. Later that night a couple of my friends and I went over to his room and we put on some music. I remember singing 'Lucy in the Sky with Diamonds.' For some reason that loosened him up, and he started talking a little bit.

"To be honest, I think his interest in me at the start had more to do with my brain than anything else. He said he needed help with his schoolwork, and I was able to give it to him. I had the feeling that was the reason he was seeing me. Then one day I told him that my roommate had set me up with someone else and I was going to go out with him. He said, 'That's fine as long as you help me with my paper,' and walked away. Then the next day he told me if I went out with this other guy, he would be very upset, that he wouldn't be able to see me anymore. I said, 'Even if I help you with your papers?' He said, 'Even if you help me with my papers.' That was the first time he really admitted that he liked me."

Kermit and Pat became inseparable soon after that. The coaches were delighted. Pat was smart and fun, made Kermit happy, and had a worldliness that he lacked.

"She was perfect for him," Tom Davis said. "It was one of those relationships you knew right away was built to last. Kermit was lucky to find her."

The coaches were feeling pretty lucky to have found Washington by the end of his freshman season. His game had developed rapidly, although it was still pretty basic: catch the ball in the low post, turn and shoot, and then go chase the rebound. His quickness made him very difficult to box out, and he probably got as many points off offensive rebounds as he did out of the offense. By the time Kermit returned for his sophomore year, his weight was up to 215 and he was 6-8.

There was no doubt in anyone's mind that he would be AU's starting center. In those days American played in the Middle Atlantic Conference, a forerunner of what became the East Coast Conference, a very competitive league that included traditional eastern powerhouse basketball schools like Temple and La Salle. The Eagles also played all the local schools in the D.C. area: Maryland, Georgetown, and George Washington. This was before the proliferation of conferences changed the pecking order in college basketball. AU was on a level similar to Georgetown and GW, though below Maryland, which was part of the Atlantic Coast Conference and was becoming a national power under Lefty Driesell.

Washington was American's best player as a sophomore. He led the team in scoring and rebounding, and the team's record improved to 13–12. The Eagles were competitive almost every night because it was almost impossible to keep Washington off the offensive boards. "Some nights our offense was simple: throw it up and let Kermit go get it," Young said. "It was an amazing thing to watch. Two years earlier he had been running around the gym at St. John's in those white shorts with no idea how to play. Now he'd become the second leading rebounder in the country."

In fact only Artis Gilmore, the 7-foot-1 center at Jacksonville, the NCAA runner-up that season, averaged more rebounds per game than Washington. The Eagles had no on-campus gym back then, just a small practice facility. They played their home games— as did George Washington until it built an on-campus gym in the midseventies—across the Potomac River in the ancient gym on the army base at Fort Myer, Virginia.

The Fort, as it was called, was like no other home court in the country. American's "locker room" was actually the weight room. Players would drape their clothes across weights and sit on various machines to listen to the coach's pregame talk. Some nights the heat worked. Other nights it didn't. Most nights there was no hot water in the showers. On one occasion the visiting coach, after a controversial call had cost his team the game, got so angry that he smashed a hole in the wall, walking off the court. A few minutes later there was a knock on the "visiting" weight room door. It was the military police, there to arrest him for damaging government property.

As the team got better, AU students and fans flocked to the Fort, which could seat about 3,000 people if the fire marshals weren't looking. (How could they look? It was a military base.) Washington became a folk hero on campus and, even more amazingly, in his old neighborhood. High school buddies of his, many of them looking for work or waiting to be drafted—America's military engagement in Vietnam had not yet ended—would show up at the games to cheer him on.

"I was their hero," he said matter-of-factly. "They came because they were living through me. I was living the dream every kid in my neighborhood had growing up. I had gotten out. I was going to college, getting an education. I was a basketball star. People who wouldn't even look at me when I was in high school wanted to be my friend now. It was a whole new world."

And a new life. After all the years of feeling inferior, of feeling unwanted in his own home, thinking that he was a nobody born to a mentally ill mother, he had become someone. To most people at AU, Kermit was the guy everyone wanted to be friends with. As he became a bigger and bigger star, he became more outgoing and confident. About the only person who could sense the hurt he still felt from boyhood was Pat, the person he spent the most time with.

"It was very hard for him to show affection," she said. "Sometimes I would ask him directly if he really cared about me, and he would say something like, 'I think you're really nice.' It was hard for him to be more open than that. He had never been nurtured, never really been loved. I came to believe that if I nurtured him, if I loved him enough, he would get past all that. But I don't believe he ever really did.

"I was important to him. He cared about me. He needed me. But in some ways I was more the mother he felt he had never had than his girlfriend or his wife. He was happy in those years at AU, very happy, but it wasn't because he was with me. I was just part of the fabric.

"We would go to a party, sure . . . after he shot his hundred jump shots. There were two things that drove Kermit in those years: the adulation he got from being the star of the basketball team and the thought that he might play in the NBA. Once that became a real possibility, it was the driving force in his life more than anything or anyone. The strange thing is, as hard as he was working, all the hours he put in, all the obsessing, all the questions about 'am I good enough, how do I get better?' I missed what was going on. Because I thought when all was said and done, we'd graduate, he might play a little bit of ball somewhere, but then he'd go on to law school and we would go on with our lives."

Most of these thoughts didn't come to Pat until much later, when the marriage began to deteriorate. Back then she saw Kermit as a work in progress, someone she loved being with, someone who was smart and kind and good-hearted. That was enough for her. And she believed that loving him all day, every day, would be enough for him. She knew then that basketball was his passion. She thought as they grew older that would change.

It never really did.

It was during his sophomore year that it first occurred to Kermit that he might be able to play basketball for a living. He had averaged 18 rebounds a game against good competition, and he knew he was still learning and improving. And growing. By the time he came back for his junior year, his weight was closing in on 240. He was also starting to get a lot of publicity, much of it courtesy of Marc Splaver, American's bright young sports information director.

Splaver, who had graduated from AU in 1970, knew a good story when he saw one. He began peppering the local media with stories about Washington; about how the coaches had discovered him almost by accident; about how he had completely remade his body in two years; about how he had come to school as a shaky student and was consistently making A's and B's. Kermit loved the media attention Splaver was able to get him, and he and Splaver became close friends.

The team continued to improve during Washington's junior year. By now some of the recruiting work done by Young and Davis was starting to pay off. Davis had left to become the head coach at Lafayette, but the recruiting roots he had laid were starting to take hold. The team was built around D.C. area kids—Wilbur Thomas and Pete DeHaven from northern Virginia and Johnny Lloyd from D.C. And the star was from D.C. too.

The Fort had now become the place to be whenever the Eagles were at home. During that 1971–72 season there were victories over Syracuse, Georgetown, Rhode Island, and Navy, and over George Washington twice. By season's end AU was 16–8, the school's best record since it had played Division II ball in the early sixties. There was talk around campus that the team might receive a bid to the National Invitation Tournament. In those days, an NIT bid was a big deal, since only twenty-five teams made it into the NCAA tournament and sixteen got into the NIT, many of them nationally ranked teams. (These days sixty-five teams make the NCAA field and forty go to the NIT.)

"If it were now, we would have had a chance to go to the NCAAs that year, and we certainly would have been in the NIT," Washington said. "But there were forty-one spots, not a hundred and five. That makes a big difference."

The Eagles went uninvited, which was disappointing. But all the key players, most notably Washington, were returning for another season.

Maybe.

The American Basketball Association had come into existence in 1967, and since the NBA did not then allow underclassmen into its draft (until the courts ordered them to, in 1973), the ABA did. Most of the players who left college early were academically suspect or were offered what was then considered mind-boggling money: multiyear contracts worth six figures a season. Washington had been spotted by scouts from the ABA and was coveted by Lou Carnesecca, the former St. John's University coach who was then the coach of the New York Nets.

This was before agents had become major factors on campus, luring players away from school. Even though Washington was now receiving national attention because of the numbers he was putting up, his life wasn't anything like a comparable student-athlete's would be now. If he were in college now, he would be surrounded by an entourage every time he left the locker room. He would have agents, or their bird-dogs, lined up to buy him dinner or a drink. He would be told repeatedly how he was wasting his time in college. Why play for nothing, he would hear constantly, when you can play for big bucks next year in The League? Even someone as level-headed as Washington might be tempted.

Washington's entourage most nights consisted of Pat, a couple of friends from the dorm, and Josh Rosenfeld, who had become a team manager as a freshman and was one year behind Kermit in school. He rarely stayed out late, and he didn't drink or smoke. Occasionally his pals would encourage him to try a beer. He had no interest.

"I never even considered it," he said. "It didn't fit in with who I was or with where I was trying to go."

By then where he was trying to go was clear: the NBA. "It became my obsession," he said. "I had become a basketball player. That was what I was and who I was, it was my identity. I did well in school because I worked at it, and it never occurred to me not to get my degree in four years—back then, everyone did—but I never gave any thought after my sophomore year to doing anything after college except play basketball. It was as if my full name became 'Kermit Washington, basketball star.' That's who I was to people who met me, and to myself."

At the end of his junior season, Kermit Washington, basketball star, had the chance to turn pro. The Nets called Tom Young and told him they would be willing to offer Washington a four-year deal for $400,000—guaranteed. Young knew that $400, much less $400,000, was a lot of money to Washington, and he would not have been the least bit surprised if Washington had been bowled over by such an offer. After all, the Nets were offering someone who had never had any money at all financial security beyond his wildest dreams to do the thing he loved best.

He called Washington into his office one afternoon and told him what the Nets were offering. He said he would understand if Kermit felt he had to take the money. Washington looked at him as if he were from another planet.

"That's a great offer, Coach," he said. "Please tell them thank you very much, I'm very flattered. But I'm not leaving school."

Young was stunned. He had expected that at the very least Kermit would want some time to think about the offer. He hugged him and told him he was convinced he was going to have a great senior season and be a high draft pick. He had not said that to him *before* his mind was made up because he didn't want to appear to be trying to influence his decision.

"It was a lot of money, no doubt about that," Washington said years later. "But leave AU? There was no way. I had never been happier in my entire life than I was there. I knew we were going to have a good team my senior year, and I was excited about that. There was no way I was going to leave my friends behind. It actually surprised me that Coach Young thought I might leave."

"Looking back, maybe I underestimated Kermit's maturity level a little bit," Young said. "I knew what his financial situation was, and I thought that kind of money would tempt him. But he was always about things more important than money—even when he didn't have any money."

Washington finished the school year with a grade point average of 3.4 and was chosen as an academic All-American. In the meantime, Marc Splaver was positioning him to take a run at being an All-American in basketball the following season. Splaver knew the chances of a player from a school like American making All-American were not great. Very few people outside the East Coast had any idea what American University was or who Kermit Washington was.

Splaver knew he had to come up with something that would get people's attention. Academic All-American was a good start, since very few players who were basketball All-Americans came close to being academic All-Americans. But he needed something more, something eye-catching. Aha! At season's end, Splaver had figured out that Washington's career averages were close to 20 points and 20 rebounds a game. There had only been a handful of players in history who had been 20-20 men.

Keeping 20-20 in mind, Splaver came up with the Kermit Washington Eye Chart, reminding people that Kermit was a

potential 20-20 man. At the very least it would get people's attention, more so than a mind-numbing page of statistics.

While Splaver was plotting his PR assault, Washington headed
off to Colorado Springs for the Olympic Trials. His play had been
good enough to get him invited to try out for the 1972 Olympic
team, which would be coached by the legendary Henry Iba, who
had won back-to-back national titles at Oklahoma A&M in 1945
and 1946. Iba was now retired, but he had been given the Olympic
job for a third straight time. The Olympics were considered a
walkover for U.S. basketball. The U.S. team had never lost a
game in Olympic competition, dating back to 1936, and had won
the gold medal in 1968 in Mexico City even though many of
the best collegiate players, including Lew Alcindor, had boycotted
in protest of the Vietnam War. Led by a (then) unknown high
school senior named Spencer Haywood, the Americans still won
with ease.

Times were different in 1972. More of the top Americans
showed up for the tryouts, including Maryland star Tom McMillen
and Doug Collins of Illinois State. Even so, a number of the country's best college players refused to participate, notably UCLA center Bill Walton, who had just led the Bruins to an undefeated
season and their sixth straight national championship. Washington
arrived in Colorado Springs thinking he had a chance to make the
team. He had surprised people in the past, there was no reason he
couldn't do it again.

But when he arrived he found himself in an unfamiliar world,
one he wasn't at all comfortable with. Iba had assembled some of
the top coaches in the country to run the tryouts. Joe B. Hall, who
was about to succeed Adolph Rupp at Kentucky, was there. Bob
Knight, who had just finished his first season at Indiana, was there.
Dean Smith, who had just coached North Carolina in his fourth
Final Four, was there. Iba gave the coaches marching orders that
were direct: He wanted a lot of discipline on this team. He wanted

tough kids who could deal with adversity. He wanted kids who would respond to being yelled at by getting things right sooner rather than later.

Washington was tough and he was disciplined. But as Young and Davis had discovered early on at American, he did not respond to yelling. "I hated it," he said. "Every day in drills, every day in scrimmages. Screaming and hollering. It didn't matter who was coaching you, you got yelled at." He smiled. "You want to know how bad it was? I thought Bobby Knight was one of the nicer guys out there."

Whoo boy. Washington was so miserable that he called Young to tell him he was thinking about coming home. "All they do is yell at me, Coach," he said. "I can't play when I get yelled at like that."

Young was chagrined. "I felt a little bit guilty," he said. "I had been so gentle with him that when someone got on him he just couldn't deal with it. Maybe if I had forced him to learn that sometimes coaches do raise their voices to make a point, it wouldn't have been such a shock to him to be in that environment. But when you have someone who works as hard as Kermit every single day, you feel like yelling at him is almost redundant. But it probably would have helped prepare him for other things if I had gotten on him a little bit more."

Young called Knight, whom he knew well from competing against him during Knight's days as coach at Army, to try to explain that this was one kid who was going to respond better to a kinder, gentler coaching approach. Knight, according to Young, told him he understood and he knew that every kid was different, but the coaches were doing what Iba wanted. "Believe it or not, Tom," Knight said, "I'm getting on them less than a lot of the other guys."

Washington stuck out the tryout camp but, to no one's surprise, didn't make the team. And thus he avoided being part of the first U.S. team to lose an Olympic basketball game, the infamous "double-inbounds," gold medal game, in which the Soviet Union was given what amounted to a do-over on a last-second inbounds pass and scored on the second attempt to win the game. The U.S. team protested, lost the protest, and refused to accept their silver medals.

The game was played in Munich. By then Kermit Washington's senior year at American had started. He was exactly where he wanted to be.

In the fall of 1972, the AU campus brimmed with anticipation. The school had only been playing Division I basketball for eleven years at that point, and the 16 victories the previous season had matched the 16 wins the 1967 team had recorded as AU's all-time Division I high-water mark. With all the key players and the superstar back, expectations were high.

The schedule was ambitious: Syracuse, St. John's, Duquesne, and Rice were some of the nonconference opponents. There would be the usual conference games with the three Big Five schools— Temple, St. Joseph's, La Salle. And there would be the local rivalry games with Georgetown, George Washington (twice), and Navy. Maryland wanted nothing to do with the Eagles. Lefty Driesell's program was about to kick into high gear, but he wasn't taking any chances by scheduling Kermit Washington and company.

The Eagles started 9–1 before a loss in the Palestra to St. Joseph's brought them back to earth. "For some reason we always had trouble in the Palestra," Washington said. "I think it may have had something to do with the fact that those teams were always good."

Chris Washington, who had just finished his rookie season as a member of the St. Louis football Cardinals, came home for a January game against George Washington. His brother responded with 18 points and 34 rebounds, but the Eagles lost, 85–80. "If you were any good," Chris told his younger brother, "you guys would have won."

The Eagles didn't lose very often after that. Splaver's eye chart and Washington's eye-popping numbers were bringing a lot of national media to the Fort. Every home game was a sellout. Washington was the Big Man on Campus both literally and figuratively. "It was," he said, "the happiest time of my life."

The race for postseason and for 20-20 went down to the last game of the regular season. The Eagles had won their twentieth game with an 88–79 victory over La Salle and thought they were in good position to get invited to the NIT. Washington was averaging just over 20 rebounds a night, but he was slightly under 20 points per game. Splaver did some calculating: to finish the regular season at 20-20, Kermit would need 40 points and 19 rebounds in the finale, which would be in the Fort, against Georgetown.

"I knew I could get the rebounds," Washington said. "But forty points—against a good team—that was going to be tough."

Washington had been joyriding most of the season. Now, for the first time, he felt pressure. He felt as if the eyes of the entire campus were on him. "I felt as if not doing it would be a letdown for so many people," he said. "I had never been nervous about a basketball game the whole time I had been at AU. You were always a little bit nervous before a game, anticipating it and all, but this was different. My stomach hurt, my head hurt, I couldn't sleep, I couldn't eat. I just felt as if everyone was counting on me, and I didn't want to let them down."

There wasn't an inch of room in the Fort that night. Everyone from AU was there. Everyone from the old neighborhood was there. Kermit's dad was there too. Everyone in the place knew, even the Georgetown players and coaches, exactly the numbers Washington needed. This was John Thompson's first team as coach at Georgetown. It was a very young team, one whose nucleus would take the Hoyas to the NCAA tournament in two years, but not the national power Thompson would later build. Still, it was a team made up mostly of D.C. kids who knew Washington and weren't about to let him make history without a battle.

Splaver, on the ball as ever, had already let the media know that Washington would be only the seventh player in history to achieve the 20-20 if he did it.

Five minutes into the game, it appeared as if all of Splaver's research, all the eye charts, all the effort, were going to be for naught. "I couldn't do anything right," Washington remembered. "I couldn't catch the ball. I couldn't shoot it. I couldn't do anything. I was so nervous I could hardly breathe."

Young called time out. "Kermit, what's wrong?" he demanded. "Calm down and just play."

Something happened during that time-out, Washington's not sure what it was. "I felt, all of a sudden, as if someone had thrown a warm blanket over me. All of a sudden I was okay. The nerves went away. To this day I can't tell you why. But when we went back on the court, I was fine."

He took over the game. Every shot started going in. He was taking—and making—shots he never even practiced, much less tried in games. The game turned into a rout, the Eagles building their lead steadily in the second half. They were running every play through Washington. He was already past the 20-rebound mark with ten minutes left in the game. He still needed more points. He got to 38 with a little more than two minutes to go on a rebound basket. The next time down the court, he caught the ball on the left wing, took one step to his left, and threw up a left-handed hook.

"First one I ever took in my life," he said.

It went in.

Pandemonium. Everyone in the place knew what had happened. The game stopped and Young took Washington out; he wasn't going to leave him in during the last two minutes of what would be a 90–68 victory once he had his points. There wasn't a soul in the building who wasn't on his feet cheering—including the Georgetown bench.

"I don't like the idea of anyone scoring forty points on us," John Thompson said later. "But if it had to happen, I'm happy it happened for Kermit. I can't think of a more deserving player."

The victory, the achievement, the entire night, set off a campuswide celebration back at AU. If the Eagles had won a national championship, it is unlikely the student body would have celebrated with much more zeal. There was a cake and a party that lasted most of the night. "The thing I remember the most about it was people thanking me," he said. "They thanked me for making basketball so much fun for them."

As he retells the story of the euphoric evening, Washington shakes his head, a faraway look in his eyes, and says for about the tenth time in his recounting of the AU years: "It was the happiest time of my life."

There was, as it turned out, one game left to play. American had finished the season 21–4 and received an invitation to the NIT, the school's first bid to postseason in Division I. In those days the entire sixteen-team NIT was played in Madison Square Garden, so the Eagles found themselves in New York matched against Louisville, a team that had reached the Final Four a year earlier in the first season of Denny Crum's Hall of Fame head coaching career, a career that ended up lasting thirty years.

Louisville was a legitimate national power, one of those schools that would easily have been in the NCAA field under today's rules. They had size and quickness that was on a different level from the teams AU had faced throughout most of the season. Even so, the Eagles hung tough. They were within 3 points midway through the second half, before a Louisville spurt put the game out of reach. The final was 97–84. Washington, needing 20-20 to maintain his 20-20 for the season, came up with 29 points and 24 rebounds. Since that euphoric spring of 1973, no college player has averaged 20-20 for a single season. Washington nearly made it to 20-20 for his career, finishing his three years at AU averaging 19.7 points and 20.2 rebounds a game.

The next couple of months were a whirlwind for Washington. There were all-star games to play in, including a trip to Hawaii to play three games out there. There was schoolwork to finish. There were agents to interview, since he was now considered a surefire first-round draft pick by most scouts. He was far enough ahead in his schoolwork that the time away from class didn't cause any major academic problems for him. Still, he was glad when the all-star games were over and he was back on campus.

He was sitting in the cafeteria one afternoon eating a quiet lunch when Josh Rosenfeld walked in with a huge grin on his face. By then, in addition to his duties as a team manager, Rosenfeld was working as a student assistant in sports information, helping Splaver deal with the PR monster he had created. Rosenfeld walked over, put out his hand, and said, "Congratulations, you did it."

"Did what?" Washington said.

"Made All-American."

"My first thought was, 'Oh, that's really nice, I made academic All-American again,'" Washington said. "I was happy about it, but to be honest, I expected it. I knew I had the grades, so why wouldn't I make it?

"So I just said to Josh, 'Oh, that's really nice. Thanks.' He looked at me and said, 'Kermit, do you know what a big deal this is?' I said, 'Sure, academic All-American is very nice . . .'"

Rosenfeld broke in. "Kermit, I'm not talking about academic All-American, I'm talking about basketball. You made *first team* All-American."

Washington was shaking his head. "No," he said firmly. "You mean All-East."

"No!" Rosenfeld insisted. "Not All-East, All-American. Here's the team: Bill Walton, David Thompson, Doug Collins, Ernie DiGregorio, and you. Does that sound like an All-East team?"

Washington was floored. He knew how hard Splaver had been working to get him on the national map, and he had hoped to make some kind of All-American team—perhaps third team; at least honorable mention. But first team?

"I just couldn't believe it," he said. "I knew I had good stats, and Mark had gotten me a lot of publicity, but I never thought of myself in the same sentence with players like that. Playing in the all-star games and doing well helped my confidence in terms of thinking about where I was going to get drafted, but I didn't think in terms of All-American. Certainly not first team. It was like the perfect ending to a perfect college career."

Actually, there was more. On graduation day, Washington was awarded a postgraduate scholarship for academic excellence and chosen for the Bruce Hughes Award for meritorious service to the AU community. He was an academic All-American again and graduated with a 3.37 GPA in sociology.

He had come a long, long way since the day four years earlier when Young and Davis had spotted him running around the gym at St. John's High School in his all-white outfit. But there was still more to come. When the NBA held its draft, the Los Angeles Lakers, picking fifth, selected him. Donald Dell, whom he had chosen as his agent from among the four Young had brought in to talk to him—"because he was the only one who acted as if I would be helping him rather than he would be helping me"—told him he was going to demand a contract guaranteed for four years for an average of $100,000 a year.

The NBA. A six-figure salary. Los Angeles. The Lakers—Jerry West, Wilt Chamberlain. He really thought he was having a long dream and would wake up any minute in the tiny room at 237 Farragut and hear Barbara yelling at him to get out of bed and get ready for school.

As thrilled as he was by everything that had happened in his life, there was an element of sadness to graduation day. Part of him wanted to stay at American forever. He felt so comfortable there, so safe, so *loved*. He knew it would all be very different in Los Angeles and the NBA.

First-round draft picks didn't become instant millionaires in the seventies the way they do now. So while Dell negotiated with the Lakers that summer, Washington stayed in D.C. and worked various jobs so he would have spending money until his contract was signed. Every night after work, he would drive (he could finally afford a car) over to American and slowly cruise through the campus, already nostalgic for his days as the Big Man on the Little Campus.

He was in Massachusetts, working at Red Auerbach's camp, when Dell called to tell him the deal was done. Four years guaranteed, salaries of $80,000; $90,000; $100,000; $110,000. There was a fifth-year option at $120,000. He was officially a wealthy young man. He called Pat and told her the news. He wanted her to meet him in L.A. once he was out there and got settled. They had never really talked much about getting married, it was more an unspoken given that they would get married sometime after college.

He went back to Washington to get all his things together for the trip to Los Angeles. School was in session by now, and he went by the practice gym at AU one day to see his old teammates. He was given a hero's welcome, but he felt more like an old man than one of the guys. His classmates weren't there; they had all graduated and gone on to grad school or jobs. Tom Young wasn't there either: AU's 21–5 record had springboarded him to a job as head coach at Rutgers. Even Marc Splaver was gone. The Washington Bullets, recognizing a brilliant young PR mind when they saw it, had hired him to run their PR department.

It was hard to believe that it had only been six months since that magic night in the Fort when his left-handed hook had put him in the 20-20 club. He certainly hadn't been forgotten at AU, but clearly he was gone. Everyone was moving on with their lives. It was time for him to do the same. The best chapter of his life was closed. He wondered what the next one would be like.

11

From Hamtramck to
Ann Arbor to San Diego

R udy Tomjanovich's trip from Hamtramck to Ann Arbor in the
fall of 1966 was a little bit longer than the trip Kermit Washington would take three years later from one side of northwest Washington to the other, but the forty-mile journey still represented a
major change of life for him.

Even though Michigan was a state school, it was—and is—the
upscale state school. Students came to the University of Michigan
from around the country, and it was justifiably proud of its national
reputation as an academic institution.

But there was no mistaking the fact that Michigan was a
big-time jock school too. The football team was one of the country's great traditional powers, although it was in a short-lived down
cycle when Tomjanovich first arrived. (By his senior year, Bo
Schembechler would start his reign as football coach and the
Wolverines would be back in the Rose Bowl.) The basketball team
had played in the national championship game in 1965 and by 1967
would be moving into Crisler Arena, a 13,000-seat showcase that
would be one of *the* places to play when it opened.

More than anything, though, Michigan was big. Even then it
had more than 25,000 students. To someone whose world had for

all intents and purposes consisted of several blocks in Hamtramck, the place was a little bit overwhelming at the start. "It was just a completely different world," Tomjanovich said. "I think I was a little intimidated when I first got there, but looking back, I was probably like most freshmen in that sense."

Most freshmen were not highly recruited basketball players. Being part of the basketball team, even if it was just the freshman team, gave Tomjanovich a niche, a place he could go, one corner of the campus where people knew him and he had a very defined role. That helped, even if the freshman team only played three games that season. Even with that built-in basketball niche, right from the beginning, Tomjanovich had that feeling inside his stomach again, the need to prove his worth. He had become a star in high school, done everything that needed to be done to prove to people in his neighborhood that he was more than the kid whose family had to go on welfare some of the time.

Now, though, he was back on square one. Sure, there were some expectations because he had been a highly recruited basketball player. But he often ran into kids with sophisticated backgrounds; kids who thought his 1200 SAT score was only respectable; kids who resented jocks, especially those on scholarship.

The Vietnam conflict was moving into high gear, and college campuses were divided into two groups, prowar and antiwar, with most students falling into the latter category. Tomjanovich had stepped from a neighborhood still steeped in the values of the fifties onto a campus that was smack in the middle of the sixties. "Talk about culture shock," he said, laughing.

He was not about to be deterred from his goals by anything, not the size of the campus or the size of the campus protests. He was going to work as hard as he needed to in order to do well in school and become a star basketball player. He played well as a freshman, but he understood the real tests wouldn't come until the next season, when he became part of the varsity.

Freshman year was important for another reason: he met Sophie

Migas. They had actually met before at a party during Rudy's senior year in high school. He had noticed her right away: she was tall and striking, with raven-colored hair and, as he would later write in his autobiography, "the best pair of legs I had ever seen."

Sophie and her three sisters had been raised in Hamtramck by their mother after their father died when Sophie was eight. Everyone in the Polish community knew the Migas sisters. Like their mother, they were all tall and striking. Sophie had been a cheerleader at St. Florian's High School. It was shortly after Hamtramck had played St. Florian's that Rudy and Sophie encountered one another at a party. Sophie mentioned that she was a cheerleader, and Rudy asked her if she remembered him from the Hamtramck game. No, she said, she really didn't.

"I was the only white starter and I scored fifty-four that night," he said years later. "And she didn't remember me?"

Actually Sophie did remember him, but she wasn't about to let on. In fact, after their second encounter at another party, she told a friend of hers, "I'm going to marry that guy."

Why? "I'm not sure," she said, thirty years into the marriage. "I think there is something to the idea of meeting your soul mate. Something about him told me he was my soul mate."

"When she told me the story after we got married, she said it was something about my eyebrows," Rudy said, shrugging. "Fine with me, as long as it worked."

He was shy then, as now, but in Sophie's words, "never quiet."

"Once he became comfortable in a situation, had a little confidence that he belonged where he was, he had plenty to say. He's always been that way. I think Rudy likes to study a room, figure out what is going on and who is in it. Once he feels as if he's got it figured out, he gets past his initial shyness. Once we were dating, he wasn't quiet with me. Just the opposite in fact."

Rudy knew nothing of Sophie's future plans when he and Sophie came across each other again when he was home from

Michigan on a weekend. He liked it that she seemed completely unimpressed with the fact that he was a basketball star, even if he was nonplussed by the notion that he had dropped 54 on her school right before her very eyes and she hadn't noticed. Once they started dating, Rudy tried making it home whenever he could, which wasn't easy since he didn't have a car.

"I bought a lot of seven-dollar bus tickets," he said.

Sophie was going to Detroit Business School and planning a career in New York. She was a year younger than Rudy, so he didn't have to worry about her disappearing to the East Coast before he finished at Michigan. He had no idea what her long-range plans were—or what his own were. All he knew was, he was about to become a sophomore at Michigan and he wanted to be in the starting lineup from day one. Even if Sophie didn't care if he was a basketball star, he wanted to show her that he was. Just as he wanted to show everyone else.

As he had hoped, Tomjanovich was in the starting lineup for Michigan on opening night of his sophomore season. The Wolverines were opening Crisler Arena, and coach Dave Strack had scheduled a game against Kentucky to give the new place a big sendoff. The only problem was that Kentucky was at a different level than Michigan and won the game easily, 96–79. The sophomore starting at power forward had a pretty good debut, though, pulling down 27 rebounds.

"It was all adrenaline," he said. "I was running around in circles. I couldn't buy a shot."

He also came out of the game with a strained arch, which made him doubtful for the next game—at Detroit. It seemed as if half of Hamtramck showed up for the game. Urged on by John Radwinski, his old high school coach, who now felt no need to play tough guy with him anymore, Tomjanovich decided to give it a try. Hobbling, he scored 30 points, and the Wolverines won, 104–99.

He was locked in as a star after that. By now Sophie knew he was a basketball player, and on the weekends when he didn't make the bus trip to Detroit, she often came to Ann Arbor, getting a ride most of the time from one of Rudy's Hamtramck buddies. Most of his boyhood friends hadn't gone to college, and a lot of them were getting drafted and being sent to Vietnam. When they were home they partied with great gusto, and they often came down to Ann Arbor in large groups to party. The only problem with that was that Rudy didn't get as much time alone with Sophie as he would have liked.

He had now become a big name in the old neighborhood because of his success in Ann Arbor. When he came home on a weekend during the winter break, he received an invitation to dinner from someone who wanted her two sons to meet the great Rudy Tomjanovich. He turned it down.

"It was the woman in the street," he said. "The one who had turned her nose up at me when she saw me playing with my black friends. I just wouldn't go to her house."

He continued to play well throughout his sophomore year. Michigan was no better than a middle-of-the-pack Big Ten team at the time. Ohio State was a power, as was Purdue. In 1968 the Buckeyes reached the Final Four; a year later the Boilermakers, led by the legendary shooter Rick Mount, made it to the final before losing to UCLA in the last game of Lew Alcindor's extraordinary college career (88–2 record, three national titles). In 1968 the Wolverines played at Houston, facing the Elvin Hayes and Don Chaney–led team that would end UCLA's 61-game winning streak in the Astrodome a few weeks after playing Michigan. Later Hayes would be a teammate of Tomjanovich's in the NBA, and it would be Chaney whom Tomjanovich would succeed as coach of the Rockets in 1992.

But that was way down the road. Back then Hayes and Chaney were seniors on a great team, one that hammered Michigan 91–65.

Red Auerbach was at the game that night, scouting Chaney, who would be his first-round draft pick that spring. But he noticed the eager, jumping-jack forward from Michigan with the sweet jump shot. He was impressed enough that he made a point of stopping Tomjanovich on his way off the court to tell him he had played well.

As he recounted the story in his autobiography later, Tomjanovich "brushed him off. . . . I had no idea who the little man with the unlit cigar was," he wrote. When he realized the next day that he had been rude to the immortal Red Auerbach, Tomjanovich was mortified. "How could I do that to Red Auerbach?" he moaned.

According to Auerbach, who remembers seeing Tomjanovich play that night, he didn't do anything wrong. "He was very polite," he said. "He thanked me for the compliment and kept walking. His team had just gotten killed. I didn't exactly expect him to throw his arms around me and say, 'Thank you, thank you, you made my night.'"

The difference in the way the two men remember that scene sums up Tomjanovich. Auerbach, who remembers every person who has ever slighted him in any way, saw a polite kid, disappointed by a one-sided loss. He never gave their brief exchange another thought until someone brought it up to him. Tomjanovich was convinced he had screwed up, that he had been rude, that he had somehow been wrong not to recognize Auerbach. He remembered the moment vividly enough that he wrote about it almost thirty years later. Always, if there was a way for Tomjanovich to be tough on himself, he found it.

Michigan finished that season 11–13. Tomjanovich ended up averaging 19.5 points and 13.5 rebounds a game, impressive numbers, especially in an era with no 3-point shot and no shot clock. He was already attracting attention from pro scouts. There was no denying the progress he was making as a player. Still, unlike a lot of star athletes, Tomjanovich worked very hard at his schoolwork. He knew there was a chance (his words) that he might play pro ball after college, but he wasn't certain, and he wanted a degree in case basketball didn't work out for him. He worked hard at the classes that interested him and did enough to get by in everything else. He was a solid B student, which made him pretty average in the Michigan student body, well above average among Michigan athletes.

Dave Strack left Michigan after Tomjanovich's sophomore year to become the athletic director at Arizona, perhaps because the Wolverines had just gone through a second losing season. The coaching job went to Strack's top assistant, Johnny Orr, one of basketball's true characters. Orr is a legendary storyteller, one of those coaches who will stay up all night swapping tales if anyone wants to stay up with him. He was one of the few coaches ever able to compete with Bob Knight at Indiana without alienating him. Most coaches who had the nerve to beat Knight with any kind of consistency ended up on Knight's lengthy hit list. Not Orr.

Orr never seemed to forget a name. That was because he called almost everyone he encountered "Coach." Most of the people he knew were coaches, and those who weren't were flattered to be called that. Only after you were around Orr for a long time did you figure out that he called most people Coach because he had no idea what their name was.

Orr's philosophy of coaching when he took over at Michigan was simple: score more than the other guys. He was Loyola Marymount circa 1990 in 1968, minus the 3-point shot. A basket by the opposition was nothing more than an opportunity to get the ball back and score again.

There's never been a basketball player born who didn't love playing for a coach who emphasized shooting and run-and-gun offense. Defense is the dirty work of basketball. Every great coach will tell you that you can't win without learning defense first (a philosophy Orr came around to in the 1970s), and most practices—especially in preseason—emphasize defense. The ultimate putdown a player can suffer at the hands of Bob Knight has always been the same: "He can't guard the floor."

If you can't guard the floor, you can't play for Bob Knight.

But you could play for Johnny Orr in 1969. One of Orr's assistants then was Fred Snowden, who later became the head coach at Arizona. Tomjanovich took an activities class that year taught by Snowden and spent much of it (surprisingly he got an A) working with Snowden on a bank shot. The first time he tried the bank shot out in a game was against Indiana, and he scored 48 points, tying Cazzie Russell's school record. From that point on, the bank shot was an important part of his repertoire.

The late 1960s were a good time to be a talented college basketball player. The American Basketball Association had come into existence in 1967 and was trying to compete with the NBA for talent. During Tomjanovich's senior year in high school there had been a total of nine professional basketball teams. By the time he started his junior year at Michigan, thanks to NBA expansion and the birth of the ABA there were twenty-two.

That meant there were more jobs and, for the top players, the asking prices had gone up, since there was competition. The ABA was willing in some cases to sign a player to a contract and then let him choose his team. That wasn't what Tomjanovich was thinking about when Johnny Orr became the Wolverines' coach. He was still focusing on all the weaknesses he saw in his game.

"I knew I wasn't particularly fast and I needed to improve my defense," he said. "We were going to score a lot of points because of Johnny's style, but I figured the pro scouts would be on to that. They would think my numbers were deceiving."

Tomjanovich was right about one thing: pro scouts don't pay a lot of attention to statistics. At most, they use them to back up whatever they have decided about a player. When pro scouts looked at Tomjanovich they saw a quick leaper, a hard worker, and a guy who was 6-8 and could roam twenty feet from the basket and consistently make shots. There was no doubt in anyone's mind that he would be a pro.

But that wasn't the way Tomjanovich looked at it. The knot in the pit of his stomach now showed up on game nights, that feeling that he had to prove himself—again and again. The team wasn't a lot better during his junior year: the record improved to 13–11 overall and 7–7 in the Big Ten. Tomjanovich's numbers also improved. His scoring average soared to 25.7 points per game, and he also averaged 14 rebounds a night.

That set up a senior year in which Tomjanovich had three goals: graduate with a solid GPA; play well enough to be a high draft pick; and convince Sophie that, wherever he was going after college, she should go with him.

"By senior year she had me, I mean totally," he said. "I had a car by then, and I would drive into Detroit and meet her whenever I could. Sometimes, if my classes were over early, I'd go in and meet her for lunch. She would always fix sandwiches for me to take back to school, and they were so good I'd eat them before I even got back."

He smiled. "Funny how you act when you're young. I'm totally hooked, but I have to be cool. So I tell her one day that if she wants to see other guys while I'm up at school, I understand, it's no big deal. That was absolutely the last thing in the world I wanted, but I had to act like it didn't really matter to me. She got all upset and said, 'Is that what you really want? You want to see other people?' And I was like, 'No, no way, that's the last thing I want.' After that, I quit trying to be cool."

He ended up going three-for-three in his senior goals. He graduated with a B average; he continued to improve in basketball, averaging 30.1 points per game and almost 16 rebounds; and when spring came he persuaded Sophie to marry him.

"I didn't know where I was going," he said. "But I knew wherever it was going to be, I wanted her to be there."

The question then was, where would he be going? Tomjanovich was certain to be a high draft pick in either the NBA or the ABA. He flew to New York to meet with representatives from both leagues and came back convinced that the NBA was the place to be. The ABA had offered more money total—except that most of it was in a back-loaded annuity. Given the shaky status of a three-year-old league, signing that sort of deal wasn't very appealing. So it would be the NBA.

As it turned out, he was the second player chosen in the draft. After the Detroit Pistons took St. Bonaventure center Bob Lanier, the San Diego Rockets took Tomjanovich. The choice was controversial. The Rockets were a struggling, third-year franchise, and the thinking in town was that Pete Maravich, college basketball's all-time leading scorer, who had averaged more than 44 points a game during three seasons at LSU, was a natural fit. He would score a lot, he would do it with flair, and he would sell tickets.

"He would sell a lot of tickets on the road, we knew that for sure," said Pete Newell, who was then the Rockets' general manager. "But that was fool's gold, because we wouldn't share in road gate receipts, so it wouldn't help us to sell out other people's buildings. I also knew he would sell tickets at home, at least in the short term, but I was looking at it long term. When I looked at Rudy, I saw a guy who could do a lot of things: he could score, he could rebound, he could run the floor, and he could shoot the ball from deep at 6-8. I had nothing against Maravich. I just didn't think you could build a championship team around a player who had to control the ball that much of the time. Pete had fabulous individual skills. Basketball's a team game. I thought long term Rudy was a better pick for us."

Newell was castigated by the local media for the pick. "Rudy Who?" was one headline. In the meantime he had also drafted Calvin Murphy, stealing the future Hall of Famer in the second round after the entire league had passed on him in the first round because of doubts about his height. Those doubts drove the 5-foot-10-inch Murphy. "I played angry my whole career," he said, "because I had so many people to prove wrong."

Tomjanovich never played angry, and he had never had any insecurities caused by his height. But by the time he arrived in San Diego, he would have as much to prove as Murphy. Just for different reasons.

The wedding was pretty close to perfect. It was held in the church across the street from Sophie's home, and just about all of Hamtramck was there. The local hero who had made good at Michigan and was on his way to stardom in the NBA was marrying the beautiful former cheerleader after a storybook romance. The newlyweds got in their Chevy Camaro when the party was over and began driving southwest, headed for their new life on the West Coast.

"It was all perfect," Sophie said. "Until we got to New Mexico."

That was where the bad movie started. Rudy got nailed for speeding somewhere in the middle of nowhere. "We were cruising along, listening to the radio out on the open road," he said. "I looked up in the rearview mirror and saw this very angry policeman gesturing at me to pull over. He didn't have a siren, and he'd been behind me for like twenty minutes. He was pissed."

Naturally they couldn't just pay a fine and move on, they had to go before the local judge. Just as naturally His Honor was at lunch and the newlyweds had no choice but to wait until he came back. While they waited, Rudy stewed about all the time they were losing. He needed to get to San Diego, get settled in, and begin preparing for training camp. After all, this was a new league and a new life, and there was so much to prove. He started talking about some kind of shortcut.

"When he pulled out the map, I knew we were in trouble," Sophie said.

The judge finally finished lunch and told Rudy the fine was $75, which was a fortune in those days. They got back in the Camaro, having lost several hours. About an hour later, something told Rudy they weren't headed in the right direction. He pulled into a gas station to find out where they were and where they needed to go.

The news wasn't good. "We had gone about fifty miles in the wrong direction," he remembered. "The guy told us we had two options: turn around and go back the fifty miles to get back to where we'd be pointed in the right direction on the interstate, or go through the mountains.

"I said, 'Okay, we'll go through the mountains.'"

Sophie's response was direct: "No way. We aren't going that way."

"We have to, we've lost a half a day."

"Don't care. Not going that way."

"We are going that way."

"Rudy, just because you got a speeding ticket doesn't mean we have to risk our lives."

"Well if I'd had a good map girl, this wouldn't have happened."

Wrong thing to say. Sophie was out of the car, crying.

"I'm going back to Hamtramck."

"Fine."

The proverbial first fight in the middle of nowhere, somewhere in the West.

"I gave in finally," he said, laughing at the memory. "I knew she wasn't going back to Michigan, but I also knew I wasn't going to San Diego without her, and she was very determined."

"I was determined," she said, "that we get there in one piece."

The mountain plan was abandoned. So were the map and any shortcuts. Rudy backtracked to the interstate and drove like a demon on the main roads the rest of the way. Fortunately he didn't get another ticket, and they arrived in San Diego without further incident.

And thought they had died and gone to heaven.

They were young and in love and had never seen southern California before. "Heck, we hadn't seen much of southern Michigan," Tomjanovich joked years later.

They got an apartment five minutes from the beach and settled into an idyllic lifestyle, different from anything either had ever imagined. Of course it wasn't quite the same in the NBA as it is now. Rudy had signed a contract for what felt like more money than he could possibly hope to spend in a lifetime—four years, $400,000—but the perks weren't quite the same. Each day he would bring his practice uniform home for his wife to wash, and before he went on the road, she had to make sure his road uniform was presentable.

Sophie was also a bit nonplussed when she was asked early in the season to speak to a group of teenagers about life as an NBA wife. "I was about two years older than most of them," she said. "And probably a lot less worldly. I had no idea what to say."

Giving that speech turned out to be easier than dealing with an NBA husband. The husband was confused and frustrated by what was going on with his new team and his new career. The Rockets were coached by future Hall of Famer Alex Hannum, who had coached everywhere in the ABA and the NBA and had won three titles with three different teams: the St. Louis Hawks in 1958, the Philadelphia 76ers in 1967, and an ABA title with the Oakland Oaks in 1969.

Hannum wasn't happy with Newell's decision to draft Tomjanovich with the first pick. These days it would be almost impossible for a player to be chosen in the first round without the approval of the team's coach, who often as not has final say on personnel matters under any circumstances. Back then there was a clear separation of church and state—except in Boston, where Red Auerbach did everything until he stepped down as coach. The general manager selected the players and the coach coached them.

Hannum wasn't even present at the draft when Newell selected Tomjanovich.

Tomjanovich was caught in the middle of a feud between Newell and Hannum. Both were strong-willed. Hannum wanted Newell to make changes, perhaps trade the first-round pick for more experienced players. As the season went on, Tomjanovich found himself playing less and less rather than more and more. Even though he suspected that his lack of playing time had little to do with anything he was doing wrong, he kept thinking that if he worked and worked he would eventually win Hannum over. What was the deficiency in his game? What could he work on to improve? Since he wasn't even getting that much playing time in practice, he would often go to a local gym at night to shoot by himself and work on his game. Most nights he took a rebounder with him. That would be Mrs. Tomjanovich. At least, she thought, she would have some stories to tell if she was asked the next season to talk again about life as an NBA wife.

"That was a long winter," she remembered. "I mean, we loved San Diego, the weather, the whole thing. But Rudy was so frustrated. He hated not playing, and he kept searching for an answer when in truth there wasn't an answer. It wasn't anything he was doing wrong, but he couldn't see it that way. He just kept working and working and working and getting nothing out of it."

Back then first-round picks weren't superstars with agents who could go in and get a coach fired over lack of playing time. They were rookies who did what they were told and didn't complain. It wasn't in Tomjanovich's nature to complain anyway, but not playing was eating him up. The last time he had felt like a failure in basketball had been after the tryouts for the freshman team in high school. In the past he had always figured he could work his way through any deficiencies in his game. Now even that wasn't working.

"I think I knew I was in trouble when I came into a game against Detroit, got a tip-dunk right away that ignited a run, and went on to have a real good game," he said. "A few days later, we were looking at film of the game [in those days there was no tape, and it took several days to get film developed], and Alex looked at that play and criticized me for it. Said I was out of position. Now, this wasn't a play you made all that often; it was really pretty good, and he's criticizing me for it. I had a feeling at that moment that he was looking for reasons to not play me."

The season ended with the Rockets going 40–42, the best record in their four-year history. Tomjanovich played in 77 of the 82 games but averaged less than 14 minutes a game, often playing most of his minutes at garbage time. He averaged 5.3 points and almost 5 rebounds a game—the latter fairly remarkable given his limited minutes. Even though the team ended up missing the playoffs by just one game, attendance changed little: the team went from an average 6,123 per game to 6,774. Whether the crowds would have been larger if Rudy Who had played more is questionable. At the very least, no one in San Diego seemed eager to see him *not* play.

Hannum quit at season's end to take an ABA job, and Newell hired Tex Winter to replace him. He was convinced that his team was turning a corner. Attendance had improved at the end of the season with the Rockets in the playoff hunt, and Elvin Hayes was rapidly becoming a superstar. Newell thought that Tomjanovich and Murphy were also going to be stars. By Memorial Day, the Rockets had sold more season ticket packages than they had sold for the entire season in 1970–71. "I felt like we were about to take off in San Diego," Newell said. "We were going to be a good team the next year, and people liked what we were doing. Then I got the phone call from Boston."

It was mid-June, and the owners were holding their annual meetings. The playoffs, believe it or not, had been over for six weeks (the Milwaukee Bucks had wrapped up the finals in a four-game sweep over the Baltimore Bullets on April 30—a date that now coincides with the first week of the endless NBA playoffs), and the draft had already been held. Newell's phone call came from team owner Robert Breitbard, telling him he had just sold the team to a group in Texas that was planning to move the Rockets to Houston, Elvin Hayes's hometown.

"It will be tough spending a year as a lame duck," Newell said.

"No it won't," Breitbard said. "The team is moving *now*."

And so, three months before training camp was scheduled to begin, the San Diego Rockets became the Houston Rockets. Newell had a clause in his contract which stipulated that if the team left California, he did not have to go along. He agreed to remain as a consultant while the team was transitioning from San Diego to Houston.

The players had no such clauses. Much to their chagrin, Rudy and Sophie found themselves packing the Camaro again, leaving behind the friends they had made in San Diego and heading east to Houston. This time they made the trip without any speeding tickets or fights over routing. But neither one of them knew anything about Texas summer, and when they arrived in mid-August it was a shock.

"I think we were sick the entire first month we were there," Tomjanovich said. "You go from a hundred degrees outside to fifty degrees with air-conditioning blasting inside everywhere. You were bound to get sick. Between that and the fact that it rained every afternoon, we missed San Diego a lot."

But they adjusted. They found a house in a quiet neighborhood on a cul-de-sac that was walking distance to the supermarket and the movies and lots of places to shop. This was especially helpful when Rudy took the car to go to practice, since they still only had one car. The new neighbors were friendly and helpful, and they quickly adapted to their new lifestyle.

It wasn't nearly as easy for the team. The new ownership seemed to think the way to make the Rockets popular was to travel them all over Texas to play. The Rockets played every place on the state map during the 1971–72 season, playing some home games in the cavernous Astrodome, others next door in Astrohall, an auditorium attached to the Astrodome. They also played a number of games in Hofheinz Pavilion on the University of Houston campus. Worse than that, there were home games in San Antonio, a few more in Waco, and even some way out west in El Paso.

The only thing the six different home courts had in common was that the crowds were small. Texas was, and is, a football state. In 1971 the Rockets were the first pro basketball team in the state—there are now three—and without a true home, they got off to the kind of awful start (3–17) a team simply can't afford when it is trying to build a fan base. The new owners had figured fans would come out to see local hero Elvin Hayes, who had been a superstar at the University of Houston in the late sixties. Fans have short memories. If Hayes wasn't starring for the Cougars, challenging Lew Alcindor and UCLA, and taking UH to the Final Four, he was just another name from the past.

For the season, the Rockets averaged under 5,000 fans per home game in all six of their "homes." They played better after the awful start but never could dig themselves out completely, finishing 34–48. For Tomjanovich, though, things were better than his rookie season, even with the team's poor play and all the bouncing around. Winter made him a starter, and he responded by averaging 15 points and almost 12 rebounds a game. He was just the kind of active inside-outside player Newell had envisioned when he drafted him, and he became more and more comfortable as the season wore on.

"I got my confidence back that season," he remembered. "I felt comfortable playing for Tex, and even though we weren't as good as we should have been, I felt as if I belonged in the league, that I could play. The year before, I hadn't felt that way."

The one saving grace about all the traveling was that he and Calvin Murphy had become completely comfortable as roommates. During their rookie season, each had been assigned to a veteran: Tomjanovich was with John Q. Trapp, who had grown up in Highland Falls, which bordered on Hamtramck. "My home boy," he said. Murphy was with Larry Siegfried, an eight-year NBA veteran who had played on championship teams in Boston earlier in his career.

Tomjanovich got along fine with Trapp. Murphy was miserable with Siegfried. "Larry kept trying to train him," Tomjanovich said, laughing. "He wanted him to take naps in the afternoon, get to bed right after games. Calvin was miserable. One afternoon John and I were going out to a movie when Calvin jumped out the door of his room in his underwear. He grabbed me and said, 'Where you going, where you going?' I said we were going to the movies, and he said, 'Take me with you, please take me with you. That man in there is driving me crazy.'"

They took Murphy to the movies. Shortly after that Murphy suggested to Tomjanovich that they room together. That was fine with him as long as it was fine with Hannum. Murphy went and asked Hannum, who said it was okay. "Murph was all excited about it," Tomjanovich said. "Then Siegfried comes over and says, 'Can you believe Alex broke us up like that? I was just starting to get you trained.' And Murph says, 'Yeah, Larry, I just can't believe it.'"

The new roomies took a while to settle in together. The first night, after they had eaten and watched some TV, Murphy asked Tomjanovich if he had trouble sleeping after games. "Always," Tomjanovich answered.

"How about some music?" Murphy asked.

"Great idea," Tomjanovich said, thinking some quiet, soothing music would help him sleep. "I thought he'd put on the Dells or the Stylistics or something like that. Next thing I know James Brown is blasting all over the room."

By the time they reached Houston, Tomjanovich and Murphy had become inseparable on the road. Exactly why the two of them hit it off the way they did is a mystery unless you believe in the theory of opposites attracting. At least outwardly. Murphy was, by his own description, the league's angry man. Every night was a crusade to prove how good he was. In college, at Niagara, he had averaged a spectacular 33.1 points per game over three years—the fourth highest scoring average in history. But he never led the nation in scoring because he was in college the same three years as Pete Maravich, whose 44.2 points per game is still the highest per game average by a landslide.

Then, in spite of his gaudy numbers, he wasn't drafted until the second round. That was because the NBA always discriminates against those who are under 6 feet tall. Like Tomjanovich, he didn't start as a rookie, but he received considerably more playing time off the bench and averaged 15 points per game. Still, he was always proving himself as a player and as a tough guy. No one in the NBA was more willing or able to fight than Murphy. Players of all sizes soon learned not to mess with little Calvin—or call him little, for that matter.

Tomjanovich was the complete opposite. He was tall, dark, and handsome and was as quiet and laid-back as Murphy was intense and feisty. Murphy never stopped talking; Rudy never seemed to really start. Except that Tomjanovich was just as focused on proving himself as Murphy. He was still the kid from Hamtramck whose dad drank too much, who remembered the looks in the streets as he and his father wheeled the welfare meals home, the kid white folks looked down on because his best friends were black.

Once again his best friend was black. And once again he was proving himself. Their wives became close friends, so unlike a lot of roommates who are always together on the road but never at home, they were together at home all the time too.

"I never had a brother," Murphy said. "Until Rudy."

And so, like a pair cut straight from a buddy movie, they went everywhere together, home and away. Some nights after games they would go back to the room and Calvin would rant about playing time or the officiating or an opponent. Rudy would listen and then tell him what he thought, whether Calvin wanted to hear it or not.

"He was about the only guy who could say to me, 'Calvin, you're wrong,' and I would listen," Murphy said. "He was never someone who just let me talk and accepted what I said because it was easier that way. He thought I was screwing up, he told me."

He also knew how to give Calvin a hard time. Once when the team was on a flight from Atlanta to Houston, the pilot flew right through a thunderstorm. Tomjanovich was not a nervous flyer. Murphy was. Naturally they were sitting next to each other. "It was a real bad one," Tomjanovich said. "It was so bad that a bunch of the guys started singing songs just to take everyone's mind off all the bouncing around."

Murphy wasn't singing. Finally he turned to Tomjanovich and said, "Just do me one favor, Rudy. Turn around and see what Jimmy Walker is doing."

Walker, who had been a superstar at Providence College in the sixties, was considered the most unflappable player on the team—on the court or in a thunderstorm. "Nothing scares him," Murphy went on. "Tell me what he's doing."

Tomjanovich turned around and looked back at Walker. "Well," Murphy asked, "is he okay?"

"Calvin," Tomjanovich said, "he's praying."

"*Oh God*," Murphy shrieked. "We're going down!"

The team was still changing. Ray Patterson, who had run the Milwaukee Bucks, was named the team's president and general manager at the end of the 1971–72 season. One of his first acts was to trade Hayes, a shocking move since Hayes was still a young player and a hero in Houston. Hayes went to the Baltimore Bullets in exchange for Jack Marin, a solid swingman but hardly a player with Hayes's star power. The deal seemed to have little effect on the team for two years: the Rockets, having won 34 games in their first season in Houston with Hayes, won 33 and 32 the next two without him.

The team's leading scorers in 1974 were Rudy Tomjanovich and Calvin Murphy, averaging 24 points and 20 points per game respectively. They had proven they belonged in the NBA. Tomjanovich made his first All-Star team that season. Clearly now he had proven himself at every level.

"But we still hadn't won," he said. "We still hadn't even made it to the playoffs." In other words, there was still more to prove. Much more.

Rudy at the University of Michigan, proving himself at the big-time college level. (Photo courtesy of the University of Michigan)

Kermit at American University: "The happiest days of my life." (Photo courtesy of American University)

When it was good: Kermit with a rare open shot. (John Zimmerman/ *Sports Illustrated*)

Homecoming: Rudy (his jaw wired shut), Sophie, and their daughter Nichole, together again in Houston a few weeks after the punch. (Bob Straus/*Sports Illustrated*)

Kermit and Pat in happier days. (Photo courtesy of Pat Carter)

The comeback that wasn't: Kermit during his brief stint with the Golden State Warriors. (Peter Read Miller/*Sports Illustrated*)

On the way to a
championship:
Rudy leading the
Rockets to their
first NBA title,
in 1994. (John
McDonough/
Sports Illustrated)

Victory: Rudy and the Rockets celebrate with NBC's Bob Costas. (John
McDonough/*Sports Illustrated*)

Red Auerbach, the man who saved Kermit's career. (Dick Raphael/ *Sports Illustrated*)

Kareem Abdul-Jabbar, the best player in the game. He tried too late to stop the fight. (John Zimmerman/*Sports Illustrated*)

Calvin Murphy, the last man anyone in the NBA wanted to tangle with. (John Iacono/*Sports Illustrated*)

Jerry West as Lakers coach. Twenty-five years later he is still horrified by what he saw. (John Zimmerman/*Sports Illustrated*)

12

The Bright Lights of L.A.

Donald Dell was relatively new to the business of agenting in 1973. He had been a star tennis player in college and had gone on to get his law degree at the University of Virginia. In the late 1960s he had been captain of the U.S. Davis Cup team and had become close friends with Arthur Ashe. When tennis became an open sport in 1968, allowing pros to play in the Grand Slam events, Dell began representing players he knew as their lawyer, Ashe among them.

To this day, after thirty-five years as an agent, Dell still winces when he is referred to as an agent. "Lawyer, representative, either one is fine," he said. "Agent implies something that I'm not."

While others might disagree with that self-assessment, Dell was still learning his way around the "sports representation" world when he signed Kermit Washington as a client in the spring of 1973. He only had a handful of basketball clients at the time, and landing someone who according to all reports would be one of the first ten players chosen in the NBA draft was a major coup for him.

"I remember when I told him I had chosen him," Washington said. "He was really excited. In fact I think that's one of the reasons

I chose him. He gave me the impression that it was important to him to represent me. The other guys I met with acted as if they were doing me a favor."

Shortly after the NBA draft, Dell and his newly minted client flew to Los Angeles for preliminary meetings with the Lakers. On the plane, Dell and Washington talked contract. Washington wanted to know what kind of deal Dell was planning to ask for.

"Given your position in the draft, I would think we can get at least four years guaranteed at somewhere around four hundred thousand dollars," Dell answered. "There might be a fifth year, but we should get at least four."

Washington nodded. "What does guaranteed mean?" he asked.

Dell explained it meant that the team had to pay him for whatever period the contract was guaranteed for, regardless of whether he was still on the team. "That's why it's guaranteed," Dell explained. "They are guaranteeing they'll pay you no matter what."

Washington's eyes went wide. "They have to pay me even if they cut me, even if I'm not good enough to play for them?"

Dell nodded.

Washington shook his head. "No," he said. "I don't want to do that. I don't want to be paid for not working. If I'm not good enough, they shouldn't have to pay me."

Dell was stunned. "I had never had an athlete say that to me before that day, and I have never since had an athlete say that to me," he said. "Kermit just believed you should only be paid for working. He felt as if that was stealing."

Kermit Washington certainly isn't the only person ever to put forth the notion that athletes shouldn't be paid if they don't perform, but he may well be the only *athlete* ever to put forth that notion.

"It just didn't seem right," he said. "The way I was raised, you only got paid for work done. What Donald was talking about just didn't sound right to me."

Dell explained to Washington that the guarantee was protection: from injury, from a coach who might not like a player, from being rushed to perform at a level a young player might not be able to attain early in his career. It was standard, something the general manager—in this case Pete Newell—would accept as a matter of course. This sort of thing, Dell explained, is the reason you hire an agent.

Washington agreed . . . grudgingly. Even later in his career, when he had come to understand that in the NBA you fought for every penny, he was never completely comfortable with the notion of being paid for not playing. By then, though, he understood that the owner—whoever it was—wasn't paying him as an act of charity. He would learn about that the hard way.

It was late in the summer when Dell and Newell finalized Washington's contract. It was pretty close to what Dell had told him it would be. The first four years were guaranteed, and there was a club option for a fifth year. His salary would go up each year, beginning at $80,000 the first year and climbing in $10,000 increments for four years.

To Washington, an annual salary of $80,000 was as good as $8 million. He was thrilled. For the first time in his life, he actually had money to spend. He flew to Los Angeles, signed his contract, found a condo near the L.A. Forum and the Lakers' training camp at Loyola Marymount, and asked Pat to come to Los Angeles once he had moved into his condo.

The plan was to get married. They had talked about doing it on the East Coast before making the move, but had agreed it would be a lot simpler to just go to a justice of the peace in Los Angeles and do it that way. Although his success in college had brought a certain degree of peace to his relationship with his father and stepmother, Washington still felt awkward and uncomfortable with them. The memory of Barbara asking him for his house key when he left to enroll at American was hard to shake. Pat was closer to her family, but not so close that getting married across the country from them bothered her. So just before training camp started, they were married in Los Angeles City Hall.

The wedding was another surprise to Dell; not the notion of Kermit's marrying Pat, but the way it happened. "I was out there for a couple of things and I stopped by to see Kermit one morning," he said. "We were sitting there talking when all of a sudden Pat started screaming from upstairs, 'Kermit, get up here and get dressed or we'll be late!' I asked Kermit what was up and he said, 'Oh, no big deal, we're just getting married in an hour.'"

There was no honeymoon, unless you count the notion of a couple of East Coast kids settling into a new home in L.A. as a honeymoon. In those days the NBA season started the second week in October and training camp started the last week in September. Kermit and Pat were married September 23. Two days later, Kermit reported to camp to begin his NBA career.

Even though he was the Lakers' top draft pick, someone the team had spent a good deal of money to sign, he felt overwhelmed at the start. The Lakers were a team in transition, but they were still the Lakers. They had reached the NBA finals in four of the previous five seasons, winning the title in 1972, and had lost seven-game series in the finals to the Celtics in 1969 and the Knicks in 1970. The previous spring, they had lost the finals in five games to the Knicks. Shortly after that series, Wilt Chamberlain surprised most people in basketball by retiring.

The Lakers' center was now Elmore Smith. The core of the team was the backcourt: All-Star Gail Goodrich and Hall of Famer Jerry West. Washington was intimidated by West; terrified, in fact.

"I had never played with a competitor like Jerry West," he said. "Anytime I made a mistake in practice, it felt to me as if he was staring holes in me. I could almost hear him thinking, 'What in the world were we thinking drafting this guy?' I was a lot more scared of him than I was of Coach [Bill] Sharman. I mean a lot more scared."

It was not an easy team for a rookie to fit in with. Most of the players were longtime NBA veterans who were well into their thirties. Bill Bridges, who was one of the toughest, strongest players in the league, blooded Washington early in camp, literally and figuratively, pushing him around, daring him to retaliate. Early in the season, the team traded for a fading Connie Hawkins to strengthen the power forward spot, meaning that Washington's playing time dwindled from not much to very little.

The worst part was feeling as if he wasn't good enough to play at the NBA level. Washington had never become a polished player in college; he hadn't needed to. Against most teams that American played, he could camp out in the low post, catch the ball there, and power his way to the basket. If he missed, he chased the rebound and scored that way. Often his best offensive move was to throw the ball off the backboard, rebound it, and score.

That wasn't going to work in the NBA, especially at 6-8. He would have to learn to play power forward, which was a position completely different from college center. To begin with, it meant playing facing the basket and away from the basket. A jump shot was a prerequisite, and Washington's knowledge of the jump shot didn't extend much beyond his ability to spell the words.

So there he was on a veteran team, trying to learn a new position and feeling as if he was going nowhere fast. He hurt himself during an exhibition game, falling awkwardly on his rear end while grabbing a rebound. Afraid he would be labeled soft if he complained about the injury, he didn't tell anyone how much it hurt and ended up doing damage to his back that would stay with him throughout his career.

The Lakers had won 60 games in 1973 with Chamberlain. Without him, with Smith at center and Washington playing a very minor role, they won 47 in 1974 and were beaten in five games in the opening round of the playoffs by the Kareem Abdul-Jabbar–led Milwaukee Bucks. West decided that, at thirty-five, he had seen enough. The team had gotten old in a hurry, and even though West still averaged more than 20 points a game that season, he decided to retire. In two seasons, the Lakers had lost two Hall of Fame players, arguably two of the best ten players in the league's history.

Not surprisingly the Lakers plummeted in 1975, dropping to 30–52, the worst record for the franchise since the move from Minneapolis in 1960. Washington's second season wasn't any better than the first. Instead of being a benchwarmer on a good team, he was a benchwarmer on a bad one. He didn't feel any more comfortable in games. He was still an offensive liability. He was an aggressive rebounder, able to use his quickness and leaping ability to get to the ball, but very unsure of himself on offense. If he was more than five feet from the basket, defenders dropped off him, daring him to shoot.

The only saving grace, he thought, was Donald Dell's guaranteed contract. "If I hadn't had that," he said, "I'd have been long gone."

By the end of that miserable 1974–75 season, it was apparent that the Lakers had to put their team through a complete makeover. Losing wasn't acceptable in Los Angeles, and it certainly wasn't acceptable to team owner Jack Kent Cooke, especially when his hockey team, the Kings, which shared the Forum with the Lakers, weren't making a dent in the standings or at the box office. The Lakers had to be fixed, and fast.

That was where Kareem Abdul-Jabbar came into the picture. He had one year left on his contract in Milwaukee and had made it clear to management there that he had no intention of re-signing at the end of the 1976 season. The Bucks had won the NBA title in 1971 and had lost a seven-game series in the finals to the Celtics in 1974. One title in six seasons was not enough to sate Abdul-Jabbar. Beyond that, Milwaukee was the heart of the Midwest. Abdul-Jabbar had grown up in New York, had gone to college in Los Angeles, and had become a Muslim after the 1971 season, a political statement that hardly endeared him to the typical Bucks fan.

Newell had been friends with Bucks general manager Wayne Embry for years. When he heard that Embry was looking to move Abdul-Jabbar rather than lose him for nothing in a year to free agency, he opened talks about a swap. First, though, he had to convince his coach, his front office, and, most important, his owner that it was worth giving up the players the Lakers would have to give up to get Abdul-Jabbar.

"When you look back at it now, it seems like the most obvious thing in the world to do," said Sharman. "But back then, none of us was all that sure. Kareem was thought of as a little bit of a troublemaker if only because he was so quiet and kept to himself so much, and we knew it was going to cost a lot to get him. But Pete kept hammering away, saying you couldn't go wrong trading for the best player in the game, and there was no doubt Kareem was the best player in the game."

The toughest sell turned out to be Cooke. It wasn't that he didn't want to make a deal, he very much wanted a superstar on his suddenly starless team. But he knew it would cost a lot, both in terms of players and dollars, to land Abdul-Jabbar. And so while Newell negotiated with Embry, Cooke was off negotiating with Portland owner Herman Scarkovsky to make a trade that would bring Bill Walton to Los Angeles.

When Newell finally learned what Cooke was up to, he was stunned.

"What stunned me was that Mr. Cooke was always going on and on about not liking Walton," Newell said. "He would say to me, 'What is wrong with that young man, Peter? What is he thinking about with that haircut and that beard and all those people he has living in his house? It's just awful, Peter, awful.'"

Cooke apparently didn't think the beard, the long hair, or the way-out friends would be so bad if Walton were wearing a Lakers uniform. Walton had been in the league for one year at that point and had experienced only mixed success, largely due to injuries that had limited him to 35 games as a rookie. He had averaged just 12.8 points per game when he had been able to play. Because of that he would cost less than Abdul-Jabbar, both playerwise and moneywise.

Newell thought Walton was a great talent but an unproven player. Abdul-Jabbar was the best player in the game. To him it was a no-brainer. "I told Wayne if we were going to make a deal, we had to move fast, because if Mr. Cooke went off and made his trade with Scarkovsky, that would be the end of it," Newell said.

There was one other factor: the New York Knicks. They also wanted Abdul-Jabbar, who had grown up in the city. His acquisition would make a heroic homecoming for a team that had fallen on hard times with the retirement of Willis Reed and Dave DeBusschere and the aging of Walt Frazier and Bill Bradley. The Knicks needed a talent and excitement injection every bit as much as the Lakers and were willing to spend a lot of money to bring the hometown kid home.

"But that was the big difference," Newell said. "They were offering a lot of money because they really didn't have any players to trade. I had players who could help Wayne's team."

Knowing time was short, Newell and Embry agreed to meet in Denver to try to hammer out a deal. Newell offered four players: center Elmore Smith (important, because the Bucks would need a center), guard Brian Winters, and two young players the Lakers had just taken in the first round of the draft, Junior Bridgeman and David Meyers. Embry knew he was going to get ripped by some for trading Abdul-Jabbar with a year left on his contract. But the Bucks had only been 38–44 that season, even with Abdul-Jabbar averaging 30 points a game.

He agreed to the deal.

Then he flew back to Milwaukee to convince ownership to make the deal. Time was so short—Cooke was ready to pull the trigger on the Walton deal if Newell couldn't close on Abdul-

Jabbar—that Newell sent his lawyer back to Milwaukee with Embry so the papers could be signed as soon as Bucks' ownership agreed.

"Mr. Cooke really wasn't sure if we weren't better off with the younger player," Newell said. "He was willing to go along, but only if I got it done in a hurry, because he didn't want Walton getting away. I had to keep reminding him that Kareem was only twenty-eight. Not exactly over the hill."

Embry called Newell at 7:00 A.M. the day after the meeting in Denver. His ownership had bought in. When Newell told Cooke the deal was done, he told him to go ahead and make it. On June 16, 1975, Kareem Abdul-Jabbar became a Los Angeles Laker.

"I remember Mr. Cooke saying, 'Peter, I hope you're right about this,'" Newell said. "I think in the end we did the right thing."

Abdul-Jabbar's fourteen productive seasons as a Laker and five championships—as opposed to the single title Walton won in Portland before injuries crippled his career—would appear to bear Newell out.

No one was more thrilled to hear about the deal for Abdul-Jabbar than Kermit Washington. On a practical level it meant he would have to spend less time filling in at center than he had in the past. Abdul-Jabbar always played a lot of minutes and rarely got into foul trouble. On a personal level it meant he was going to be teammates with his hero and role model.

"Kareem was a great player," he said. "He always seemed to conduct himself with dignity, and I knew he had graduated from UCLA in four years. I thought if I could be like him, I'd be doing okay."

Washington was never going to be 7-foot-2 and was never going to possess one of the most potent offensive shots in the history of

the game, Abdul-Jabbar's unstoppable skyhook. But he had graduated from American in four years and carried himself with dignity,
so there were parallels.

Being Abdul-Jabbar's teammate was thrilling, but not always
easy. The Lakers' new star had never been outgoing, and coming
back to Los Angeles didn't change that. Occasionally he got angry
with Washington in practice for being too physical with him when
the two would go head-to-head. And while his presence made the
Lakers better, he didn't provide the kind of immediate turnaround
that had been hoped for. The Lakers finished 40–42 and out of the
playoffs for a second straight season. Abdul-Jabbar played in all 82
games and averaged 27.7 points per game, but it wasn't enough.
The team hadn't yet been able to find anyone who could begin to
replace West. Goodrich was still a good player but starting to fade,
and there was little help for Abdul-Jabbar up front.

Specifically there was very little help from the 1973 number one
draft choice, now in his third lackluster season. "I was as miserable
as you can be," Washington remembered. "I wasn't playing, when I
did play I didn't play well, and my knee was giving me fits. Other
than that, it was a wonderful season."

He only got into 36 games and played half as many minutes as
he had the previous season. His points and rebounding only
slipped a little, because they couldn't go down very much from 4.5
and 4.1. By the end of the season, Washington knew he was one
year away from being out of a job if something didn't happen. "I
think they had pretty much given up on me," he said. "They just
looked at me as a mistake. Once the changes happened, I was convinced I was gone—at the end of the next season, unless they could
somehow trade me before that."

The changes came at season's end. Even though Walton had
been limited to 51 games and the Blazers had finished three games
behind the Lakers, Cooke had not been happy about the fact that
his team had finished under .500 after he had spent so much

money to get Abdul-Jabbar. Jerry West wanted to coach. So Cooke made West the coach, promoted Sharman to general manager, and "reassigned" Newell to a consulting job. Washington, who had been terrified of West when they had been teammates for a year, was convinced that West would do everything in his power to trade him or even try to convince Cooke to buy out the last guaranteed year of his contract.

"Kermit was right," West said years later. "Based on what I had seen of him, I thought the best thing we could possibly do was make a trade for him before the season started."

Washington was at a loss. He went home to D.C. for a few days and had lunch with Mike Cardozo, who was then handling contracts at the newly renamed ProServ.

"What am I going to do, Mike?" he asked, almost rhetorically. "I just can't play the way they want me to play. If I don't get off the bench this season, I'm going to be out of the league."

Cardozo knew Washington was right, he wasn't just another rich basketball player bemoaning his fate. "Why don't you go talk to Pete Newell," he suggested. "He's got a lot of time on his hands right now and he was a great college coach. Maybe he can help you learn how to play the forward position."

Washington was convinced that a big part of his problem was that he had never been coached on how to play the power forward position. Back then the NBA wasn't aswarm in assistant coaches the way it is now, and there was very little time for coaches to work individually with players. Washington was only vaguely aware of the fact that Newell had been a great college coach, but when Cardozo suggested going to him it sounded like as good a proposal as any other he had heard. So one morning he went to Newell's new office and presented him with the idea.

"Basically I said, 'Help me,'" he remembered. "I told him I'd work as hard as he wanted as long as he wanted. Of course I had no idea what I was getting myself into."

Newell had always been loathe to interfere with players while he was the general manager, feeling he was treading on the turf of the coaching staff. The only time he had ever worked individually with players as a general manager had been in the summer of 1971 in San Diego, when Alex Hannum had left the team and no new coach was in place yet. The players he had worked with that summer were Stu Lantz and a talented but frustrated kid who had just finished his rookie season: Rudy Tomjanovich. "Stu needed to work on going to his left, Rudy needed to work on creating his own shot," Newell remembered. "I really enjoyed working with them, but I only did it because we didn't have a coach at the time."

Now, though, he wasn't the general manager. He had always liked Washington and felt responsible for him since he had drafted him. But he wanted to be certain Washington was serious about doing the kind of work that would be necessary to make it worth both their whiles.

Most mornings they went at 7:00 A.M. to the gym at Loyola Marymount, which was where the Lakers trained during the season. LMU was also the home of the L.A. summer league at the time, and there were some days when they couldn't get the gym, even early in the morning.

"When that happened we would just get in the car and drive to a high school gym someplace and convince the custodian to turn the lights on for us," Newell said. "One way or the other, we found a place to work."

And work they did. It was, as Washington always likes to put it, "a living nightmare."

Newell knew he had to change Washington's game technically at both ends of the floor: get him to play facing the basket on offense, to develop some kind of jump shot so he would be a threat away from the basket, and get him to be able to guard quicker people with some proficiency on defense. The defensive part was the hardest, because Newell insisted on repetition to make Washington stronger: slide drills, hands-up drills, every drill that players despise. Washington hated every second of it but never backed off, never missed a day, never came up with an excuse not to show up.

"There was one drill he had done in college," Washington remembered. "You got down in a stance, put both hands up, and started sliding. First to your left, then to your right. Every thirty seconds or so he would call out, 'Change,' and you would have to go in the other direction. It was the most brutal thing I've ever done."

The first day Newell had Washington do the drill he collapsed in a heap after three minutes. "Kermit," Newell told him, "by the time I'm finished with you, you're going to do this drill for twenty minutes."

"Not possible," Washington answered.

"I remember one morning we were finishing up and we were doing the slide/hands-up drill and I was all over Kermit, screaming in his face not to quit, not to give up, not to back off," Newell said. "A couple of younger guys who were coming in to warm up for a summer league game walked in and saw me screaming in Kermit's face. They recognized Kermit as a Laker, a real live NBA player. I heard one of them say to the other as we were finishing, 'Wow, I guess that old man has no idea who it is he's yelling at.'"

By the end of the summer Newell could see that he was yelling at a different basketball player. Washington did the slide/hands-up drill for twenty minutes every morning the last two weeks. The work was paying off, Newell was convinced of it. Washington felt a lot more confident and knew he was in the best shape of his life, but the payoff wouldn't come until training camp. He would have to go in there, overcome his fear of Jerry West, and show the new coach that he was a different player than the one who had never averaged more than 5 points or 4 rebounds a game during three years in the league.

"I knew I had an uphill battle with Jerry," he said. "But at least when I finished the summer with Mr. Newell I felt like I was going into the battle with some weapons. I was better all alone in that gym. The question was, would I be better with other NBA players on the court with me?"

The answer was an emphatic yes. West could see it almost from the first day of camp. It wasn't as if Washington hadn't been in shape in previous years—that had never been his problem—but now he was in better shape than anyone on the team. And clearly he had new basketball skills.

"He was a different player, especially on offense, but on defense too," West said. "I had thought of him before as someone you couldn't play for long stretches, because it was like playing four-on-five on offense and you couldn't do that. But he had moves now, he could make something happen facing the basket. He had made himself into a power forward."

Washington's confidence grew with each passing day at training camp. By the time the season started, he had gone from the end of the bench to the front of the bench; from an average of eight minutes per game—when he got into a game at all—to playing half the game, every game. Soon after the season began, he became either the sixth man or a starter, because West recognized that he brought the kind of ruggedness to the floor that made life much easier for Abdul-Jabbar.

Often West had Washington cover the opponent's best inside player. He could now afford to keep him on the floor for long stretches because his offense, while hardly spectacular, was good enough that the other team had to guard him. At Newell's insistence, he had worked for hours on a jump shot that he could take to fifteen feet, something he had never been able to do in the past. Beyond that, given the added minutes he was playing, Washington was a force on the boards, averaging almost 10 rebounds a game even though he only played about half the game most nights.

Buoyed by Washington's improvement and the addition of Cazzie Russell, a proven scorer at the small forward spot, the Lakers were the best team in the league during the first half of the season. Up in

Portland, Bill Walton was finally healthy and beginning to become the dominating center everyone had expected him to become when he first came into the league in 1974. For the season, he would average almost 19 points per game, more than 14 rebounds a night, and 4 assists, using his superb passing skills to find the open man in the Portland offense. With Walton healthy almost the entire season—he did still miss 17 games—the Blazers emerged as a force.

But they couldn't beat the Lakers. Three times during the first few months of the season the teams met, and three times the Lakers won. Abdul-Jabbar was still a better player than Walton, thanks in large part to his experience, and Washington was one of the few players in the league strong enough to not be dominated by power forward Maurice Lucas, who was the Blazers' leading scorer and the league's number one intimidator. At 6-8, 240 pounds, with a mean streak that literally scared opposing players, Lucas often took over games with one snatched rebound or even a fierce stare. Washington wasn't nearly as skilled as Lucas, but he was every bit as big and strong. He wasn't about to back down to him.

"The first half of that season was my dream come true," Washington said. "All the work in the summertime was paying off. I felt more confident, and I knew everyone else had more confidence in me too, especially Jerry and Kareem. That meant a lot to me. We were playing well, and I knew I was one of the reasons. I kept thinking to myself, 'All of this is too good to be true.'"

The only negative connected to all the newfound minutes Washington was playing was the chronic ache in his right knee. He had first damaged the knee as a rookie, but rest had always been a tonic when it began to really bother him. During those first three seasons, he had gotten plenty of rest. But now, after a summer of hard work and an NBA schedule that meant playing four or five nights a week for lengths of time he hadn't even thought about since college, the knee began to hurt again.

Washington didn't want to go to the doctors and have it checked, because he was concerned they would find something and insist on surgery that would end his season. No way would he chance that. His plan was to play through the pain until the end of the season and then find out what—if anything—could be done.

The Lakers' last game before the All-Star break was at home against the Denver Nuggets. Driving to the Forum that night with Pat, Washington knew the knee was worse than it had ever been but was hoping the four-day All-Star break would give him the rest he needed. "I thought if I could stay off it for those four days, I'd be okay," he remembered. "That had worked in the past. I knew the pain would come back once we started playing again, but I was thinking it would come back in stages the way it always did and if I made it to the playoffs, where you have more nights off than during the regular season, I'd be okay. The season was already two-thirds over. I was convinced I could do it. Pat thought I was crazy, that I needed to see the doctor."

He ended up seeing a doctor—that night, because he didn't make it through the game. Late in the second quarter, running the lane on a fast break, he caught a pass, went up for a layup, came down, and *heard* his knee shatter. "That's what I remember most, the sound of it," he said. "When I went down, the pain told me I was in trouble, but more than that the sound left no doubt that I had done something really, really bad."

The fragile knee had simply collapsed from the wear and tear of playing when there was already damage done. Lying on the floor of the Forum, Washington looked down and saw his kneecap pushed over to the side of his leg. "I knew right then," he said, "that at the very least my season was over."

At the very least was right. He had torn a tendon and done damage to both his cartilage and his ligament. Even today, with all the advances made in orthopedics, that would mean major surgery. In 1977 it meant surgery that had to be considered career-threatening.

They operated the next morning. The next few days are hazy in Washington's memory except for the pain. It was bad enough that when Pat came to the hospital with Dana, who was a little more than a year old, he couldn't bear to have his daughter sit on the bed with him. "Every time she moved or bounced or did anything, pain shot through my entire body," he said. "It killed me to do it, but I finally had to ask Pat to take her home. I was in agony."

Things weren't very good for the Lakers either. They were a different team without Washington, not as strong on defense or on the boards. They did manage to hang on to finish the season with the league's best record, 53–29, but Portland was closing fast at the finish. Without Washington to deal with Lucas, the Blazers beat the Lakers in their last meeting of the regular season and then swept them in the Western Conference finals.

It is unlikely that the Lakers would have beaten the Blazers at that stage of the season even with a healthy Washington. Portland had matured into a superb team that would go on to upset the supposedly unbeatable Philadelphia 76ers in the finals. But it is just as unlikely that the Lakers would have been swept if Washington had played. "They had real trouble with us when Kermit was healthy that year," Abdul-Jabbar remembered. "Would we have won? I'm not sure. But four straight? No way."

Jack Ramsay, who coached that Portland team, doesn't argue with Abdul-Jabbar's assessment. "We were on a roll by then," he said. "But if we had played the Lakers with Kermit, they would have been far more dangerous than they were without him. They simply didn't have anyone on that team other than Kermit who could handle Maurice."

The finals that year were still a prime-time event. This was just prior to the start of the so-called dark period, when the NBA's ratings had slipped so badly that CBS began televising the finals on tape delay at 11:30 P.M. In 1977 the 76ers were a true glamour team, led by the spectacular Julius Erving, who had joined the team after the merger with the ABA the previous fall. George McGinnis was a superstar, Doug Collins was a perennial All-Star, and Darryl Dawkins, the 7-foot-1-inch center who had never gone to college, was thought to be one of the next great players. The opponent was the upstart Blazers, a team from the NBA's smallest market, an expansion team just seven years earlier. Now they had Walton and Lucas and a group of hard-nosed role players who weren't intimidated by the 76ers.

The first two games were in Philadelphia, and the Sixers, after winning a close game one, routed the Blazers 107–89 in game two. Near the end of that game, Dawkins and Lucas got into a fight. It wasn't one of those throw a few punches and dance around NBA fights, it was a serious brawl, with players jumping in to try to pull the two immensely strong men apart.

Brent Musburger, doing play-by-play for CBS, remembers being frightened that a full-scale riot was going to break out. Dawkins and Lucas were both so strong and riled up that it took a bevy of players and security people to finally get them off each other. While the fight was going on, many in the crowd began pushing toward the court, including friends and family of Dawkins.

"It was a frightening moment," Musburger remembered. "And the timing of it was important. This wasn't just another fight in another NBA game. This was two big, strong men who were really angry taking swings at one another, and no one could stop them. Plus, it was the finals, it was prime-time national TV. It could not have made Larry O'Brien happy to see this happening in the middle of his showcase. It left you with a very bad taste in your mouth."

Musburger was right about O'Brien's reaction. The commissioner had been concerned all season with the escalating number of fights in the league. He felt powerless to stop the fighting, since the most he could fine a player for getting into a fight was $500 and the longest suspension he could mete out was five games. The Dawkins-Lucas fight *was* scary. O'Brien and everyone in the league knew it could have been much worse.

Perhaps energized by the fight, the Blazers turned the series completely around, taking the next four games to win the title four games to two. They clinched the championship on a Sunday afternoon in Portland, setting off a wild postgame celebration. In a decision long remembered by both the NBA and CBS, the network honchos chose not to stay in Portland for the postgame celebration or even for the trophy presentation—which was taped to be shown later—because they wanted to switch immediately to the final round of the Kemper Open golf tournament.

By the time Musburger got out of the locker room after the trophy presentation, fans in the arena had figured out that CBS had cut away as soon as the game was over. "They were furious," Musburger said. "I was the symbol of CBS to them. I was wearing the blazer, I was the voice they heard, the face they saw. They probably thought I had something to do with the decision, which of course I didn't. It got ugly. I needed a security escort to get out of the building and a police escort to get out of the parking lot to the airport. They hid me out in the airport until my flight took off. It was a scary scene."

O'Brien was convinced his league had become too violent in every way. Most of the owners agreed with him. That summer, at the league meetings, responding to the forty-one fights during the regular season that had each led to at least one ejection—usually more—and to the specter of the Dawkins-Lucas fight, the owners voted to give O'Brien much broader powers to penalize players who fought during a game. The maximum fine for fighting was increased to $10,000—roughly equivalent, given the difference in salary levels, to a $100,000 fine today—and, more important, the commissioner now had the right to suspend players indefinitely without pay. That was a long way from $500 and five games.

"It was an important thing to do," David Stern, then the league's outside counsel, said. "The message had to be sent to the players that what had gone on before was no longer tolerable. We needed to stop it before it got worse. That was our goal."

Kermit Washington paid little attention when the new penalties for fighting were announced. He was deep into the process of rehabbing his knee and preparing for another summer of torture with Pete Newell. His only concern was getting back to where he had been as a player before his knee had collapsed on him on that February night in the Forum.

The last thing on his mind was being suspended for fighting during a game. All he was thinking about was getting himself back into games.

13

Turnaround

While the Lakers were hitting bottom during the 1974–75 season, an old team that needed to make major changes to contend again, the Houston Rockets were a team finally headed in the right direction.

The team had spent its first three years in Houston running in place. Consistently lousy was the best way to describe the Rockets. They had won 34, 33, and 32 games, and their attendance, a paltry 4,966 the first season, when they played in half the cities in Texas, had actually dropped to 3,855 by the third season. The team had already been sold once since the move to Texas and was about to be sold a second time. Tex Winter had coached for a season and a half and then been replaced by Johnny Egan. Ray Patterson had come in as president and general manager and promptly traded Elvin Hayes, the team's most popular player.

But by the end of the 1973–74 season, there were some signs of life. The heart and soul of the team was now made up of three young players: Rudy Tomjanovich, Calvin Murphy, and Mike Newlin, who had come to the Rockets one year after Tomjanovich and Murphy. Two-thirds of the way through that season, Patterson had made what appeared to be a minor deal, sending Matt Guokas and Jack Marin to Buffalo and getting Dave Wohl, a guard, and Kevin Kunnert, a 7-foot center out of the University of Iowa, in return. At the time, the trade appeared to be nothing more than Patterson conceding that trading Hayes to Baltimore to get Marin had been a mistake.

But Kunnert proved to be more than just a throw-in to a deal that would be little noted nor long remembered. The Rockets were in desperate need of help inside. They were a team that did not play good defense in the post and a team that was consistently outrebounded. Kunnert had a major impact in both areas. He wasn't the quickest or prettiest player in the world to watch, but he wasn't the least bit afraid to mix it up inside and was willing to use his size to push opposing centers out of the low post. He was also a very capable rebounder, leading the team during his first full season with an average of 8.4 a game. Coincidence or not, the Rockets went from minus 130 rebounds versus the opposition for the season to plus 256.

"Off the floor, you never met a nicer guy than Kevin," Tomjanovich said. "He was quiet but very funny and enjoyable to be around. But on the floor, he wasn't afraid of anything or anyone. He was a physical player but not a dirty one. On the other hand, if someone messed with him, he responded."

The Rockets were a young and improving team that season. The core of the team—Tomjanovich, Murphy, Newlin, Kunnert, and Ed Ratleff—were all in their midtwenties. Needing to finish the regular season strong after a four-game losing streak had put them in jeopardy, they won three straight to reach the playoffs for the second time in team history (they had made it in 1969, with a 37–45 record, when eight of fourteen teams qualified) and went into postseason with a record of 41–41, the first time in the team's eight years that it had finished at .500.

The first-round playoff opponent was the New York Knicks. The Knicks were at the end of a glorious run during which they had won two NBA titles (1970 and 1973) and had been a league force every year, reaching at least the conference finals for six straight seasons. But Willis Reed, their center and captain, and Dave DeBusschere, their heart and soul, had retired. Walt Frazier and Earl Monroe were still a potent backcourt and Bill Bradley was still the starting small forward, but the centers, John Gianelli and Hawthorne Wingo, weren't exactly Reed's caliber.

Generating interest in the team for the first time ever in Houston, the Rockets won the three-game miniseries 2–1. They won the deciding game in a blowout, 118–86, with Tomjanovich leading the way with 25 points. That put the Rockets into a conference semifinal series against the defending champion Boston Celtics. Tomjanovich and Murphy were both superb, each averaging more than 25 points per game, but the Celtics, with Dave Cowens and John Havlicek and Jo Jo White, had too much experience and firepower. They won the series four games to one.

Still, it appeared that a corner had been turned. Tomjanovich and Murphy were now established stars in the league firmament. The team was about to move into a new building in the fall of 1975, the Summit. After four years of feeling as if they were on the road regardless of where they played, they would have a true home in an NBA-quality building. The days of treks to El Paso and nights playing in front of thousands and thousands of empty seats in the Astrodome were behind them.

The new building and the playoff run did boost attendance. The average went from just over 4,000 per game in 1975 to just under 7,000 in 1976. That was better, but it still meant the team was being outdrawn on most nights by a lot of the state's high school football teams.

"We were making progress, but it was slow progress," said Ray Patterson, then the team president. "It was exactly the same as with the team on the court. People got excited in the playoffs in '75, but until we showed that we were more than a .500 team, we weren't going to get people running to the box office. Rudy and Calvin were exciting players, but we needed to be more than what we were if we were going to truly turn the city on."

The 1975–76 season was almost identical to 1974–75, the team hovering at .500 and trying to find a way to sneak back into the playoffs. The problem was that Houston played in the Eastern Conference, which had most of the power in the league that year. In the Western Conference, the Milwaukee Bucks and Detroit Pistons made the playoffs with records of 38–44 and 36–46. The Rockets finished at 40–42 but were six games behind the last playoff qualifier in the East.

The core of the team had put up numbers almost identical to those they had posted in 1975. In fact Kunnert had improved his numbers, averaging better than 12 points and just under 10 rebounds a game. Talented forward John Johnson had been added through an early-season trade, but still the Rockets were a .500 team. Changing coaches—Tom Nissalke replaced Egan at season's end—probably wasn't going to change the team's performance that drastically.

"It wasn't as if they had a bunch of guys who didn't play hard," Nissalke said years later. "Coaching wasn't their problem. No one played harder than Rudy and Calvin, Newlin or Kunnert. Those guys were all competitors. The team needed another star if it was going to make the jump to the next level."

Patterson knew this. Just prior to draft day he made a trade with Atlanta that gave the Rockets the number one pick in the draft. He then used that pick to take John Lucas, a talented point guard who had been a four-year starter at the University of Maryland. Lucas was the kind of pure point guard that the Rockets lacked. Murphy was more a shooter than a passer. Lucas was an explosive player, a versatile athlete who had performed the unique double of being a collegiate All-American in both basketball and tennis.

"He was perfect for us," Tomjanovich said. "We had players who loved to run the fast break, and Luke was the guy who would find you on the break. If you were a shooter, you had to love playing with him."

Patterson wasn't finished dealing. Two games into the new season, with his team having started 2–0, he made what appeared to be an audacious deal with the Buffalo Braves. He traded his team's next *two* first-round draft picks and sent a large chunk of cash to Buffalo in return for twenty-one-year-old Moses Malone.

Two years earlier, Malone had made headlines when he decided not to become a teammate of Lucas's at Maryland. Instead, having committed to coach Lefty Driesell, having already arrived on campus to enroll for classes, he decided at the last possible moment to forgo college completely and sign with the Utah Stars of the ABA. Malone was a 6-foot-10-inch basketball prodigy who would have been a dominant college player. Nowadays players skipping college to turn pro is routine, something that happens in several cases every single year. In 1974 it was a brand-new phenomenon. It had only been one year since Spencer Haywood had gone to court to force the NBA to allow him to play before his college class graduated. Now a new step had been taken: a player bypassing college altogether.

His decision not to suit up at Maryland stunned Driesell. Without Malone, the Terrapins reached the NCAA tournament's round of eight in 1975, leaving Driesell to wonder forever what his team might have done with Malone. A case can be made that Driesell never completely got over Malone's defection. He never forgave Donald Dell, who became Malone's agent and negotiated the ABA deal for him. Years later, whenever Dell's name came up in conversation, Driesell would shake his head and start talking about "the man who took Moses away from me."

In fact for many years Driesell included Malone in his media guide on a page titled "Lefty's Players in the Pros." There, along with players like Lucas and Tom McMillen and Len Elmore, was Malone, who never once wore a Maryland uniform. Only after being chided for years about the picture of Malone did Driesell finally remove it.

As talented as he was, Malone found the transition to life in the pros difficult. He was a boy living among men. And although he was big and strong, he didn't really know how to play the game, certainly not at the pro level. He struggled in Utah and continued to have difficulties after signing with the Buffalo Braves in the NBA after two seasons in the ABA. At times his potential was apparent. At other times, he appeared to be years away from being a competent player.

There was also a perception that Malone wasn't very smart. That may have come in part from his decision to skip college, but it had more to do with the fact that he was so shy that when he spoke he almost never raised his voice much above a whisper. When he did speak, he spoke rapid-fire, as if trying to get the ordeal over with. His nickname around the league for many years was Mumbles Malone.

Malone wasn't stupid by any stretch, and as the years went by and he grew more confident, that became apparent to those who played with him. But he was always difficult to understand because he spoke so quickly. Even when he got over his shyness, he was a nightmare in a crowded locker room for reporters, because if you weren't standing right next to him, you couldn't hear a word he was saying.

Ray Patterson didn't much care about Malone's speech patterns. He saw a young player who would fit in perfectly with his team. As solid as Kunnert was on the boards and on defense, he was never going to be a low-post scorer. In fact, he was at his best on offense roaming the perimeter, shooting his funny-looking but effective (it looked more like he was launching a rocket than shooting a basketball) jump shot. The Rockets had all the perimeter scoring a team could want. They needed a force in the low post. Patterson believed Malone could become that force. He was willing to gamble his first-round draft picks because he saw Malone as someone who would have been taken with the first pick in the draft if he were coming out of college at age twenty-one or twenty-two.

The Malone trade was as big a success as the Hayes-Marin trade had been a bust. Malone gave the Rockets the inside presence they had lacked, averaging 13.5 points and 13.4 rebounds a night that first season in Houston, even though he was still learning how to play the low post. What's more, he freed up other players to do other things. Tomjanovich didn't have to worry about rebounding as much, and Lucas and Murphy both felt they could release on the fast break earlier because Malone was likely to come up with most defensive rebounds.

When Nissalke began playing Malone and Kunnert together, the big lineup proved effective. Kunnert could now play the perimeter, since Malone was camped inside, and the Rockets became an excellent rebounding team with Malone, Kunnert, and Tomjanovich up front. They went from 23–19 halfway through the season to 49–33 and won the Central Division, the first division title in the history of the franchise.

At last the team was starting to catch on in Houston. Attendance kept improving throughout the regular season, and it took off in the playoffs, with the 16,000-seat Summit finally playing to sellout crowds. By now the Tomjanovich family had become full-fledged Houstonians. Their first child, Nichole, had been born in 1973, and Melissa had followed in December of the 1976–77 season. They had moved into a house in a comfortable middle-class neighborhood. Rudy had gone from wondering if he was good enough to play to being the team's leading scorer, a perennial All-Star, and, along with his pal Murphy, the symbol of what the Rockets had become.

"That was a great ride that spring in the playoffs," he remembered. "Even though we'd been there in '75 and had gotten a taste of it, this was different, because we really thought we belonged. In

204 · JOHN FEINSTEIN

'75, winning that series against the Knicks was almost enough. It was as if we proved we were a legitimate team, and when we lost to the Celtics, even though it was disappointing, heck, it was the Celtics. How bad could you feel about losing to the Celtics?

"In '77, every loss hurt. And every win felt great. What hurt the most about losing the series to the 76ers was we were convinced if we got to the finals we could beat the Blazers. We were a lot like them in that we had kept improving during the season [and finished with an identical record] and were peaking in the playoffs."

If there was any doubt that the Rockets were coming into their own, it was wiped out during the conference semifinals against the Washington Bullets. Washington was a deep, experienced team led by the great Wes Unseld and Elvin Hayes, who was still a scoring force. The Bullets had reached the finals in 1975, the start of a run that would see them get that far three times in five seasons and win their only NBA title in 1978. When they went up two games to one in the series with game four to be played in Washington, it looked as if the Rockets might exit early.

But with Malone holding his own against Unseld and Tomjanovich and Murphy bombing from outside, the Rockets pulled out game four 107–103 and proceeded to shock the Bullets by winning the next two games to take the series 4–2. That put them into the conference finals against Philadelphia, a team that had all but been awarded the NBA title in October when it had acquired Dr. J, Julius Erving, to go with George McGinnis, Doug Collins, and Darryl Dawkins.

"Me and Doc together," McGinnis had said at the time. "Lights out."

The Sixers hadn't been lights out in the regular season, finishing a solid but hardly overwhelming 50–32—one game better than the Rockets. Still, everyone believed that when the time came to turn it on in the playoffs, they would. That had not proven to be the case in the conference semis, when they had to go seven games to beat an aging Boston team. Now they were facing the young and supremely confident Rockets.

Home court ruled for three games, the 76ers winning twice in Philadelphia, the Rockets once in Houston, before Collins came up with a monster night in game four, pouring in 36 points to lead his team to a 107–95 win that gave Philadelphia a 3–1 lead with game five in Philadelphia. That appeared to be the end of Houston's dream season. But the Rockets went into the Spectrum on a Sunday afternoon and with Lucas playing his best game of the season—21 points and 12 assists—and Tomjanovich making key shot after key shot, they stunned the 76ers and their fans, who were already preparing to start the finals against the Blazers (who had swept the Lakers) two nights later.

Instead, the two teams went back to Houston for game six. By now Erving had taken over on offense for Philadelphia. He had scored 37 in the loss on Sunday and in game six he had 34 more. But the Rockets kept answering and the game went to the wire, just as the game on Sunday had.

In the waning seconds, the 76ers had the lead, 111–109. Lucas, brilliant again throughout the night, drove the lane and went up for what would be a game-tying shot with one second left. The ball banked in and the whistle blew. Collins, famous throughout his career for taking charges, had put himself between Lucas and the basket and the two had collided. If the call was a block, the shot would count and Lucas could win the game with a free throw. But one man's block in basketball is another man's charge.

Jake O'Donnell called charge: no basket. Suddenly, stunningly, the series was over. Instead of going back to Philadelphia for a game seven in which all the pressure would have been squarely on the shoulders of the 76ers, the Rockets were going home.

"Maybe the single most disappointing game of my life," Tomjanovich said years later. "We were absolutely convinced we were going to win that series." He smiled. "I guess you have to say Doug made a great play, because he got away with it."

Twenty-four years later, Ray Patterson still wasn't quite over it. "You know, I've been asked a lot through the years if I hold a grudge against Kermit Washington for what he did to Rudy," he said. "My answer has always been that it was a terrible, terrible act but I don't think there was real malice involved. He made a horrible, horrible mistake. But Doug Collins I'm still upset with. He took a dive and got away with it. I really felt as if he and the officials took a potential title away from us."

Murphy, who always sees things a little differently from most, will force a laugh when the subject comes up. "Doug had nothing to lose," he said. "He couldn't stop Luke, so he did the only thing he could do, hope to get a call. And he did."

As much as the loss hurt, the Rockets didn't see it as an ending but a beginning. They were a young team just coming into their own. None of the key players was thirty yet, and Malone was emerging as a major force. He had averaged better than 20 points per game in the playoffs and looked ready to take his place as one of the league's stars. Lucas had also made it clear during the playoffs that he was a star on the rise. Even though Collins had gotten the call on the critical play, the fact that Lucas had been willing to take the shot at that moment—and in the eyes of the Rockets had made it—was another piece of evidence that he was going to be the team's point guard for years to come. For the season, he had averaged 11.1 points and just under 6 assists a game. Like Malone's, his numbers had gone up in the playoffs.

Tomjanovich-Malone-Murphy-Lucas was about as good a core group as anyone in the league could put on the floor. Kunnert had adjusted well to his new role, and the team had responded well to Nissalke's coaching. The only person who wasn't terribly happy with the way the team had evolved was Newlin, who had lost his starting spot to Lucas and seen all his numbers drop precipitously: minutes per night had gone from 39 to 25, shooting percentage from 51 to 45, and points per game from 18.6 to 12.7. There had been rumors during the season that the team was trying to trade him, which didn't please Newlin at all. To his credit, he had hung in, not pouted, and had played well when called upon in the playoffs.

"I always admired the way Mike handled that situation," Tomjanovich said later. "A lot of guys would have become a real problem because of what had happened. Mike never let that happen. He was as good a guy to be around when he was coming off the bench as when he was our second leading scorer."

"I wanted to play—badly," Newlin said. "But there was no way I was going to let any of those guys down by being a whiner or a baby about it. They weren't doing it to me anyway. Nissalke was."

Nissalke and Newlin were oil and water, a problem that would continue in the future. But the team was a young close-knit group that got along well. They were a classic melting-pot team: Tomjanovich had grown up poor in the Midwest; Kunnert had grown up well-to-do in the Midwest. Murphy was from Connecticut, Malone was from southern Virginia, Lucas from North Carolina, and Newlin from the West Coast. Lucas and Murphy, the guards, were the extroverts, the other starters were quieter, though Tomjanovich, now the team captain, had become more assertive with each passing year. They were the core of a team on the rise.

They couldn't wait for the 1977–78 season to start.

14

The Punch

As the new NBA season began in the fall of 1977, most experts were predicting that the finals at season's end would be a rematch of the series that had concluded in June with the Portland Trail Blazers beating the Philadelphia 76ers for the title. The Blazers were clearly a team destined to do big things for a long time, with Bill Walton now a star on the same level as Abdul-Jabbar. The 76ers were so certain that their loss in the finals had been a fluke that their season-ticket pitch to fans for the new season included the slogan "We Owe You One."

In both Los Angeles and Houston, they had different ideas. People seemed to have forgotten that the Lakers had finished the previous season with the league's best record, one that would have been even better if Kermit Washington hadn't missed the last 27 games of the regular season. The Rockets had won as many games as the Blazers and had been one questionable call from playing a game seven with the Sixers. If they had won that game, one can only imagine what Philadelphia's slogan for the new season might have been. Perhaps "We Owe You An Apology."

No one was more eager to get to training camp that fall than Washington. He had been through another long, difficult summer with Newell. "It was actually tougher than the previous summer, because now he wasn't just working on technique, he was making me get back into shape," Washington said. "There were days I thought I'd die out there."

Washington finally decided midway through the summer that his misery needed company. He had played some summer ball in the past with Kiki Vandeweghe, who had just finished his freshman season at UCLA. He convinced Vandeweghe to come work with him and Newell, telling him how much Newell had helped him the previous summer. "I kept telling him to look at how much I'd improved," he said, laughing. "What I didn't tell him was that the man almost killed me."

Vandeweghe became a regular in the early mornings, and occasionally Jerome Whitehead or Kenny Carr, two more young players, would also show up. But the focus for Newell was still on Washington, who had now become a project for him. "I felt as if letting him work less hard would be letting him down," Newell said. "Because it was hard work that had gotten him that far."

By the end of the summer, Washington's knee felt strong and he thought he was ready to step back into the lineup. In spite of his injury, the Lakers had picked up the fifth-year option on his contract after the doctors had told them he should be able to make a complete recovery. That meant he would make $120,000 for the season while auditioning for a potentially huge contract when he became a free agent at the end of the season.

The team had made some changes. Cazzie Russell and Lucius Allen, who had been a big part of the success the Lakers had enjoyed the previous season, were gone. Ernie DiGregorio, who had been the rookie of the year in Washington's rookie season, had been acquired from Buffalo. Norm Nixon, a rookie from Duquesne, was the team's number one draft pick and West's choice to run the team at point guard over DiGregorio. Lou Hudson, a veteran shooter, had also been acquired, as had Jamaal Wilkes.

"I wasn't sure why they had made so many changes to a team that won fifty-three games," Washington said. "Cazzie had a great season the year before and he was gone. They traded for Ernie, then Jerry didn't want to play him. They brought in all these big names. The year before, every guy knew his role and had been happy with it. Kareem was the star and then there were the rest of us, no ifs, ands, or buts about it. No one whined or complained. We just played. With all the new players, it just seemed as if we were never on the same page as a team the way we had been the year before. Of course, if Kareem hadn't gotten hurt, maybe we wouldn't have even noticed any of that."

Abdul-Jabbar's injury occurred on opening night when, frustrated by the physical play of Milwaukee rookie Kent Benson, he went after the Bucks center and ended up breaking his right hand on Benson's jaw. It was another example, as the L.A. *Times*'s Ted Green would later think, of Abdul-Jabbar not being willing to tolerate someone he thought to be an inferior player trying to stand up to him.

"Kareem never liked it physical, and it infuriated him when someone pushed and shoved him who he didn't think could play," Green said. "Benson was in his first game ever in the NBA. He was probably scared to death, holding on for dear life, and then Kareem turned around and nailed him."

Abdul-Jabbar contends that physical play didn't bother him, but dirty play did. "I never played against a more physical player than Wes Unseld," he said. "He was strong and he would push you, and getting around him for a rebound was almost impossible. But he never tried to hurt you. He never crossed the line between physical play and dirty play. He had athletic skills in addition to being strong and tough. There were other guys who crossed the line, some more than others. Benson crossed the line. If I thought someone was trying to hurt me, I took that personally. I thought he was trying to hurt me and I reacted."

That reaction was heard around the NBA. O'Brien wasn't the least bit happy that on the first night of the new, get-tough-on-fighting regime, the league's best player had started a fight. He fined Abdul-Jabbar $5,000 and said he would have suspended him if he hadn't been injured. Nowadays Abdul-Jabbar would have faced a suspension after he recovered from his injury. Back then it was all new in terms of suspensions. When O'Brien heard that Abdul-Jabbar would be out a month to six weeks because of the broken hand, he decided to let that be his suspension.

With Abdul-Jabbar out, Washington's importance to the team was greater than it had ever been. New starting center James Edwards wasn't nearly the force on offense or on the boards that Abdul-Jabbar was, and Washington was asked to do more than he ever had in the past. He responded well. By the time Abdul-Jabbar returned after missing 20 games, Washington was averaging 11.5 points per game and was fourth in the league in rebounding, at 11.2 per game.

Not surprisingly, the team struggled without Abdul-Jabbar. Everything the Lakers did at the offensive end was built around him, and he was a defensive and rebounding presence at the other end. Without him, teams were able to focus their defenses on the Lakers' perimeter shooters, since neither Edwards nor Washington was close to being the kind of threat Abdul-Jabbar was. Additionally, Norm Nixon was learning to play in the NBA at the point guard position, and even though he was talented, a rookie was still a rookie.

"It wasn't a lot of fun those twenty games," Washington said. "It was frustrating. But I think we all tried to take the attitude that once Kareem came back, we could be the team we were last year before I got hurt. We certainly weren't happy with where we were when he got back, but we had only played twenty-one games. We had three-quarters of the season still left."

The Rockets hadn't lost any of their star players to injury at the start of the season, but they had also gotten off to a disappointing start. The nucleus of the team that had come so close to making the finals was still intact, but the league had adjusted to playing against the Rockets' big lineup—Malone, Kunnert, Tomjanovich, Murphy, and Lucas. John Johnson, a quiet veteran presence off the bench, had been traded, and his place had been taken by Robert Reid, a rookie learning the NBA ropes. The dislike between Newlin and Nissalke continued to simmer, but it wasn't as if the two were ripping each other publicly.

For whatever reason, the team was losing almost every close game. Playing at home on opening night, they lost a lead and the game to the Chicago Bulls, 107–103. Two nights later they lost in Kansas City by one. There was a 2-point loss at Milwaukee, a 4-pointer to Buffalo, followed by another 2-pointer three nights later against the New Orleans Jazz. The losses to the Braves and Jazz, both at home, started a six-game losing streak that culminated in a rout (finally) at the hands of the Knicks in New York, 106–84.

"I think we were more baffled than anything else," Tomjanovich said. "Most nights, it wasn't as if we were getting killed or had no chance. We just weren't making plays at the end of games. We weren't as confident as we had been in the spring."

Nissalke made some changes. He put Reid into the starting lineup, upped his minutes, and sat Kunnert down. He used Kunnert to spell all three starters up front and didn't play him as much with Malone, because the lack of speed in that lineup was causing defensive problems. He put in some new plays on offense designed to get the ball to Tomjanovich more often.

"We were so slow when we played the big lineup that [the *Houston Post's*] Tommy Bonk had nicknamed us the water buffalos," Nissalke remembered. "He was right. We had caught people by surprise the previous year. No surprise lasts very long in the NBA. They were on to us. We had to make changes."

The changes appeared to be working. The Rockets won three in a row, breaking the losing streak with a "got you back" romp over the Knicks in Houston followed by an easy win in Cleveland and (at long last) a close win, 120–116 in overtime, at home against the 76ers. The Sixers game, played before a near sellout crowd, brought back happy memories of the previous spring, when the Rockets had been the hot team in town.

That victory got them to 9–12 heading into a brutal West Coast trip. It would start on Tuesday in San Francisco against the Warriors and then, after two days off, would continue with three games in three cities in three nights: at Los Angeles, at Phoenix, at Seattle. These days NBA teams never play more than two nights in a row. But in the 1970s three in a row, though unusual, was not uncommon, especially since weekend games drew better than weeknight games. Since this was still in the days before team charters, the three games, three cities, three nights meant the Rockets would be up before dawn on both Saturday and Sunday to catch a commercial flight to the city where they would play that night.

They lost another close game, 107–105, to the Warriors to begin the trip, then headed to L.A., where they would be well rested for the game Friday night with the Lakers. "When you were going to play three in a row on the road you always wanted to try like hell to win the first one, because you knew your chances to get a win diminished each night," Tomjanovich said. "Plus, I remember it had been a while since we had won in L.A., so we went into that game really wanting to get one there."

It had been almost four years (December 23, 1973) since the Rockets had won in the Forum. Their road record for the season was a miserable 1–8. But the Lakers were equally motivated, since they had already dug themselves an unexpected hole in the Pacific Division with their poor start, a hole that looked even deeper since the Blazers had picked up right where they had left off the previous season and had opened up 20–4. In the still-strong Western Conference, the Lakers needed to get their season headed in the right direction or run the risk of missing the playoffs.

Ted Green, the Lakers' *L.A. Times* beat writer, summed up the contest best: "It was a run-of-the-mill December NBA game between two teams that, whether they wanted to admit it or not, were on their way to run-of-the-mill seasons. The building was half-empty and the play was, to put it politely, less than glorious."

Except for Tomjanovich, who was brilliant in the first half, making 9 of 14 shots. With Jamaal Wilkes and Don Chaney both out with injuries, West was forced to put second-year pro Tom Abernethy on Tomjanovich. Abernethy had been an excellent defender in his college days at Indiana, and it was his work ethic as much as anything that would keep him in the NBA for five years.

"I always thought I played pretty good defense," he said. "You couldn't play for Coach [Bob] Knight and not play defense. But Rudy Tomjanovich on a shooting roll was not something I was in any position to stop." Years later, Abernethy laughed at the memory. "It wasn't as if I wasn't trying, but it didn't seem to make much difference."

Bolstered by Nissalke's new plays and by the feeling shooters get on a night when they think everything is going to go in, Tomjanovich was excellent the first 24 minutes. The game was a rough one, and Malone missed a large chunk of the second quarter after picking up his fourth foul. That was why Nissalke started Kunnert at the beginning of the second half, hoping to keep Malone out of foul trouble and fresh for the fourth quarter.

Even though the game was rough and they had been forced to call quite a few fouls, referees Bob Rakel and Ed Middleton had no major concerns about the way the evening was going. The score was tied, 55–55, at halftime. Looking back on the night, everyone who was involved says almost exactly the same thing: it was just another routine night in a long season.

And then, in a few seconds, everything changed. Murphy began the half by hitting a jump shot to give the Rockets a 2-point lead. It was on the Lakers' next possession that Kunnert and Abdul-Jabbar began skirmishing under the basket. Washington, doing his job, stepped into the fray because the Lakers certainly couldn't afford to lose Abdul-Jabbar again either to injury or suspension. Exactly what happened during the next few seconds between him and Kunnert remains in dispute. Kunnert blames Washington and Washington blames Kunnert.

Twenty-five years later it really doesn't matter who elbowed whom or why Washington turned around and punched Kunnert. What matters is what happened next: Tomjanovich saw Kunnert in trouble and ran back downcourt to help his teammate. The next thing he remembers is thinking the scoreboard had landed on his head.

His life had changed forever. So had Kermit Washington's. And so too had the life of everyone else on the court that night. In fact the NBA itself would never be quite the same.

15

A New Life

Trey Washington was born on January 26, 1978. Seventeen days later, Trey's father was born again as a basketball player.

Larry O'Brien announced Kermit Washington's reinstatement on February 1, eleven days before the sixty-day suspension period would end and two days after he had met with Washington and Donald Dell. Even though O'Brien hadn't brought in a stenographer to record Washington's hearing, he had taken enough notes that in announcing the reinstatement he put out a detailed five-page statement explaining what had led him to allow Washington to resume playing. The statement made it apparent that this was not a decision made without great thought.

"The basis of Mr. Washington's application [for reinstatement] as set forth in both his letter to me and a personal meeting I had with him in my office on January 30th 1978 can be summarized concisely," O'Brien wrote.

> 1. Mr. Washington acknowledges that his acts were inexcusable, deeply regrets what he did, assured me that he will never again behave in a similar fashion and recognizes the

need for strong penalties, such as the one imposed on him, to demonstrate that such actions will not be tolerated in our sport.

2. Mr. Washington urges that portrayals of him as a "tough" or "intimidating" player, or as an "enforcer," are unfair. In fact, says he, his entire experience as a student, husband, father and participant in community programs for the benefit of children, as well as his relationships with all who know him well, belie any attempt to describe him as one who would deliberately injure another human being.

3. Mr. Washington asserts that the record fine, the 60-day suspension without pay and the present and future effects of these penalties on him are ample punishment for his misbehavior. He says that, apart from the lengthy interruption of his career and the substantial financial loss, he has daily been subjected to expressions of hate and anger and has voiced his concern that such expressions will not quickly subside.

Mr. Washington has also re-emphasized his sympathy for Mr. Tomjanovich's suffering and has expressed his support for my strong stand against physical violence in the NBA.

I have no reason to doubt Mr. Washington's statements in this matter. His regret of the incident, his sympathy for Mr. Tomjanovich, his understanding of the seriousness of his act and his acknowledgement that such conduct must not be repeated by him or engaged in by any other NBA player are, I am persuaded, genuine. Moreover, his descriptions of himself, as a concerned member of society who abhors violence, have been confirmed by persons who know Mr. Washington well.

This brings me to consideration of whether Mr. Washington should be reinstated at the end of the 60-day period or whether his suspension should be continued for the remainder of the season. My search for guidelines to be applied in answering this question has not yet yielded any simple criteria. There are those who would argue that there is, in fact, a simple guidepost: that Mr. Washington should not be permitted to play as long as Mr. Tomjanovich is unable to play. Whatever appeal this "eye for an eye" justice may have held for ancient civilizations, I cannot comfortably embrace it as the controlling rule for decision in his case because I, as the person with the duty of decision, must shoulder the responsibility of determining both the adequacy of the punishment and its effectiveness as a deterrent.

As to the adequacy of the punishment, I determined the fine and 60-day suspension to be sufficient. I do not presume to pronounce it as the *only* appropriate punishment, since such questions must necessarily yield a wide range of appropriate decisions. On both a personal and professional basis, I am deeply concerned about the seriousness of the injuries to Mr. Tomjanovich, but no punishment that I administer can reduce those injuries or speed his return to the NBA. Furthermore, were I to allow my deliberations to be guided solely by Mr. Tomjanovich's extreme misfortune, I fear I would necessarily be led to an injustice in dealing with Mr. Washington's application.

On the question of whether the fine and the 60-day suspension of Mr. Washington will have the necessary deterrent effect, I would state the following:

First, I would hope the most effective deterrent to emerge from this entire incident would be the recognition of the severe damage which players are capable of inflicting upon one another. If the injuries suffered by Rudy Tomjanovich cannot finally convince NBA players that violence is simply unacceptable in our game, then I fear that actions from this office alone will not achieve that result.

Second, if it must be known that punishment for such conduct will be swift and severe, in my view the punishment of Kermit Washington—the most stringent ever for such an occurrence in the NBA—meets these criteria. Moreover, lest my rejection of "eye for an eye" justice in this case can be taken as an indication toward leniency, all who are willing to listen have now received ample notice of the consequences that will be meted out to future transgressors without regard to the extent of the injuries they actually inflict. In short, let it now and henceforth be understood that I will weigh heavily the recklessness or intent of the culprit, in addition to the damage (if any) caused by the attack.

Third, it goes without saying, but I add it for complete-
ness, that my admonitions against violence are not intended
solely for players. If I find any coach, general manager or
owner of an NBA team to be guilty of encouraging violence by
his players, he will be penalized as the situation dictates.

Accordingly, the application of Kermit Washington to be
reinstated as a player in the NBA as of February 12, 1978, is
granted.

Cutting through O'Brien's flowery rhetoric, a number of things
are apparent:

• He had listened to people like Pete Newell, Red Auerbach,
and Josh Rosenfeld, who had told him that Washington was not the
thug he might appear to be based on one incident.

• Washington, for all of his objections and anger, had said and
done the right things during his hearing.

• O'Brien wanted it made clear to everyone in the league that *any*
raised fist, whether it wreaked the havoc that Washington's punch
had wreaked or never landed, could lead to serious punishment.

• The Houston Rockets were not going to be very happy when
they got to O'Brien's final sentence.

In fact the Rockets were furious. O'Brien's "eye for an eye"
theory didn't wash with them. They thought it only fair that Washington sit out the rest of the season. "At that point, we didn't know if
Rudy would *ever* play again, much less the next season," team president Ray Patterson said. "If there was any doubt before the ruling
about going ahead with a lawsuit, it went away after the ruling."

Patterson was quoted after O'Brien's reinstatement of Washington as saying that O'Brien had failed to recognize the "magnitude"
of what had happened. O'Brien was incensed enough by Patterson's comments to issue another press release, nine days after the
original one, responding to Patterson's criticism.

"I note from your press statements," he said, in a telex sent to Patterson but released to the media, "that you have announced that Houston 'has no alternative but to commence litigation,' and has chosen to assert an alleged failure on my part to recognize the 'severity' of the problem.

"If there is any failure here, it lies in your mischaracterization of recent events, which serves only to exacerbate an inherently difficult situation."

Strong stuff, especially out in the public domain. If there was any doubt that the issue was still volatile, it was put aside after the public exchange between Patterson and O'Brien. The two men in the eye of the storm really weren't concerned about who was angry with whom. Tomjanovich was just trying to get healthy. Washington was just trying to get ready to play basketball again.

O'Brien's announcement gave Washington ten days to get into some semblance of shape before he met his new team in San Francisco. Red Auerbach had told him not to bother coming to Boston. The city had been immobilized by a blizzard, he couldn't work out with the team while still under suspension, and it would be easier for him to meet the team 500 miles from Los Angeles rather than 3,000 miles from there.

"The problem was, I was in the worst shape I had been in since high school," Washington said. "I had completely gotten out of my routine. Part of it was that I honestly believed I wasn't going to play again that season. But the other part was that I was just too depressed by everything that had happened to work. Once I knew I was going to play, I went to work. But I had a long way to go."

He arrived in San Francisco full of questions about what his new life with the Celtics would be like. Tom (Satch) Sanders, the Celtics' coach, had one question for him: "How much do you think you can play?"

Washington answered him honestly: "I have no idea. It's been too long to tell."

Sanders understood. "We'll see how it goes," he said. "I'll try not to play you much more than ten minutes. We'll go from there."

Washington played 30 minutes against the Warriors.

"I felt fine during the game," he said. "I was going on adrenaline. But when it was over, I thought I was going to keel over and die."

In all, though, he felt good. He felt good to be playing again, to be back on the court. His new teammates welcomed him. They asked no questions about what had happened in Los Angeles. They didn't bring up the name Rudy Tomjanovich.

That didn't mean the incident was behind him, not by any means. Auerbach and Sanders explained to him that there would be extra security assigned to him in the arena. He was briefed by security people before he joined the team. Be careful signing autographs, look carefully to see what people have in their hands. Use an assumed name in hotels—a lot of athletes do this, but Washington had never had to in the past—and avoid room service. Try not to go out alone unless absolutely necessary.

Washington took the advice seriously. The mail he had received during his suspension made it clear he was a marked man. Even with all of that, it felt good to be back in a locker room, back in basketball. Since college, the basketball court had been his home, the place where he felt most comfortable. There, and the weight room. Even though he was loathe to admit it and had said repeatedly that he would be just fine if he couldn't play basketball again, that hadn't been true. He *needed* basketball to feel complete as a person. Now, after two months, he had it back.

From San Francisco the Celtics traveled to Los Angeles. The good news was that Kermit got a couple of bonus days at home with the family. The bad news was that his return was, not surprisingly, a huge story. He tried to say all the right things, but it was difficult. He still felt as if the Lakers had let him down in the aftermath of the fight, even though he knew being traded to the Celtics was a good break for him.

The next stop after Los Angeles was Houston. But not for Washington.

"Go back to Boston," Auerbach told him. "You'll have a couple of extra days to get settled there."

Washington wanted to go to Houston. He didn't want to be intimidated by what might be waiting for him there. Auerbach wasn't hearing any of it. "It's not worth it, Kermit," he said. "There are plenty of games left. You'll miss one game. No big deal."

"Did the league tell you not to take me to Houston?" Washington asked.

Auerbach's answer was direct: "No, Kermit, *I* told me not to take you to Houston."

Years later, Auerbach said the same thing. "If I had wanted to take him there, maybe the league would have stepped in and said no," he said. "But it was pointless. I did it to protect him, but I also did it for the team. We didn't need that kind of circus. We were struggling enough as it was."

The Celtics flew to Houston. Washington packed his bags, kissed his family good-bye, and headed to snowed-in Boston. "It looked like a ghost town when I got there," he said. "It had been snowing for so long, almost nothing was moving anywhere."

He took a taxi from the airport to the Sheraton-Prudential, located a few blocks from Copley Square. He checked in and tried to make himself at home. He and Pat had debated whether she and the children should make the trip to Boston. Kermit thought traveling cross-country with a two-year-old and an infant and then living in a hotel room for two months bordered on suicide.

"There was no point in finding a place to live," he said. "We had no idea if I was going to be with the Celtics for just the rest of the season or longer. That meant we were going to all be cooped up in a hotel room, and I thought that would be a living nightmare. Part of it was selfish: I needed to concentrate on getting myself back in shape and playing basketball again. My contract was up at the end of the season, and I needed to show people I could still play, that I could put the incident behind me and be worth someone giving me a contract. But I also didn't think it was best for Pat and the kids. I knew they'd miss me, but I also knew they'd be a lot happier and more comfortable in our house in Palos Verdes than in a hotel in Boston with no place to go and snow falling every day."

Pat understood Kermit's thinking but still wasn't happy about the decision. "I just thought we should be together right then," she said. "I know Dana missed him, and I missed him too, and it wasn't exactly easy being alone with the two kids in Los Angeles, even in our house. To me it was a question of basketball or family. In the end Kermit was always going to choose basketball."

Having made his choice, Kermit threw himself into basketball completely. There were games to play and practices to go to and road trips to make. But that wasn't enough. "I needed to get myself back into a regimen, a routine. I needed to get back into the kind of shape I was used to being in. So I ran the hotel steps—every morning and every night."

The Sheraton-Prudential was twenty-nine stories high. Every morning before breakfast, Washington ran all the way up and all the way down—five times. Every night he ran all the way up and all the way down—five more times. "It got to the point where I dreaded waking up in the morning because I knew I had to run," he said. "I dreaded getting ready for bed because I knew I had to run. But I made myself do it. I would never look at the floor numbers, because I knew if I did I'd never make it to the top.

"So I would just keep my head down, and instead of thinking about how many floors I had left, I'd think about other power forwards. Every couple of flights I'd think about someone different. I'd start with Maurice Lucas and then go to Larry Smith or Danny

Roundfield or Truck Robinson or Moses [Malone]—all people I knew I was going to have to guard. I knew if I gave up, they'd destroy me. In fact one of the first games after I came back we played the Suns and Truck just killed me. I think he had twenty-nine. That was my motivation, not wanting to be humiliated by those guys because I wasn't in shape."

Washington was fortunate that Don Chaney, one of his closest friends, had been included in the trade. Chaney had played in Boston for six years and still owned a home there. Since Washington didn't have a car, Chaney picked him up most days at the hotel and drove him either to practice or the games.

"My whole life in Boston was practice, play games, and the hotel," Washington said. "The people at the hotel were great to me. When I'd get back late from a game or a trip, they always had food for me. The housekeeping people would do laundry for me and not charge me, because we'd all become friends. In a sense, for those two months they were my family.

"And, of course, Red."

Auerbach understood when he made the trade for Washington that life wasn't going to be easy for him, especially on the road. He felt an obligation to keep an eye out for him as much as he possibly could. So whenever he was in Boston, he tried to spend time with Washington if he could.

"He would come into the locker room after a game and say, 'Hey kid, you wanna get something to eat?'" Washington said, laughing at the memory. "I was always exhausted, and I knew I had to go back to the hotel and run the steps. I'd say, 'Mr. Auerbach, thanks so much, but we have to go to New York tomorrow. I think I'll just go home and go to bed.' And he'd stand there with that cigar, flick an ash on me, and say, 'Okay then, the hell with you.' But the next game, he'd be right back. One time he wanted me to go to some tennis match after an afternoon game. I think Chris Evert was playing. I just said, 'Tennis match? You?' And he said,

'You got something against tennis?' He was probably the one person during those days who could actually make me laugh."

Like everyone else, Auerbach was concerned about Washington's mental state. "Kermit was fighting a battle he couldn't win," he said. "Nothing he could say or do was going to change the way people perceived him because of that one moment. I wanted him to feel at home with us, to feel wanted."

Chaney, who had known Washington longer and better than any of the other Celtics, had noticed major changes in his personality since the incident. "His smile disappeared," he said. "My kids always loved Kermit because he was so much fun for them to be around. He would come over to our house in L.A. and get in the pool with them and pick them up and throw them into the deep end. They thought that was more fun than anything in the world. And he was always laughing and smiling and clearly enjoying himself.

"After the fight, that all changed. Before we got traded, he was over to the house a few times, but he didn't want to play with the kids. I mean, he tried, but you could tell it wasn't fun for him anymore. I'm not sure anything was fun. I was hoping when he started playing again, the old Kermit would come back. But it never did. He was different. So much more serious, as if he was carrying a great weight on his shoulders. That great smile of his just disappeared."

Auerbach knew Washington was carrying a weight on his shoulders. He tried hard to get the Boston media to accept, even embrace, Washington, to try to tell his side of the incident. This was especially important in a town not known for racial tolerance. "The key guy was [Bob] Ryan," Auerbach said. "Everyone in town respected him. When he wrote a story saying that Kermit was really a good guy who had been involved in one horrible incident, I think it really helped us with our fans."

Ryan, the longtime *Boston Globe* columnist, took the time to research Washington's history to lend some perspective to who he was and make him into more than just the thug who almost killed Rudy Tomjanovich.

"You couldn't not like the guy when you sat down and talked to him," Ryan said years later. "To me, it was clear that this was a good man who had really been, as much as anything else, horribly unlucky. He never wanted to hurt Rudy the way he did. That was obvious. It was also obvious that he was still in a lot of emotional pain because of what happened. I felt bad for him."

Ryan's piece in the *Globe* certainly helped. What helped more was that Washington was playing well. Even though he didn't feel as if he was in shape, he was playing and contributing almost exactly as he had in Los Angeles prior to December 9. For the Lakers, he had been averaging 11.4 points and 11.2 rebounds a game. In 32 games in Boston, he averaged 11.6 points and 10.5 rebounds. The Celtics were having one of the worst seasons in their history— they would finish 32–50 and miss the playoffs just two years after being NBA champions—but Washington was a bright spot. The fans in Boston quickly accepted him because of his work ethic and his effectiveness.

"I don't think he ever got booed in Boston Garden," Chaney said. "Right from the start, the fans seemed to be on his side. Of course if he hadn't played well, I'm sure it would have been different."

On the road people weren't quite so hospitable. Even though Auerbach kept him out of Houston, he still ran into hostile crowds most places he went. In both Cleveland and Detroit—the latter not surprising, since it was Tomjanovich's hometown—he received enough death threats to warrant extra security everyplace he went and uniformed officers sitting right behind him on the bench.

In a sense Washington was in denial about what had happened to his image in the aftermath of the fight. He had the cocoon of the team and Auerbach and his sheltered life of hotel, arena, practice to keep him from full exposure to the outside world. He knew the threats were there and that he needed the extra security. But his daily life during those two months was so narrow and so focused that he had little time to think about what the future might hold.

"I really was in my own little world," he said. "Except for missing my family, I enjoyed those two months. The most important thing was that I was playing again. I had my life back. Basketball was my life. If I had ever doubted it, the time away when they wouldn't let me play confirmed it. Everyone I came into contact with—real contact, not some fans booing me in an arena—was great to me. Satch [Sanders] was great to play for, and the Celtics were great too. I was actually very happy during that time."

But storm clouds were forming outside the cocoon. The Rockets and Tomjanovich had filed suit against the Lakers, claiming that the Lakers were responsible for Washington's behavior and Washington's behavior had endangered Tomjanovich's career and done tangible damage to the Houston franchise. In the meantime, the tape of the punch seemed to be on TV somewhere, twenty-four hours a day. It didn't get any less chilling with each replay and, more and more, when he ventured outside the cocoon, Washington would encounter people who would stop and point and say, "Aren't you the guy?"

The answer was yes, he was the guy. What Washington wanted to tell those people, though, was, "But that's not the whole story. I'm much more than that."

Most people didn't wait around for the rest of the story.

By the time the season ended, Washington was convinced he wanted to stay in Boston. He had performed well under difficult circumstances and he was sure that Auerbach would rebuild what had become a very old team. John Havlicek was retiring at age thirty-eight after one of the great careers in the history of basketball. The roster was filled with players crowding or over thirty:

Jo Jo White, Dave Bing, Curtis Rowe, Sidney Wicks, and Chaney were all a lot closer to the end of their careers than the beginning. Cowens wouldn't turn thirty until October, but his body had taken a pounding after eight seasons in the NBA as a 6-9 center.

The age of the team made Washington, who was not yet twenty-seven, an important part of the future as far as Auerbach was concerned. "When I made the trade it was with the thought that we'd re-sign him and he would be with us for ten years," Auerbach said.

That plan was fine with Washington. His play down the stretch had made him a marketable commodity in the NBA. Dell received feelers from a number of teams willing to sign him to contracts that would pay him considerably more than the $120,000 he had made the previous season. Washington was in the prime of his career and had proven to most that the Tomjanovich incident had not changed him as a player. Only those who knew him well could see that it *had* affected him.

"I don't think he was ever the same on the court after the incident," Chaney said. "He was still effective because he was strong and a quick leaper and nobody worked harder than he did or was in better shape. But Kermit before the punch had an edge to him on the court. He was an intimidator and he was intimidating. I think after what happened he wasn't as willing to mix it up with people as he had been, and that changed his game. I think always in the back of his mind was the fear that he might hurt somebody again."

Jerry West agreed. "Neither man was ever the same," he said. "That doesn't mean they weren't good players; they were. But I don't think either one of them ever played with the same abandon after what happened. That they did the things they did on the court is a tribute to their toughness and their competitiveness."

"He became careful," said Jack Ramsay, who would coach him at the end of his career, in Portland. "Kermit's game was about being physical. After the fight he wasn't nearly as physical. He didn't want anything to happen."

Washington has never bought the notion that he wasn't as aggressive a player after as he had been before. "If anything, in a strange way, it helped me on the court," he said. "People gave me more room, they didn't want to mess with me. I can remember in games when things did start to get physical hearing other players say, 'Don't fool around with Kermit, he might Rudy T you.' I didn't enjoy hearing that, but I knew it meant that guys were scared of me."

Washington was never in another fight the rest of his NBA career. Given that friends, teammates, and coaches all expressed concern about his penchant for getting into fights prior to the punch, it probably isn't a coincidence that he was not in another fight afterward. No doubt it was a two-way street: Washington didn't want to fight, and no one wanted to fight him. But those closest to him noticed the change, on and off the court.

"There was a sadness in his eyes after it happened," said Stu Lantz, a teammate and later a business partner in what became the Pete Newell Big Man's Camp. "It was almost as if the specter of Rudy and what happened that night shadowed him everywhere he went. He's just never been able to escape it."

But in the spring of 1978, Washington thought the worst was behind him. He had told Dell to keep him apprised of other offers but made it clear that unless someone came in with an offer that absolutely blew Dell away, he wanted to stay in Boston. He was comfortable there, and he felt he owed it to Auerbach to remain if Auerbach wanted him.

Auerbach wanted him. At the same time, he was also negotiating with another free agent he felt could help the Celtics at both center and power forward: Kevin Kunnert. Auerbach wasn't concerned about any past history between Washington and Kunnert. He just felt that each, in a different way, could help make his team better.

Late in the spring Dell called Washington. The Celtics had offered four years at $250,000 a year. Washington was thrilled.

Wait, Dell said, there's more: you can go to Denver for four years and make $300,000 a year. Back then a difference of $50,000 a year in salary was not a minor issue. Over the life of the four-year contract it would mean an extra $200,000—close to an extra year in salary. Dell asked Washington if he wanted to see if the Celtics would match. Washington said no. He knew Auerbach well enough to know that the money on the table was the best Red thought he could offer and that he would probably be insulted if Dell went back and asked for more. Washington wasn't leaving the security and comfort he felt in Boston, not even for an extra $50,000 a year. He told Dell to accept the Celtics' offer.

"If nothing else, I owed it to Mr. Auerbach to stay," he said. "And I wanted to stay, because I liked everything and everyone involved with the team."

Once the contract was signed, Washington flew to Boston to find a place to live. He was about to make a deal to buy the house Charlie Scott had lived in while playing for the Celtics when he got a message to call Auerbach. There was also a message that Dell had called. They both had the same news: don't buy a house yet. Something was going on that might change things.

What was going on was one of the stranger ownership maneuvers in the history of sports. Irv Levin, the owner of the Celtics, was a California guy. He wanted to live on the West Coast, not in Boston. But the basketball team he owned played in Boston. There was no way he could move the Boston Celtics—not and live to tell about it. The Buffalo Braves, on the other hand, could be moved. They had been in Buffalo for eight seasons, and while they had experienced some success, they were hardly an immovable franchise. They had finished the season 27–55, and attendance had dropped considerably along with the team's win total.

It was David Stern who suggested the idea of a swap to Levin: Levin would swap the Celtics to John Y. Brown, the owner of the Braves (and the future governor of Kentucky). Then Levin could move the Braves to California, specifically to San Diego, which had not had a team since the Rockets' exodus to Texas in 1971. The league liked the idea of getting back into the San Diego market and was not brokenhearted to leave Buffalo. Brown got the prestige of owning the Celtics, and Levin could have his team less than a hundred miles away from his home in Los Angeles.

Levin and Brown finalized the deal at the league meetings (held in San Diego) in June, just as Washington was about to buy his house in Boston. As part of the deal, in order to strengthen the new franchise in San Diego, several of the Celtics contracts were assigned to the newly minted Clippers. They included a backup guard named Bob Bigelow, forward Sidney Wicks, and two recent free-agent signees: Kermit Washington and Kevin Kunnert.

Washington was stunned when he heard the news. He called Auerbach and asked him how this could have happened. "If I had known this was going to happen, I would have signed with Denver," he said. Auerbach knew that was true. But this was out of his control. The deal had been made by the two owners, with the approval of the league. For once he was out of the loop. "I was devastated by the whole thing," he said. "For one thing, I didn't want to work with John Y. Brown. For another, the players we lost were really going to hurt us—especially losing Kermit."

As it turned out, the Celtics were even worse the following season than they had been in 1978, going 29–53. But during the 1978 draft, Auerbach had taken a gamble, drafting a player with the number six pick even though he knew the player planned to return to college the next season. The rules then were different. A team could draft a fourth-year college player who had one year of eligibility left as long as he was signed before the next draft was held. Otherwise his name went back into the draft. Few teams took advantage of this rule, especially in the first round, because it meant committing to someone without knowing if you would be able to sign him and knowing for certain you wouldn't have him for at least a year.

Auerbach decided this player was worth the risk and took him. His name was Larry Bird. He signed Bird a year later, just prior to the deadline, and in Bird's rookie season the Celtics were 61–21. A year later they won their fourteenth NBA championship. All was well again in Boston.

By then Kermit Washington was long gone.

16

Recovery

Christmas 1977 in the Tomjanovich house was one of mixed blessings.

The most important thing was that Rudy was home. He cried when he saw Nichole and Melissa, which wasn't easy since he was still going to need surgery to open up the tear duct in his right eye. Just being back in his own home, in his own bed, with his family, wasn't another of Dr. Toffel's little victories. It was a big one.

But the reality of what had occurred sixteen days earlier was very much a presence. Before he left to fly back to Los Angeles, Toffel had to show Sophie how to use the wire cutters to pry open Rudy's mouth in case of emergency. The act of learning how to work the cutters and the thought of what might be at stake if she had to use her new skill gave Sophie the shakes. "And I knew that if I needed to use them, I would have to stay calm and not panic in a situation in which I would want to panic," she said.

The girls weren't so much frightened by what their father looked like as baffled. Melissa just stared, almost as if she were seeing a different person. Nichole kept asking questions like, "Why did the man hurt you like that, Daddy?"

Being home was a major step in the right direction. Toffel had already performed surgery several times. He had set the jaw, and he had performed plastic surgery on the multiple broken bones in Tomjanovich's face. In all, he would perform surgery five times before he was finished, the last procedure—to repair the tear duct—coming several months later. For now, that could wait.

There was still a part of Tomjanovich that thought the whole thing was a nightmare he would wake up from. But each meal taken through a straw, each time he picked up the paper in the morning and read about another Rockets loss, was a reminder that it was all very real. For the first time since he had told his uncle Joe that he wanted to quit baseball, basketball was being played without him.

"That was a very tough thing," he said. "Plus, I think I was still in denial a little bit. Dr. Toffel had made it clear that I wasn't going to play again the rest of the season. At first I wondered if he was trying to ease his way into telling me I'd never play again. Gradually, though, that fear went away. Then I started thinking that maybe once the wires came out of my jaw, I might be able to play again before the season was over. As time went on, I realized that wasn't going to happen. That was tough to take. Watching the team, especially when I started going to games again, was even tougher to take."

Things hadn't gone well for the Rockets in the aftermath of December 9. After Murphy had carried them to the win that night in Los Angeles, they had dropped their next five, including a 113–91 loss to the Lakers in the Houston rematch five days after the fight. They had finally won a game, in New Jersey, before losing in San Antonio the night before Rudy and Toffel flew back to Houston. That made them 1–6 postfight and 11–19 overall.

Perhaps by coincidence, perhaps not, they won the first two games they played after Rudy's return home. They made it three of four on the night of January 4, the first night Rudy ventured back to the Summit. He hadn't wanted to make a big deal out of coming to watch the team play. But almost as soon as he started walking across the court to take a seat near the bench, someone spotted him. The applause grew louder and louder until all the fans in the building—including that night's opponent, the Indiana Pacers—were on their feet clapping.

Tomjanovich's response to that reception was mixed. "I was grateful and touched that people cared," he said. "I liked that, and I was emotional when they did what they did. But there was a part of my brain saying, 'This is about pity. They're cheering me because they pity me and they think I'm never going to play again. I'll prove them wrong.'"

Once again, now at the age of twenty-nine, he was back in Hamtramck proving himself. "I wasn't going to be the guy who everyone remembered for being knocked out of basketball by a punch," he said. "I was absolutely determined not to let that happen."

He was convinced, especially after that night back in the Summit, that no one would remember the four All-Star appearances or the 10,470 points he had scored in the NBA. They would remember The Punch. In many ways, he was absolutely correct.

The nightmare, actually a sort of waking dream before he was completely asleep, started happening shortly after he came home. It didn't happen that often at first, and he assumed it would eventually stop. Only it didn't.

It almost always occurred when he was really, really tired. Later, when he started coaching and would put in the brutal hours coaches put in at times, it would happen more frequently.

Always, the sequence was the same. He would be trying to sleep. Overtired, he would toss and turn for a while and then finally he would start to drift into sleep. But just before he actually fell into a complete sleep, the fear would invade his brain. He was slipping into darkness. Every moment, things got darker and darker, and he knew what was happening: he was dying. Just as everything went completely black, at the moment when he died, he would sit up with a start, usually in a cold sweat. He would jump out of bed and run down the hall, trying to get hold of himself, terrified that he was going to die.

Only years later was he able to understand that the dream's starting soon after the punch was no coincidence. He had faced death in the hospital that night. A doctor had looked him in the eye and told him he might die, and he had spent that entire night terrified that if he went to sleep, he would never wake up again. He had always feared death in the abstract. Now it had become far more real to him. Even though that very real, very tangible fear of that first night had passed, the memory of it had not.

"For a long time I told myself it would just go away sooner or later," he said. "After a while, when it didn't, I just thought it was something I had to live with, to deal with. The thing of it was, it was just as scary every time. It always took me a while to get hold of myself and calm down after it happened."

Through the years Sophie saw a pattern. Yes, it happened when he was overtired. But it almost always happened, she said, when he had been drinking.

Tomjanovich remembers having his first drink in a bar in Hamtramck when he was fifteen. Drinking in Hamtramck when you were a teenager was a ritual, something everyone did, just as their parents before them had done. All the bars routinely served underage kids, because they all knew if they didn't serve them, someone else would.

Tomjanovich was aware of his father's drinking, but in the early 1960s, almost none of the information about alcoholism that is now available existed. The term "alcoholic" wasn't very common then. Tomjanovich heard people say that his father was a drunk, and that hurt. He vowed he would never reach that point, but his father's problems with alcohol never stopped him from drinking. "It was just something that you did back then," he said. "I was no better, no worse, about it than most of my friends." He had no idea, of course, that most experts would come to consider alcoholism a hereditary disease.

Alcohol was still the drug of choice for many when Tomjanovich was in college, especially among the jock set. He never experimented with any of the drugs that became popular in the sixties because most in the crowd he ran with never did anything at parties other than drink. More often than not it was beer, occasionally hard liquor.

The lifestyle of a professional basketball player almost always involves late nights. No athlete can just go home and go to sleep after a game. Inevitably they are too keyed up from the adrenaline, and just as invariably they are hungry, since most don't eat for several hours prior to a game. Going out to eat and have a few pops after a game is part of the ritual. Some eat more, some drink more, some chase women more. Some do all of the above.

Tomjanovich liked blues bars. He would go out with a couple of teammates, get something to eat, and often stay up late listening to music and drinking. He never got passed-out drunk or blackout drunk, and it never affected his play, because like most athletes, he could sleep late most mornings. If the team had to get up early on the road to catch a flight, he wouldn't stay out late on those nights. No one he played with considered him to be an unusually heavy drinker. Certainly there were players who drank more and others who were involved with different drugs.

"What happened, though, was like most people who drink on a regular basis, I developed a very high tolerance for alcohol," he said. "I could drink a lot and not realize I had been drinking a lot. It never really was a problem."

Or it didn't seem to be a problem. Only later would he realize that he had gone down the same path as his father. And only then did he realize that Sophie was right: the terrifying visions of his own death almost always happened when he'd had a lot to drink. The older he got, the more frequently he had the waking dream.

While Tomjanovich was slowly recovering from his injuries, the Rockets' season was turning to dust. After the three-of-four mini-spurt, they began sliding again. Even putting aside the psychological traumas brought on by Tomjanovich's injury, the simple fact that their best player was gone was making things difficult.

Patterson's plan to try to make a trade for Newlin, whether truly serious or not, had gone up in smoke on December 9. Other teams now knew that Patterson was dealing from weakness, not strength, and no one put a package on the table that made moving Newlin worthwhile. Individually the Rockets still had talent: Murphy, Lucas, Malone, Newlin, Kunnert, and the rookie Robert Reid were all good to very good NBA players. Two of them—Malone and Murphy—would end up in the Hall of Fame. But the team's heart had been torn out when Washington had punched Tomjanovich, and everyone knew it.

"There was a period when being a part of that team was just great fun," Kunnert said. "We had a really good group of guys who all got along, and we were pretty good. But Rudy was the heart of it. He was the guy we all looked up to, all respected. He wasn't the captain of the team for nothing. When he got hurt, especially the *way* he got hurt, I think all the fun went out of it for all of us. We missed his game, and we missed his personality."

Murphy, who had become the leading scorer in his friend's absence, struggled more than anyone. Always emotional, he found himself crying at night on the road when he would return to the empty hotel room. "Rudy was gone," he said. "And I had no idea if he was ever coming back. In fact there was a good chance that he wasn't coming back. I tried to come to grips with that, and I just couldn't. It was awful."

Many players assumed Tomjanovich wasn't ever coming back. "It was all so mysterious," Lucas said. "Especially those first few weeks. We were told almost nothing. Occasionally Murph would give us an update, because he would talk to Sophie. Even when he came back home and we saw him a couple times, nobody said much. We all feared the worst."

The organization was also coming to grips with the notion that Tomjanovich might not come back. Patterson and Nissalke were convinced they had to base their plans on his never playing again, because they believed the odds were that he wouldn't.

"The doctors had told us he *could* play again, but there certainly weren't any guarantees," Patterson said. "There was no way to measure his chances of coming back, because we had nothing to compare the situation to. No one had ever had an injury like this, so we were flying blind."

By the time the season finally came to a merciful close, the team was in complete disarray. Newlin had gone down with a knee injury after 44 games, and Malone had missed 23 games. Any thought of rallying in the second half of the season had gone out the window with Newlin's injury. The Rockets were, plain and simple, a mess in every possible way. They finished the season 28–54, miles away from the playoffs and a lifetime away from their near miss in the conference finals a year earlier.

"Worst season of my coaching career, because it came out of nowhere," Nissalke said. "We went into the year with such high hopes. Once Rudy went down, everything just fell apart completely after that."

Still unsure about Tomjanovich's future, Patterson began negotiating with Rick Barry, who had become a free agent at the end of the season. Barry was thirty-four, but he had still been Golden State's leading scorer, averaging 23 points a game. What's more, he was still one of the league's big names, having led the Warriors to the NBA title in 1975. He had won scoring titles and he had become famous for jumping from the Warriors to the ABA and then landing back with the Warriors before leading them to the title.

Barry fit the profile Patterson was looking for. He played Tomjanovich's position, he was a scorer like Tomjanovich, and he would sell tickets because people knew who he was. His signing would be big news in Houston.

"There's no way we ever would have even talked to Rick Barry if Rudy hadn't been hurt," Nissalke said. "I understood what Ray was thinking when he started talking to him. What scared me was the compensation. If we had ended up having to give the Warriors a number one draft pick or a couple of our secondary players, okay, that would have been fine. But this was Rick Barry, and he was their leading scorer. I was afraid we were going to get hit hard."

Patterson knew that was a possibility but felt he had no choice. "We had no way of knowing if Rudy was coming back at all, or if he did come back, what kind of player he was going to be. We had a terrible season after Rudy got hurt, even before Newlin and Moses were injured. We needed to make a move."

And so, on June 17—eight days after Kunnert had left to sign with Boston—they made the move, signing Barry to a two-year contract. When Tomjanovich got the call from Nissalke to give him a heads-up that the signing was about to happen, Tomjanovich's first thought was that he would be going to Golden State as compensation. Of course that wasn't going to happen; the Warriors weren't about to take a player whose future was a question mark as compensation for Rick Barry.

As soon as John Lucas heard that the Rockets were negotiating with Barry, he was convinced he was going to be the one to go. "They were going to want someone young," he said. "That meant me or Moses, and there was no way Houston was going to give up Moses. They'd have canceled the deal first. I just knew it was going to be me."

It wasn't until September 5 that the league finalized compensation: the Rockets were told to send John Lucas and $100,000 to the Warriors. To Tomjanovich and others on the team, that seemed like an awfully high price to pay, giving up a twenty-three-year-old point guard who seemed to have a huge future in front of him for a thirty-four-year-old superstar who was clearly on the downside. "On the surface it looked like we were giving up a future All-Star for a past All-Star," Tomjanovich said.

Lucas never lived up to his full potential in the NBA because he developed a drug problem that stunted him as a player and shortened his career. "I am not going to tell you that I had never experimented with drugs before I went to Golden State," he said early in 2002, midway through his first season as coach of the Cleveland Cavaliers. "I have to take responsibility for what happened, no one else. But San Francisco was a lot different town than Houston was. I was a long way from home, in an environment unlike anything I had ever encountered in my life. Things happened that I wish hadn't happened.

"Would my life have been different if Rudy hadn't gotten hurt? Yes. How different I don't know. But I think I can honestly say that Rudy and Kermit were not the only ones whose lives changed that night in Los Angeles. I'll always believe that."

No one on the Rockets had any way of knowing at the time of the Barry signing that Lucas would find the trouble he found in San Francisco. All they knew was that their point guard was gone and that the reason he was gone could be traced directly back to December 9.

"If Rudy never gets hurt," Patterson said, "there is almost no chance that we ever sign Rick Barry."

Or lose John Lucas.

In early May, Tomjanovich flew back to Los Angeles for one last round of surgery performed by Dr. Toffel, to repair the damaged tear duct. Once that was done, he felt he could start thinking about playing again. He felt better with each passing day and was convinced he was going to play again and play well. He was determined to prove the naysayers wrong, and for once he wasn't imagining the questions. This time they were quite real.

The doctors cleared him to play early in June, and Tomjanovich began playing right away. He wasn't in any kind of basketball shape, but just being back on the court, first in informal pickup games, then as a part of the Rockets' summer league team, felt great. He was a basketball player again. For the longest time he had wondered if he would ever be able to say that.

Even though he didn't want to admit it, each day was a test for Tomjanovich. He had insisted to anyone who asked that there was absolutely no reason for him to be gun-shy when he returned to the court. His feeling was that he hadn't been injured playing basketball. He had been injured in a fluke moment in a fight. So why should he feel gun-shy (the term he kept hearing everyone apply) boxing out for a rebound or chasing a loose ball? Those were things he had done all his life, and he hadn't gotten hurt doing any of those things.

One afternoon he caught an accidental elbow in the face during a pickup game. When he bent over in obvious pain, the college kid who had nailed him went into a near panic. "Are you okay, are you okay?" he asked repeatedly. All activity stopped as everyone gathered round. Tomjanovich felt the bones in his surgically repaired face. Everything seemed to be in place. He stood up and smiled. "Thanks," he said, trying to make light of the situation, "I needed that."

In truth, he had been as scared as everyone else, because he had no idea how his face was going to react to contact. Toffel had told him it should not be a problem but he couldn't know for sure until it happened. Once it happened and he lived through it, he was relieved. But he had to admit to himself that he'd been nervous.

Once training camp was under way, Tomjanovich began to understand the kind of scrutiny he was going to be dealing with. Every time the team scrimmaged there was analysis of how he had played, how he had looked. Had he been aggressive? Had he shied away from contact? Some days he would pick up one newspaper and read that he looked as aggressive as ever. Then he would pick up the other paper and see his favorite phrase: gun-shy.

"It made me realize right away that it was going to be like this all season," he said. "Wherever I went, it was going to be a story. How does Rudy look? How does Rudy feel? How is Rudy playing? I didn't want to be the center of attention for *that* reason. It seemed as if everything in my life that had happened before the punch had never happened. To most people, I had become The Guy Who Got Nailed. I can't begin to tell you how much I hated that."

Just as Kermit Washington now felt as if he had to deal on a daily basis with people coming up to him and saying, "Aren't you the guy who threw the punch," Tomjanovich also began to cringe when strangers would approach him, pointing a finger of recognition.

"I got recognized a lot more, that's for sure," he said. "Before, if I did get recognized, it was just as a basketball player. Now I had people coming up and saying, 'You look familiar.' Then a look would come over their faces and they'd say, 'Wait a minute, aren't you the guy who got nailed?'"

Washington was in San Diego; Tomjanovich was in Houston. But in a very real sense, they were living with each other. Both hoped that would change with time.

The team that Tomjanovich returned to in the fall of 1978 was different from the one he had left the previous December. John Lucas and Kevin Kunnert were gone and Tomjanovich's new partner at the forward spot was Rick Barry. At first Tomjanovich wondered how he and Barry would fit in with one another, since both were scorers. But he was pleasantly surprised to find that Barry was a gifted passer and had reached a point in his career where he didn't mind using his passing skills as much as his shooting skills.

Even so, the team wasn't the same. His buddy Calvin Murphy was still there, and so were Moses Malone and Mike Newlin, who was still miserable playing for Nissalke but, like everyone else, thrilled to see Tomjanovich back, looking different but healthy.

"Rudy *did* look different after all the surgeries," Newlin said. "His features were, I think, sharper before. It was as if his face had been rounded off in places. He sounded a little different too. I think that had something to do with the damage to his nose. But he was still Rudy, and he was still a good player."

The team's big problem was simple: with Lucas gone there was no true point guard. Lucas was the kind of pass-first, shoot-second point guard whom players like Murphy, Tomjanovich, and Malone thrived with. They all knew that if they could get open, the ball would get to them. Knowing he had to have someone to replace Lucas, Ray Patterson made a deal with Seattle that brought Slick Watts to the team. Watts was very strong and could get in the lane and create openings that way, but he wasn't Lucas.

Tomjanovich's concern about being under constant scrutiny was legitimate. He kept telling people that as far as he was concerned, the incident was behind him. He had dealt with all the physical pain, he had gone through all the surgeries and all the rehab, and he just wanted to be a basketball player again. But it wasn't that simple. The court case still loomed in the future. Tomjanovich and the Rockets had decided to go ahead and sue the Lakers, and the case was due to reach the courts the following summer. There was also the issue of Washington and Tomjanovich being back on the same court again. That initial meeting was scheduled to take place in Houston in November. This time there were no plans for Washington to pass on the trip.

Tomjanovich had almost consciously *not* thought about Washington for months after the injury. He had taken Toffel's advice to heart and had tried not to concern himself with anything but his health. What's more, whenever he was asked if he had any comment on Washington's reinstatement by O'Brien or on the incident itself, he could honestly say that because of the ongoing litigation, he wasn't in a position to comment.

The basketball court, however, would be different. Washington was starting for the Clippers, so there would be no getting around the two of them coming face-to-face at some point. Neither man was looking forward to the meeting, because neither had any idea what to say. Both knew there would be loads of media attention paid to their first on-court reunion and there was no way to avoid that.

"It was more like something that I just didn't have time to deal with or think about than anything I was actually dreading," Tomjanovich said. "I felt kind of caught in between. On the one hand, I was moving on with my life, I was healthy and playing again. On the other hand, this kept coming up in different ways over and over. I knew there was no way to avoid dealing with the lawsuit, but I was hoping once that was over, that would be it—regardless of the outcome, that would be the final sentence to the story."

Washington felt the same way. He knew the lawsuit was still out there, but he had hoped once the suspension was lifted that he could resume his life as it had been before the incident. To a large degree, that was the way it had been in Boston. Yes, there were warnings about being careful in crowds and extra security, but none of his teammates brought it up, and after the initial flurry upon his arrival in Boston, it had become a nonfactor with the media there.

But now Tomjanovich was back playing basketball, and their paths had to cross. "I almost wished," Washington said, "that there was some way for us to go off and meet in private, talk the whole thing out, get it over with that way. That way when the media asked us about it, we could say that we'd talked, I had told Rudy how sorry I was he got hurt, and we were both ready to move on with our careers and our lives. But it wasn't going to be that simple. Life is never that simple."

17

Life Goes On

Kermit Washington was devastated when he heard he wasn't going to be a Boston Celtic for the 1978–79 season. He had felt so comfortable with the Celtics, and he knew he had a protector in Auerbach, who would see to it that he was treated as fairly as possible, especially in Boston.

But if he couldn't be with the Celtics, San Diego was about as nice an alternative as he was likely to find. The city was less than a hundred miles from Los Angeles, where he had lived for five years. The winter weather was nicer than L.A.'s and, of course, light years from Boston's. "The city, I knew, would be great," he said. "It was the team I wasn't sure about. It was all unknown—all over again."

One known was that he and Kevin Kunnert were going to be teammates. Kunnert was as surprised as Washington when he learned that he was going to be a Clipper and not a Celtic. There had been no rumors at all of any kind of swap before it was announced. Kunnert had signed with the Celtics for the simple reason that they had made the best offer—five years at $300,000 per year. Since he had never played for the Celtics, Kunnert had less reason to be upset about landing in San Diego. He didn't know any of the players or the coaches or Auerbach.

"Signing with them was just a business deal," he said. "It was the best opportunity for me. If I ended up in San Diego, that was okay too."

Neither Washington nor Kunnert was thrilled to end up on the same team as the other, but neither thought that much of it at the time. Both were occupied with trying to relocate their families and with getting used to a new city, a new team, and a new coach. The incident was nine months behind them when they got to training camp, and both assumed that the worst was over.

"I never dreamed," Kunnert said years later, "that it would still be an issue more than twenty years later. The guy has never been able to let it go."

"I haven't let it go," Washington said, "because the world hasn't let me go."

Back then everything was new for everyone in San Diego. Gene Shue had been hired to coach the team, given the job of blending the old Celtics and the old Braves into the new Clippers.

Things did not start well, as might be expected when remnants of two teams were suddenly forced to behave like one team. No one seemed certain of their role. The team had talent, especially in the backcourt, with All-Star Randy Smith and scoring machine World B. Free, who never shot unless he actually had the ball in his hands. Swen Nater was a solid center, Washington and Kunnert both contributed rebounding and good defense, and Nick Weatherspoon brought experience to the small forward spot.

But that didn't prevent an awful 2–12 start. Washington was miserable. He didn't feel as if he fit in with the new team, and he was convinced things weren't going to get better anytime soon. He was so discouraged that he actually called team owner Irv Levin and told him to cut him. "You don't have to pay me," he told Levin. "Forget about the contract. I'll just walk away. None of us deserve to be paid."

Levin may have appreciated the gesture, but he wasn't cutting his starting power forward. He told Washington things were going to get better, that he just needed to be patient and give the team time to jell. Washington calmed down.

"Maybe I was just jumpy because of everything that had gone on," he said. "Remember, in less than a year I had been on three teams, been suspended, wondered if I'd ever play again, and been made into this villain. The good news was, Mr. Levin was right—we did get better."

Things didn't get better right away. There was still the not-so-small matter of being on the same court as Rudy Tomjanovich and the Rockets. Washington was almost relieved that the first meeting would be in Houston. "I figured we might as well get the whole thing over with," he said. "I thought, maybe, just maybe, once that game was over, we could finally put the whole thing behind us. Wrong."

Tomjanovich had made his official return to action in New York on October 13, against the Knicks. He had received a standing ovation when he was introduced—and cringed when he heard the cheers—and then had played well, scoring 20 points and getting 6 assists (which had to be close to a career high) and 5 rebounds in 40 minutes. The Rockets won, 111–107, and Tomjanovich felt he had passed another test.

"Being back in an actual NBA game made it real," he said. "Now no one could say that the punch had ended my career."

On the night that the Clippers came to Houston—November 11—Tom Nissalke was in his locker room early when Gene Shue came to see him. "Maybe there's a way to defuse this a little bit," he said. "Maybe after they're introduced, before the tip, we could get Kermit and Rudy to shake hands, kind of symbolically put an end to the whole thing for everyone to see."

These days, the five starters from each team routinely shake hands with one another as they gather around the center jump circle. (The tradition reached a unique height of absurdity during the finals in 1989, when Magic Johnson and Isiah Thomas exchanged pre-tipoff kisses.) In the seventies, if the two centers shook hands it was unusual. Players simply weren't as collegial then as now.

"If you knew a guy from having played on the same team with him or something, you might do it," Washington said. "But otherwise you just lined up and played. Period."

Nissalke wondered if the handshake idea came from Shue or Washington (Washington says he knew nothing of it), but he was almost certain that Tomjanovich wouldn't go for it. "My first thought was that Rudy probably wasn't ready to shake hands with the guy," he said. "My second thought was that by doing it, we'd be calling attention to it all over again, and that was the last thing in the world Rudy wanted to do. My third thought was that doing it might be a little bit phony, especially since there was still a lawsuit pending, and Rudy would never be involved with anything that was the least bit phony."

Nonetheless, Nissalke told Shue he would ask Tomjanovich how he felt about it when he arrived at the arena and let him know. He did just that. The conversation was brief. "No," Tomjanovich said. "Shake hands? I just don't think we should do that. I just don't think I want to do that."

Nissalke didn't press the issue. He simply went and told Shue what Tomjanovich had said. To this day, Tomjanovich swears he remembers nothing about that night. He doesn't remember Nissalke asking about the proposed handshake, what he thought about in pregame, what the crowd was like, or what happened in the game. "It's all a blank," he said. "Maybe I was so pent up about it when it happened that I blocked it from my memory. I honestly don't remember a thing."

Washington's memory is clearer. "I remember," he said, "that he killed me and everyone else on the team all night. He was great. In a way I was happy for him. I was just unhappy with myself, because for the first time in my life I was intimidated. I let the whole circumstance get to me: the crowd, facing Rudy, knowing that everyone was watching us. I've had games in my life where I've been outplayed badly. But that night I was embarrassed."

The numbers back Washington up: Tomjanovich had 24 points and 11 rebounds in 33 minutes. Washington had 6 points and 2 rebounds in 23 minutes. Shue didn't play him much in the second half because he could see that he wasn't himself. Tomjanovich sat out most of the fourth quarter because the game was a rout. The Rockets, with the crowd creating an atmosphere not seen in the Summit since the conference finals in 1977, dominated the game, winning 136–123. "It was a long night," Washington said. "I think the best way to sum it up is to say I couldn't do anything right and Rudy couldn't do anything wrong. I guess in a way there was some poetic justice in that. I didn't like getting hammered on that way, but I was glad to see that he seemed to have all his game back."

Tomjanovich was in fact playing very good basketball, better than almost anyone could have reasonably hoped. Everyone in the league was aware of what had happened to him, and wherever the Rockets went on the road, he received a standing ovation when he was introduced. Tomjanovich had been prepared for—had looked forward to—a warm reception in the Summit. He had not expected, or wanted, anything along those lines on the road. He had hoped to be treated like any other visiting player, much the way Washington hoped to be treated like any other visiting player, although for entirely different reasons. As the season wore on, it became apparent to both men that no one had forgotten what had happened and that, try as they might, they weren't about to put the punch behind them just by telling people it was behind them.

Most people would have found the warm reaction from road crowds flattering or touching or both. Not Tomjanovich. "I always thought they were clapping for me out of pity," he said. "That was the last thing I wanted. When I heard the applause, all I could think was, 'They're clapping because I got nailed, because they saw the tape. I don't want this. I just want to play.'"

No one else saw it that way. "My thought was that they were applauding his courage," Nissalke said. "They *had* seen the tape, and they knew how awful his injuries were. The fact that he was back playing and playing well was a remarkable achievement. A lot of guys in his situation would have just taken the insurance and given it up. Rudy probably would have made more collecting insurance than he did by coming back to play. It would have been a lot easier. But that was never his way. He never took the easy way on anything."

And he was never easy on himself—to put it mildly. A few people in basketball had publicly criticized Tomjanovich for coming up behind Washington in the middle of a fight, saying he had made a mistake in thinking that someone engaged in a fight the way Washington was would *not* turn and throw a punch at someone coming from behind. Most notable in this group was Wes Unseld, the great center for the Washington Bullets.

"I was the peacemaker in a lot of fights," said Unseld, who was one of the strongest men to ever play the game and could end a fight simply by stepping between the combatants. "I always took the approach that if you are going to be a peacemaker, you have to be prepared to be involved in a fight, because you are dealing with people who are wound up and angry. They may not stop just because you want them to stop. There's no one I respect more in the game than Rudy Tomjanovich, but he got himself into something he wasn't prepared for. He made a mistake running in the way he did. That doesn't mean he deserved to pay the price he paid—no one deserves anything like that. He was certainly the victim of something horrible. But regardless of his intentions—and I assume they were good and peaceful—he isn't blameless in what happened."

Most people who either witnessed the fight or saw the tape of it would disagree with Unseld. "He was the captain of the team," Red Auerbach said. "He saw one of his guys in trouble and he went to help. I don't blame a guy for that."

"He looked up and saw Kunnert caught in between the two biggest, strongest Lakers on the floor," said Ted Green of the *L.A. Times*. "What was he supposed to do—nothing? His guy is clearly in trouble. He came in to help. People talk about Kermit reacting instinctively—I have no doubt that he did. So did Rudy."

There's one person who tends to side with Unseld: Tomjanovich. "When I've thought about it, I've thought that I made a mistake running into a fight with my hands down," he said. "I know why my hands were down—because fighting wasn't on my mind, breaking it up was. But it was an adrenaline situation, and I didn't take that into account. I should have been better prepared to defend myself, just in case."

Tomjanovich had been in one fight in his NBA career prior to that night, and it had shaken him. It was in his second season, the team's first in Houston, in a game in the Astrodome against the Atlanta Hawks. He got tangled up with Hawks center Bob Christian, and the next thing he knew the two of them were swinging at each other.

"I had the ball and he tried to reach around me in a kind of bear hug and take it away," Tomjanovich remembered. "I held on, and he started kind of pushing and shoving and then took a swing. We were right in front of their bench, and I remember thinking, 'I gotta get out of here.' The next thing I knew, I'd thrown about two or three punches and he was swinging at me and I could hear the crowd oohing and aahing like we were gladiators or something. Then people came in and broke it up.

"It was amazing to me how quickly you kind of lose control in a situation like that. Your adrenaline gets going and you are doing things you know you shouldn't do. When it was over, I felt ashamed of myself for losing it that way. That memory stayed with me quite clearly. I didn't want it to happen again."

Tomjanovich's fight with Christian was nothing more than a minor NBA skirmish. Neither player was ejected. "Back then, no way you'd be ejected," he said. "Today, ejection, suspension, and fine. Automatic."

The sight of Kunnert and Washington skirmishing on the fateful night in 1977 did not conjure up any memories of his own fight. "It was nothing like that," he said, "except in the sense that my reaction was instinctive, not thought out. I saw a fight, I thought my guy was in trouble, and I ran in to try to help break it up."

He smiled sheepishly. "There's one other thing. I've always thought to myself, 'Only you, Rudy, could figure out a way to run into a guy at the one perfect angle to almost get yourself killed. Any other angle and maybe he breaks my nose or my jaw. But I managed to find the angle to run into the punch so it could do the absolute maximum possible damage. For a long time, I had trouble getting that thought out of my head: 'Only you, Rudy.'"

Which is, of course, ludicrous. It was blind, dumb, horrible luck for both men that Tomjanovich's face managed to collide with Washington's fist in the seemingly only way that could possibly lead to such horrific injuries. In his masterful book on the NBA, *The Breaks of the Game*, David Halberstam describes a scene in a Celtics-Rockets game in which Dave Cowens was called for a charging foul on Mike Newlin after Newlin took what Cowens thought was a dive in the lane. On the ensuing play, Cowens raced down the court, stuck an elbow hard into Newlin's face, turned to the official, and yelled, "Now *that's* a fucking foul!"

Halberstam tells the story to illustrate Cowens's intensity as a player. Years later, reminded of the story, Newlin laughed and said, "Oh yeah, I remember it. That was just the way Cowens played."

Exactly. Cowens wasn't a dirty player by any stretch of the imagination. He played hard and he played aggressively, which helped make him a Hall of Famer. But what if, by some fluke, that elbow had caught Newlin in the eye and shattered a bone? What if it had landed in such a way as to destroy part of his face? It didn't, of course, and so the incident is no more than an anecdote retold years later to remind people of Cowens's fierce competitiveness.

Washington's punch was not an innocent act by any means. He was in an agitated state and was already going to be ejected from the game for the punches he had thrown at Kunnert. The punch wasn't an accident, and no one has ever claimed that Kermit Washington was a pacifist on the basketball court—including Kermit Washington. But the punch could just as easily have grazed Tomjanovich or missed or landed an inch higher and simply broken his nose. (To this day Sophie Tomjanovich can't stand it when someone describes Rudy's injury that night as a broken nose. "The only thing on his face that *wasn't* broken," she said, "was his nose.")

The punch was an act of malice, and Washington would have been punished for it by Larry O'Brien regardless of how badly Tomjanovich was or was not hurt. In fact, if he had never punched Tomjanovich, he probably would still have been fined and suspended for the punch he delivered to Kunnert. A week earlier O'Brien had fined and suspended Adrian Dantley for *trying* to throw a punch that never landed.

But the damage the punch inflicted was an absolute fluke. Washington's strength played a part, but the devastating effect arose from an awful confluence of factors that led to the punch landing exactly where it did with both puncher and punchee supplying momentum. If the punch had landed in a slightly different way, it would have been nothing more than a footnote, if that— "Just another stupid NBA fight," as Tommy Bonk, then of the *Houston Post*, put it.

But it didn't land that way. And even though time has blurred the public's perception of the facts, both men have lived with the consequences from that moment forward. Every person who was on the court that night remembers the moment and the scene today as if it were yesterday, not twenty-five years ago. Just talking about it is upsetting for most of them. Calvin Murphy, generally considered the toughest man in the NBA, refused to discuss that night with anyone for more than twenty years after his testimony at the trial in the summer of 1979. When he did talk about it, he cried at length as he remembered the sight of his pal on the court in a pool of blood.

Jerry West, the coach of the Lakers at the time, put it simply: "One of the reasons I got out of coaching was that night," he said. "I just didn't feel as if I wanted to be part of the game on the floor anymore after that happened. The more I thought about it, the more convinced I was I didn't want to coach. These were two good men who happened into a truly horrible situation. To this day, I don't think either one of them has found closure with it."

Both had hoped that meeting on the court again, regardless of the outcome, would bring closure. Put simply, it didn't.

Although the game against the Clippers was exceptional, it was not all that different from most nights that fall and winter for Tomjanovich. The team had changed in his absence. Most of the offense now went through Malone, who was becoming a big-time star and would end the season averaging just under 25 points and 18 rebounds a game. In the absence of a true, creative point guard, Barry was now the team's best passer, and he and Tomjanovich learned to work very well together.

Even though he was no longer the first option on offense, Tomjanovich was playing remarkably well. The only health scare came just after Christmas in Detroit, when he caught an accidental finger from M. L. Carr squarely in the nose. Carr was trying to throw an outlet pass, and as he released the ball his finger caught Tomjanovich, who was trying to prevent the pass, right in the nose. The momentum of the follow-through and the fact that the finger landed squarely on the bone cleanly broke the nose. Feeling the blood gushing from his nose, Tomjanovich panicked for a second, wondering if he had been seriously injured. He hadn't been. He had finally suffered a broken nose, but nothing else. He missed six games and then came back wearing a mask to protect the nose. But his restructured face took the blow without any problem, just as Toffel had told him it would.

"In a way it was almost a relief to get hit that hard and walk away with nothing but a broken nose," he said. "I don't think I ever consciously worried about something happening, and I had a lot of faith in Dr. Toffel's work, but having it all confirmed wasn't a bad thing."

Under the constant scrutiny he was receiving, Tomjanovich kept reading differing reports on his play. Some people insisted he wasn't the same player; others said he was good as new. The numbers he was putting up seemed to indicate the latter: he was shooting better than 50 percent and averaging 19 points and 7.7 rebounds a game. When the fans' voting for the All-Star game was announced, it was clear that they thought he had come all the way back—he had been voted onto the Eastern Conference team as a starter.

Which did not make him happy.

"I didn't think I deserved it," he said. "I thought it was another example of people feeling sorry for me, giving me a vote because they remembered what had happened to me. I didn't want to go to the All-Star game because people were thinking, 'Poor Rudy.'"

He seriously considered not going at all but was talked into it by Sophie, by teammates, and by members of the media, who told him he deserved to be on the team based strictly on his play. It wasn't as if he had never been an All-Star before the punch and all of a sudden was elevated to All-Star status.

"A lot of guys told me that if I hadn't been voted onto the team I would have been chosen by the league as a backup," he said. "I still didn't think I should start, but I knew I had been playing pretty well and I had the sense that other players really wanted me to be there. So in the end I went."

And was glad he did. The game was played in Detroit, which made it a homecoming. Playing in front of longtime friends and family, he ended up having his best All-Star game ever, scoring 12 points and getting 7 rebounds.

The acquisition of Slick Watts proved to be a boon to the Rockets. Even though he wasn't nearly the scorer Lucas had been, averaging fewer than 4 points a game, his strength and ability to get into the lane opened things up for the other four starters—Tomjanovich, Malone, Barry, and Murphy—and turned the Rockets into a dangerous team again. They were 10–11 when Watts moved into the starting lineup and finished the regular season 47–35. Unfortunately, that left them one game behind the San Antonio Spurs for the Central Division title. Instead of having a first-round bye, they had to play one of those best-of-three miniseries against the Atlanta Hawks. The Hawks came into the Summit and managed to steal game one, 109–106, then wrapped the series up in Atlanta three days later. Just like that, what had become a very promising season was over.

As disappointed as he was, Tomjanovich had to feel good about his comeback. He had come all the way back to being an All-Star–caliber player and had fit in with his team even though it had changed considerably during his absence. He was only thirty years old and there was every reason to believe he still had a number of productive years as a player ahead of him.

Kermit Washington felt the same way. After the Clippers' horrendous start and his near walkout, they too had turned their season around. As the players began to get used to one another and accustomed to Shue's system, they played better and better, closing with a rush. After the 2–12 start, the team was 41–27 the rest of the way, finishing 43–39. Unfortunately, in the loaded Pacific Division that was only good for fifth place. Even though they won six more games than New Jersey, the last of the Eastern Conference's six playoff qualifiers, the Clippers had no chance to qualify in the West.

That didn't keep Washington from feeling strongly about San Diego's future. He had enjoyed the best season of his career. For the first time in six seasons in the league, he had played in all 82 games, becoming an everyday starter. He had averaged 11.3 points and 9.9 rebounds a night. Things had even quieted for him in most of the road venues, Houston and Detroit being the predictable exceptions.

He and Pat had bought a home in San Diego near where Swen Nater lived and the two families had become close. Dana had started school that fall, and there was no reason as far as Washington was concerned to think about playing anyplace else. After his year as a nomad—Los Angeles to purgatory to Boston to San Diego—he felt as if he was finally home.

And then, during the summer, he started to hear whispers again.

Team owner Irv Levin wanted to sign Bill Walton and bring him home to San Diego. Walton had been injured—again—late in the 1977–78 season, breaking bones in his foot. The Trail Blazers had been 50–20 when Walton got hurt. They were 8–4 the rest of the regular season and then lost a six-game series in the Western Conference semifinals to the Seattle SuperSonics. Walton didn't play a single game the following season, still injured and by now involved in a public battle with the Portland medical staff, whom he held responsible for his recurring problems.

Walton very much wanted out of Portland, and returning to the city he had grown up in seemed like a natural fit. Levin, looking to add glitz to what was a solid but decidedly unsexy team, was willing to gamble with his team's future in order to land Walton. The reason it was a gamble was the league rule, which put compensation into the hands of the commissioner if the two teams couldn't reach an agreement prior to a free agent signing. Naturally, Portland would want the compensation to be based on the team's losing a young player (age twenty-seven) who had been the league MVP just two seasons earlier and had led them to an NBA title. San

Diego, for its part, would want to emphasize that it was getting a player who was a medical risk and hadn't played a basketball game in eighteen months.

Washington was horrified when he heard that Levin was trying to sign Walton. Initially his concern was that compensation would hurt the team, especially if Walton wasn't healthy enough to play. Then when he thought about it further, he became more upset: What, he thought, if *I'm* part of the compensation?

"Then I thought, 'Wait a minute, they won't do that to me for a second year in a row,'" he said. "They had sent me to San Diego when I had signed with Boston, they wouldn't ship me to Portland as compensation a year later, would they?" Washington shook his head and laughed. "Boy, was I a fool."

Of course they would ship him to Portland. Among all the players mentioned to Portland coach Jack Ramsay as possible compensation, the two players he wanted most were All-Star guard Randy Smith and Washington. He knew that Washington was dependable, a hard worker, and very coachable. Since the championship, the Blazers had become a difficult team. Even with Walton gone, Maurice Lucas would continue to demand a new contract for a lot more money. Some of the players who had been important parts of the championship team—Larry Steele, Dave Twardzik, Bob Gross—were battling injuries and age. Lionel Hollins, the superb shooting guard, also wanted out of Portland. Washington would be someone he could depend on to show up and play hard every night and not cause trouble.

Ramsay also needed a center since he was losing Walton. Tom Owens had played very well the previous season, and Mychal Thompson had been on the all-rookie team. But Thompson had broken a leg during the off-season and was going to be out for the season. Ramsay needed another big body inside. The league offered him two choices: Swen Nater or Kevin Kunnert.

There were a couple of reasons for Ramsay to lean toward Nater. First, he was a better scorer than Kunnert, a more natural low-post player. Second, Kunnert had undergone off-season knee surgery. Ramsay liked the way Kunnert played, though; he liked the fact that he could shoot from outside. That meant he could pair him with Owens at times to spell Lucas. Also, as a coach who emphasized defense, he liked Kunnert's toughness. Before telling the league whether he preferred Nater or Kunnert, Ramsay wanted Kunnert's knee examined by the Portland team doctors.

"They looked at it and told us he was fine," Ramsay said years later. "They gave him a clean bill of health."

And so Ramsay told the league Portland would accept Washington, Smith, and Kunnert as compensation. Remarkably, one year after they had been sent together from Boston to San Diego, the two men, who had barely spoken to each other throughout the season in San Diego, were again packing to move to the same city. The league went along with Portland's claim that it was losing a superstar and awarded the Blazers the three players, cash, and future draft picks as compensation for Walton.

"Unbelievable," Washington said. "It made me think they were conspiring to keep us together no matter what. They were worried I was going to sue him the same way Rudy had sued the Lakers. But if they kept us on the same team, I wasn't likely to sue, was I?"

Kunnert laughed at that notion. "The league had nothing to do with me signing in Boston. I did that all on my own because it was the best deal I could get," he said. "The league didn't decide which players went to San Diego, the two owners did. And if Jack Ramsay had wanted Swen Nater, he would have gotten Swen Nater. I think the guy is just a little bit paranoid."

While their husbands barely spoke to each other, Pat Washington and Mary Kunnert had become friends in San Diego. "We just liked each other," Mary Kunnert said. "Pat was outgoing and very sweet. Sometimes when the team was on the road we would get together and watch the game together. When my daughter was born that year, she went with me to the hospital."

"It was awkward at times," Pat Washington said. "I remember the day after the baby was born, I called Mary at the hospital to see if she needed anything. When I hung up Kermit asked me what that was about and I told him. I knew it didn't make him happy, because he blamed Kevin for the fight. But I didn't blame Mary for what had happened, and she didn't blame me. I guess that was between the two of them."

It was largely unspoken between the two of them. One night on the road, they found themselves outside a hotel waiting for a cab in the snow to go eat. A lone cab pulled up. Washington looked at Kunnert. "Come on," he said. "We'll share it. We can go eat together."

Kunnert agreed. At dinner the subject of the fight never came up. They just talked about the team and basketball and their kids.

Neither player was thrilled at the thought of going to Portland. For Washington it would be a fourth team in less than three seasons. He still hadn't sold his house in Palos Verdes. Rather than buy yet another house in Oregon, he decided to rent a house and keep the one he had bought in San Diego. He was balancing a lot of real estate, hoping he would end up selling at just the right time.

As it turned out, the Walton signing helped neither franchise. Walton managed to play a total of 14 games in San Diego during the 1979–80 season. That was 4 fewer than Kunnert played in Portland. His knee continued to hurt him, and he would never be completely healthy again for the rest of his career.

The one player in the group who continued to thrive was Washington. With Lucas injured a good deal of the time and eventually traded to New Jersey, Washington was not only a starter but someone the team looked to on offense. "It was the first time in my pro career that there were actually plays drawn up for me," he said. "I enjoyed it. When Maurice came back, that stopped for the most part, but I still got the ball a good deal."

He had the best year of his career statistically, averaging 13.6 points and 10.5 rebounds a game. The Blazers actually started

10–0 that season, but injuries and turmoil brought them back to earth, and they finished the season 38–44, barely making the playoffs, where they lost a three-game opening-round miniseries to Seattle.

That was the season that David Halberstam spent with the Blazers researching his book. Halberstam is as good a reporter as has ever lived, and it didn't take him long to recognize that Kermit Washington's arrival in Portland had dumped a fascinating story in his lap. He spent a great deal of time with Washington, and when the book was published, it included a lengthy section on Washington's life: his background, his rise at AU, and then the punch and its aftermath.

In Kunnert's mind, Halberstam completely bought into Washington's version of the events of December 9, 1977. In the book, Halberstam reported that Kunnert had thrown the two elbows at Washington's head but didn't include Kunnert's very different account of the encounter. Kunnert still has the autographed copy of the book Halberstam sent him and has underlined a number of passages that bother him.

"The one that really gets me is this one," he said, pulling the book off a shelf. He pointed to a marked passage. In between commas, talking about some of Ramsay's frustrations with the team, Halberstam wrote: "Washington, a fast learner, and Kunnert, a slow learner."

"Reading this book you would think that Washington was completely innocent that night and that I was this big dope from Iowa who picked a fight with him," Kunnert said. "To this day every time I look at that book, I feel sick to my stomach. He just bought into the entire Saint Kermit story. Please."

Whether Halberstam bought in or not doesn't really matter at this point. What matters now—as it did then—is that the book ratcheted up the harsh feelings between Kunnert and Washington. By the time the book appeared, the incident was four years old. But it still wasn't over.

18

Time to Move On

If you accept the history of the Houston Rockets according to Calvin Murphy, the beginning of the end for "his" Rockets came on June 7, 1979. That was the day Del Harris succeeded Tom Nissalke as the team's coach.

Harris had been Nissalke's assistant and was the players' choice to succeed Nissalke, who had been fired by George Maloof, the Rockets' fifth owner since 1971. Maloof came in intending to make sweeping changes but eventually decided to retain Ray Patterson as general manager. Nissalke wasn't as lucky. According to Tomjanovich, Maloof initially wanted to hire Norm Ellenberger, who had been the coach at the University of New Mexico when the Lobos had been the target of a major NCAA investigation. But after talking with a number of players, he was persuaded to hire Harris, in large part because he was given a lot of the credit for turning Moses Malone into a star.

Tomjanovich had been able to get through his first season back after the punch with only one injury problem, the broken nose. But the following season, injuries began plaguing him. He had some groin miseries and a recurring problem with his right arch.

"The only way for it to heal completely," he said, "was to stop play-ing. I wanted to play." He could feel his body slowing. He had never been quick, but now he felt a half-step slower. He couldn't jump the way he once had. Whether the injuries he had suffered in Los Angeles were connected is impossible to tell. But at thirty-one, a player with Tomjanovich's work ethic should have been at the peak of his career, not on the downside.

"You'll never be able to tell me that everything his body went through trying to recover from all those injuries didn't shorten his career," Mike Newlin said. "The fact that he came back to play the way he did is a tribute to Rudy. But sooner or later it was going to catch up to him."

That had been the crux of the testimony almost everyone associ-ated with the Rockets had given during the civil trial that was held in Houston in the summer of 1979. One by one players and coaches who had been involved in the game were called to testify. One by one they recounted the harrowing facts. Sitting in the courtroom, looking at the six-person jury, Kermit Washington had one thought: "We have no chance."

Kareem Abdul-Jabbar agreed. Abdul-Jabbar was probably the only witness in the case whose testimony backed Washington in any way. He testified that he had seen Kunnert punch Washington before Washington squared off and punched Kunnert. "I was very concerned about how the trial would come out for Kermit," he said years later. "I just didn't feel a black man in the state of Texas being sued by a white man stood much chance of getting a fair trial."

Technically Washington wasn't being sued; the Lakers were. While that gave Washington relief from any financial liability, it made sitting in the courtroom and listening to the lawyers that much harder to take. "The whole trial was about the Lakers' failure to control me, to train me, to keep me from injuring people," he said. "It sounded as if they were describing the behav-ior of some kind of animal. Then whenever I would see their lawyers in the hallway they would say, 'Hello, Mr. Washington, how are you, Mr. Washington?' It was infuriating. I'm not even sure why I was there at all. The whole thing was a sham."

One reason he was there was to testify. On the second day of the trial, Tomjanovich testified. Over objections from the defense, the jury was shown film of the punch and slides of what Tomjanovich looked like when he arrived at the hospital that night. While the film and the slides were shown, Tomjanovich sat in his chair and looked into the distance, away from the screen. "I didn't need to see it again," he said. "That was a long two weeks. I knew why we were there, but I didn't like being there anyway."

Toffel testified in detail about the nature of Tomjanovich's injuries. Most important, he testified that in spite of the surgeries and pain he had already been through, Tomjanovich was likely to face recurring sinus headaches in the future, could lose his sense of smell, and would probably have serious dental problems because of the damage done to his gums. He also said that Tomjanovich's face, though repaired, would never be the same again.

"It will never be the same the rest of his life," he said. "The scar tissue will never be quite as strong as it was in its original state."

Toffel and Tomjanovich were followed by all the players and coaches present that night. Most damaging to Washington may have been the testimony of referee Bob Rakel, who said he had not seen Kunnert throw an elbow or a punch before he and Washington squared off. He remembered skirmishing, first between Abdul-Jabbar and Kunnert and then between Washington and Kunnert, but he said he had not seen either the punch Abdul-Jabbar described or the elbows Washington described.

Not surprisingly, the angriest testimony came from Kunnert, who, under questioning from Robert Dunn, the Lakers' lawyer, said he had not thrown an elbow at Washington's head or a punch of any kind and that any testimony to that effect was a lie. When his turn came, Washington repeated his story about Kunnert elbowing him. He also said he had no idea who it was running at him from behind and he had reacted instinctively and was very sorry for the injuries Tomjanovich had received.

At no point during the two-week trial did Tomjanovich and Washington make eye contact or exchange so much as a hello.

It took the jury five hours to return a verdict. Tomjanovich had asked for a total of $2.6 million in actual and punitive damages from the Lakers. The jury decided that wasn't quite enough. It awarded Tomjanovich just under $3.25 million—$1.746 million in actual damages and $1.5 million in punitive damages.

"I was shocked," Tomjanovich said, shaking his head twenty-two years after the trial.

"I wasn't," Washington said, smiling.

Whether Abdul-Jabbar's assessment of a Texas jury was correct or Washington's initial belief that he and the Lakers had "no chance," it certainly didn't make anyone on either side happy when U.S. District Court judge John V. Singleton informed the lawyers shortly after reading the verdict that "at least" two of the six jurors had asked if Tomjanovich could autograph their copies of the court's legal instructions.

There would be an appeal, and even though the $3.25 million figure was imposing, there was no way of knowing if or when Tomjanovich would collect any of the money. As it turned out, the two sides eventually agreed to a $2 million settlement before the case was heard on appeal. Under the agreement, most of the money was placed in an annuity that was set up for the Tomjanovich children.

Starstruck jurors or no starstruck jurors, there was no doubting the seriousness of Tomjanovich's injuries. Toffel's calm, detailed account, and the film and the slides and the parade of witnesses who all essentially said it was the worst thing they had ever seen in their lives, certainly worked against Washington. The jury was asked to decide damages, not intent.

There was absolutely no doubting the damage that had been suffered.

By both men.

In his autobiography Tomjanovich ends the chapter on the 1977–78 season with this summation: "The Washington incident cast a shadow over the entire 1977–78 season, and when Malone and Newlin were injured in the second half of the season, we plummeted to a 28–54 record. . . . The Washington saga didn't really end until the fall of 1979, when I was awarded a multimillion-dollar settlement following a court case in Houston."

That reference to the "Washington saga" appears on page 107. In the 178 pages that follow, Kermit Washington's name appears one more time—when Tomjanovich discusses people wanting to bring up the "Washington episode" throughout his comeback season. "I learned," he wrote, "to tolerate these sorts of comments."

No doubt both he and Washington had hoped the court case would be the end of the saga. Both soon learned that it wasn't. By the end of the 1980 season, Tomjanovich suspected his career was beginning to wind down. He hoped the injuries that had slowed him during the season would prove to be just an interlude, not a beginning. But he knew that he had only been able to start 50 games, and as Toffel had predicted, he was still dealing with pounding sinus headaches and pain in his teeth. Beyond that, he had gone from being a great sleeper to a poor one. Part of that was the recurring vision of his own death; part of it was general discomfort.

Washington had found comfort in Portland, even more so than in Boston or San Diego. Portland was the smallest market in the NBA, with a population of slightly more than 500,000. The Blazers' championship in 1977 had cemented them as icons in the community. If you played for the Blazers, you were almost automatically a hero in Portland. Washington's hardworking style of play, his easygoing manner away from the court, and his willingness to show up and play every night without complaining about his role or his salary made him popular with the fans, who sold out the Portland Civic Center—12,666—every single night the Blazers played.

It wasn't as if the Tomjanovich incident had gone away. But at that stage of his life, Washington felt as if it was receding and assumed that sooner or later it would be all but forgotten. "I had paid the price for making a mistake," he said. "I had been suspended and fined; I had been threatened and cursed. I had been through the humiliation of the trial and walked away with whatever label the jury's verdict could put on you. It still came up when we went on the road, and it still came up in the media. I began to think my actual name was 'Kermit Washington, who in December of 1977 threw the punch that almost killed Rudy Tomjanovich . . .'

"But in Portland, I was just Kermit Washington, basketball player. People were nice to my family, I felt as if I belonged in the community. It was a happy time."

During that first season in Portland, after injuries had knocked a couple of players off the Western Conference All-Star team, he was chosen to play in the All-Star game. Remarkably, just as Tomjanovich had gone home to Detroit for the 1979 game, Washington went home to Washington for the 1980 game. When American University learned he was going to be in town for the three-day All-Star weekend, it made arrangements to retire his number 24 uniform in a ceremony at the Fort the night before the All-Star game.

Slowly but surely, it seemed, Washington's life was being put back together, piece by piece. In 1980–81 he was named team captain. He had what had become for him a typical season, averaging 11.4 points per game and 9.4 rebounds on a solid Portland team that finished 45–37. The only negative was the recurring pain he was feeling in his back and knees. The more he played, the more pain he felt, but that, he knew, was inevitable. "I would rather deal with the pain and play," he said, "than not play."

He had to sit out nine games during that season but was nonetheless an integral part of the Blazers. Kevin Kunnert was also playing in pain: his reconstructed knee had never completely healed. Even so he managed to play in 55 games that season, although his minutes (16) points (4.4) and rebounds (5.1) were way down from his healthy, halcyon days in Houston.

"I could never really jump, run, or move the same way after I had the surgery," he said. "I had the long-term contract, so I was going to be paid regardless of whether I played or not. But I felt an obligation to at least try to play, to earn the money I was being paid. I never saw myself as a quitter."

The frosty relationship between Washington and Kunnert had grown even colder after the trial. That was understandable, since each had testified under oath that the other was a liar. In a sense, both were poster boys for the difficulty of NBA life. Both were only twenty-nine during the 1980–81 season (Washington would hit thirty in September 1981, Kunnert eight weeks later, in November), and yet both were hobbling around on the knees of old men, wondering how much longer they could play effectively, if at all.

Rudy Tomjanovich, who was three years older, was dealing with the same thoughts and frustrations that season in Houston. Various injuries had slowed him too. Some nights he couldn't play. That wasn't the worst of it, though: as the season wore on, there were nights when he could play but, for the first time since his rookie year, the coach chose not to play him.

The revamped Rockets had finished 41–41 in 1980. The following season, they continued to be a .500 team. Rick Barry had retired, leaving Tomjanovich without the guy most likely to get him the ball when he got open. In 1980 the Rockets had acquired 6-foot-11-inch Billy Paultz, nicknamed The Whopper, one of the sharpest, funniest men in the league. Paultz was one of those players who never overwhelmed anyone with his grace on the court or with his numbers but always seemed to play on winning teams. As the 1980–81 season went on, Del Harris began playing him more and more, paired inside with Moses Malone. Needing some speed up front, Harris usually went with young Robert Reid as the small forward. Often that left Tomjanovich out of the rotation.

Calvin Murphy was going through similar frustrations in the backcourt. Lucas's departure had started a lengthy search for a point guard. Slick Watts had been a stopgap in 1979. That summer Tom Henderson had been signed as a free agent and Allen Leavell had been picked up in the draft. Searching for the right combination, Harris began playing Henderson and Leavell together at the guard spots and bringing Murphy off the bench. As the season wore on, both Tomjanovich and Murphy saw their minutes dwindling. Murphy still played often as a regular part of the rotation but was not the least bit happy and—surprise—made it clear to everyone that he was not. Tomjanovich played much less and wasn't happy either. Not surprisingly, he never complained.

"That doesn't mean it didn't hurt," he said. "Del was very straight with me about it when he decided to play Billy more and me less. I appreciated that, but it was killing me to not play. Now, twenty years later, I can sit here and talk about it unemotionally and understand why Del did what he did. But back then it was brutal."

He found himself almost a full-time spectator for the first time since the Alex Hannum days in San Diego. The Rockets were again struggling to make the playoffs. Tomjanovich was in the uncomfortable position of wanting his team to win while knowing that any success they had made Harris's decision to sit him look like the right one. He wondered what his future in Houston was going to be. He had two years left on his contract. At thirty-two, he was convinced he was too young to be finished as an effective basketball player.

"It was a Catch-22," he said. "I couldn't stand not playing. But I couldn't argue with the results we were getting with the new lineup."

His teammates didn't like seeing him out of the rotation either. They went so far as to bring it up in team meetings. At one point during the playoffs, Tom Henderson stood up, pointed at Tomjanovich, and said, "Del, how can he not be playing? There's no way I can believe he can't help us."

Maybe he could have helped. But he didn't get the chance. The 1981 playoffs made it clear that Tomjanovich's days as a member of the Rockets' regular rotation were probably behind him. Houston, now in the Western Conference, sneaked in by winning three of its last four games to finish 40–42 and then, led by Malone, got on one of those hot runs a low-seeded team occasionally experiences. First they shocked the Lakers—who had finished 14 games ahead of them in the standings—in the three-game miniseries, winning game three in Los Angeles. At the same time, the Kansas City Kings, who had also finished 40–42, upset Portland in their miniseries. Then, the two sub-.500 teams each pulled an even more shocking upset in the conference semis: the Rockets beat Midwest Division champion San Antonio in seven games, while the Kings stunned Phoenix, the top seed in the West after a 57-victory regular season, also in seven games.

That set up the all-sub-.500 conference final. The Rockets, full of confidence by now, won the series in five games. Remarkably, they were in the NBA finals, facing the Celtics, who had been rejuvenated a year earlier by the arrival of Larry Bird.

Tomjanovich and Murphy didn't quite know what to think. Each had dreamed about playing in the finals and at last they had arrived. "I loved being part of the finals," Tomjanovich said. "But I didn't really feel as if I *was* a part of them. I felt as if I had a very good seat."

With Malone playing wonderfully, the Rockets made the series a difficult one for the Celtics. They split the first four games before Bird took over in a dominating game five win and then made all the big shots down the stretch in game six at the Summit to wrap up the Celtics' fourteenth NBA title. Auerbach's gamble in the spring of 1978—drafting Bird in the first round even though he was planning to play in college for another year—had paid off in spades. And in a banner.

Even in defeat Houston was euphoric. All the home playoff games in the last two rounds were sellouts. Scalpers were even seen outside the Summit, which had to be a first. When it was over, Tomjanovich wondered what his future with the Rockets was going to be.

He only knew one thing for certain: it was time to prove himself all over again.

What he needed to do, Tomjanovich was convinced, was get himself into the best shape of his life. The nagging injuries of the past two seasons had slowed him. He hadn't played any summer ball since the comeback summer of 1978, and he knew he needed to do that to get himself into game shape coming into training camp. He was still young enough to have plenty of good basketball left in him.

"I was going to show them," he said. "Just like I had always done."

The first hint of real trouble came in early June, three weeks after the 1981 finals had concluded. The Rockets traded two future draft picks to Washington to bring an aging Elvin Hayes back to the team. Hayes was thirty-five but had still averaged almost 18 points a game for the Bullets. He played the same position as Tomjanovich played and like Tomjanovich was a deadly shooter.

"It was pretty clear to me then that if I wanted to keep playing, I mean really playing, I was going to have to go someplace else," Tomjanovich said. "The one thing I knew I didn't want to do was sit on the bench and collect a paycheck."

His contract called for him to be paid $300,000 a year for two more years. If he wanted to be dealt, Ray Patterson would make a deal for him. And there would be teams that would be willing to take him, given that he could still score and would provide leadership and a role model for younger players on any team he played for. Tomjanovich was ready to make the move. He wanted to prove that he could still play. Calvin Murphy understood his reasoning but hated the idea of seeing his buddy leave town.

"It would have killed me to see him in another uniform," he said. "It would have been awful. I didn't blame him, not one bit. In fact I probably should have gone in and told them to trade both of us someplace. I just didn't want him leaving town."

It never came to that. On a hot late-summer afternoon (as if there is any other kind in Houston) Tomjanovich was relaxing in his front yard, watching his kids play with some close friends from the neighborhood. Nichole was nine, Melissa six. Both loved their school and had grown up with the same friends since birth.

"I looked at them and thought to myself, 'What am I doing here?'" Tomjanovich said. "I had worked hard all summer and I knew I was in good shape. I was absolutely convinced I could go to a team and help them. But how much? Would I be a sixth, seventh man? Would I play a lot or not a lot? I couldn't be sure, even though I knew I still had some good basketball in me. There was no question in my mind about that.

"So I finally had a talk with myself. I said, 'Okay, Rudy, this is the deal: you're going to uproot your family for a year, maybe two, take them to someplace brand-new, put the girls in a new school, make them start all over, and then probably move them *again* in a year or two, all so you can satisfy your ego and prove one more time you can still play?'

"I realized I was being ridiculous. I didn't need to play again. I'd had a wonderful career. My family was in good shape financially. I had proven I could come back after the punch and play well again. It hadn't knocked me out of basketball. It was time to move on to the next thing. I didn't want to just be one of those guys who hangs on until he gets dragged out the door kicking and screaming."

Tomjanovich called his lawyer and asked him to set up a meeting with the Rockets. He told them how he felt; that he didn't want to be traded and he didn't want to sit on the bench for two more years collecting dust and paychecks. A deal was struck: Tomjanovich would retire as a Rocket. The team would pay him his player salary for one more season rather than two. And the team would try to find a role for him in the organization.

The question was, what would that role be? This was 1981, long before the current era, when most NBA benches have more guys sitting on them wearing suits than uniforms. In 2001 the Rockets' media guide listed thirteen people on the basketball staff, not counting the additional four listed as basketball support staff. Not only is that not atypical, it is relatively small. The Rockets today have *two* video coordinators.

But twenty-one years ago that wasn't the case. The Rockets' coaching staff consisted of Del Harris and assistant coach Carroll Dawson. It was Dawson who did most of the advance scouting, and he, Harris, and general manager Ray Patterson split up the bulk of the college scouting. Tomjanovich didn't want to start his nonplaying career in some community relations job in which he spent most of his time handing out schedule cards and media guides at basketball clinics.

Initially, Harris and Dawson set up a meeting for him at the University of Houston with coach Guy Lewis. The UH coach, a legend in Houston, was willing to bring Tomjanovich onto the staff as a volunteer assistant—which would work financially, since the Rockets were still paying him—to give him a chance to learn the nuts and bolts of coaching and scouting. That was fine with Tomjanovich.

"I had never really given much thought to what I was going to do after playing," he said. "And then all of a sudden it was there, right in front of me. I hadn't thought of myself as a coach, but I had always been someone who liked coming up with plays, even when I was a kid playing in the schoolyard. So that appealed to me.

"But then one day we got to talking, and Carroll told Del that he thought they could really use me doing some scouting—college and advance. So we decided I'd try and do that and see how it went."

On October 2, 1981, with training camp about to begin under the new NBA calendar, which had pushed the start of the season back to the end of October, the Rockets called a press conference. Rudy T, the most popular player in the history of the franchise, was retiring. He had played in 768 regular-season games and scored 13,383 points in eleven NBA seasons, averaging 17.4 points per game. He had 6,198 rebounds—8 per game—and 1,573 assists. He had shot better than 50 percent from the field—.501—a statistic unheard of nowadays for a perimeter player. He had played in five All-Star games. Less than four months after his retirement, he would become the first Rocket to have his number (45) retired.

He had been a great player, a leader, a pillar of the community. And when he found himself traveling alone as a scout in the ensuing months and years and strangers would see him folding his 6-foot-8-inch frame into an airplane seat and ask him if he played basketball, he would nod and say that he had. And then, invariably, they would ask him his name. He would tell them. Their eyes would flicker with recognition and then, almost without fail, they would say, "I know you, you're the guy who got punched."

While Rudy Tomjanovich was announcing his retirement, Kermit Washington was preparing to go to training camp. He was concerned about the aches and pains he was feeling in both his knee and his back. He had been forced to cut back his summer workload with Newell because of the pain, even though he and Newell now had a full battery of players participating in what had once been their one-on-one workouts.

After missing large chunks of every one of his first five NBA seasons—the first three because he was riding the bench; the fourth

because of his knee injury; the fifth because of his suspension—
Washington had missed almost no time at all during the next three.
He had played in all 82 games in San Diego and then had played 80
games and 73 games the next two seasons in Portland. The nine
missed games in 1980–81 had been caused by his knee being too
sore to play. He had hoped that going a little easier during the summer would allow him recovery time so he could start the new season fresh.

But he knew as soon as camp started that he was in trouble.
Every practice was torture. He needed long stretches in the training room, icing his knees, getting into a hot tub for his back, just to
recover. About the only person on the team who was as physically
miserable as Washington was Kevin Kunnert, whose surgical knee
seemed to get worse with each passing day. They were both just
thirty years old, but their bodies felt a lot older than that.

"I knew we were in trouble with Kermit right from the start that
season," Jack Ramsay, the Blazers' coach, said. "Just running up
and down the court was difficult for him. You knew he wasn't dog-
ging it, because he would never do that, so if you saw him running
slowly it was because his body wouldn't let him go any faster. And
he'd lost that great, quick leaping ability of his. You hoped it might
come back, but it didn't seem likely."

Kunnert began the season on the injured list. Washington was
trying to play, but it was difficult. Mostly he played in short bursts
off the bench, because he couldn't run up and down the floor more
than a few times without feeling pain. November became December and December became January. If anything, the pain he was
feeling was worse than it had been in training camp. He had played
in 20 games, averaging 20 minutes a game and just 5 points and 4.7
rebounds a game. None of those numbers were close to what he
had produced when he was healthy.

Washington kept hoping he would get better. He tried resting
for a while. Then he tried not practicing but playing in games. It

wasn't working. "I finally woke up one morning and realized my time had come," he said. "I didn't want to stop playing, but my body was telling me I couldn't play anymore."

He went and told Ramsay that he was going to retire. Ramsay was disappointed but not surprised. Washington asked if he could talk to his teammates before the announcement was made. Of course, Ramsay told him.

He talked, that day, about loving basketball and how much he would miss it, but there came a time to step aside, to give younger players a chance. He said he didn't want to hang on and collect a paycheck and take up a spot on the roster if he couldn't play anymore.

Kevin Kunnert sat and listened and seethed. He was convinced Washington's speech was directed at him, an older player trying to come back from serious injury. "I was going to get paid whether I played or not, just like Kermit," he said. "If he didn't think he could play, that was fine, I understood. But there was no reason for him to come in there and act as if he was doing something heroic. I wanted to still try to play, thought I might be able to contribute something. That was my decision. His decision was his decision."

On the afternoon of January 25, 1982, Washington announced that he was retiring from basketball after eight and a half seasons in the NBA. His career statistics were not nearly as imposing as Tomjanovich's, but given all the games missed, they were more than respectable. He had played in 501 games and averaged 9.3 points and 8.4 rebounds per game. His shooting percentage from the field, .526, wasn't much lower than his shooting percentage from the foul line, .656, thus proving correct the referees who had told him they were doing him a favor by not sending him to the line more often.

He had played for four NBA teams and had made one All-Star team. He had been considered a pillar of the communities he had lived in and a violent thug in many other communities. In Portland his retirement was big news. In Washington, D.C., and Houston, Texas, it was news. Everywhere else it was either a short note or a part of the agate—small type—on the sports page.

On the morning of January 26, most newspapers across the country ran the wire service notice on Washington's decision. "Portland Trail Blazers forward Kermit Washington announced his retirement. The Trail Blazers activated center Kevin Kunnert to take his spot on the active roster."

19

Starting Over

The transition from basketball player to non–basketball player was decidedly easier for Rudy Tomjanovich than for Kermit Washington. Not only was he getting paid for his first year out of the game at a player's salary—$300,000—he had walked into a job that he absolutely loved right from the start.

"As soon as I started scouting, I thought it was something I had been born to do," he said. "I enjoyed everything about it, especially evaluating players and trying to figure out who was most likely to do well at the next level. Plus I really felt as if I was making a contribution to the team. The travel was tough, but really no tougher than when I was playing in terms of time away from home. I can honestly say that if I had kept doing that sort of work for the next twenty-five years, I think I would have been completely happy."

It wasn't as simple for Washington. He wasn't nearly as certain what he wanted to do with the rest of his life. His financial situation wasn't bad, but it wasn't overwhelmingly good either. He still owned his house in San Diego, in part because when he had wanted to sell, the market hadn't been very good, but also because his brother, Chris, and his family had lived there for a while.

Like his younger brother, Chris Washington had beaten the odds and made it from Farragut Street to the pros. He had made the St. Louis Cardinals as a defensive back in 1972 after being drafted in the tenth round out of Texas–El Paso (the school had changed its name from Texas Western while Chris was there) and had become a starter during his rookie season. "Chris was a great football player because he never had any fear," Kermit said. "His life had been so bad when we were young that he didn't worry about getting hurt. Nothing could happen to him that would be as bad as our life had been."

During his second season in St. Louis, Chris Washington tore up his knee. He underwent major surgery and was never able to regain the toughness and aggressiveness that had marked his play before the injury. The Cardinals released him at the end of the 1973 season.

Like many athletes—but unlike his brother—Chris Washington had left college without a degree. He tried to find work in St. Louis after he stopped playing but was never able to find anything he really enjoyed or that made him the kind of money he needed to support his wife and son, who had been born in 1974. According to Kermit, the calls asking for money started not long after his brother stopped playing football.

"I know he didn't want to ask," he said. "But his wife liked nice things. She was beautiful, really beautiful, and when they met, Chris was still playing football, making good money and able to take care of her the way she wanted to be taken care of. I didn't want to say no to my brother, so when he called I sent him money. Looking back, I probably didn't do him any favors."

Shortly after Kermit was traded to Portland, Chris called to say that he and Janice and their son, Eric, were thinking of moving to California. Could they stay in the San Diego house until they found their own place? This was during the off-season in 1980, Kermit said. "We were in San Diego during the summer, and I didn't think that was going to be a good setup, but I agreed. Chris said he wanted to enroll in engineering classes at San Diego State. So I said okay."

The two Washington families shared the house until Kermit and Pat and Dana and Trey went back to Portland in the fall. Chris Washington did enroll at San Diego State. Kermit agreed to pay his tuition, loaning him the money until Chris had a job and could pay him back. Chris and his family stayed in the house for two years, until Chris dropped out of school again. Shortly after that, they returned to St. Louis. By then the relationship between the brothers and the two families was tense. Kermit told Chris he had to get a job or finish school but he couldn't—and wouldn't—lend him any more money.

"By then our mom was really sick and I was paying for her care back in Washington," he said. "I wasn't playing ball anymore, so I wasn't making the kind of money I had made. I told Chris I'd give him the shirt off my back if it would help him. I like helping people, and there was no one I wanted to help more than my brother. But there's a line between helping and being taken advantage of.

"I never should have let him leave California. I should have stopped him. I should have made him stay out here and finish his degree and get a good job. Then it might have been different."

After he retired, Kermit decided to stay in Portland. He finally sold the San Diego house. He was able to get part-time work as a strength coach with the Blazers. By the fall of 1983 he felt so good and so strong from working out in the weight room constantly that he was convinced he could make a comeback. He asked Ramsay to let him come to training camp and try to make the team.

"Of course I said yes," Ramsay said. "If he was healthy or even close to healthy, he could help us. The fact that I liked him was a factor, but I really looked at it as something that could potentially help the team."

The comeback could have been a storybook sort of thing had it worked out. Washington told team president Larry Weinberg that rather than be paid, he wanted his salary donated to a group he had started after his retirement called the Sixth Man Foundation. Washington's goal was to raise money to help kids in need in the Portland area. When David Stern, by then the commissioner of the NBA, found out about what Washington was proposing to do, he called Donald Dell.

"He can't play without a contract," Stern told Dell. "It is against our collective bargaining agreement for a hundred different reasons. If he wants to take the money and give it to his foundation, that's fine, but the team has to pay him."

Dell, Weinberg, and Washington finally agreed to a contract for the NBA minimum. Sadly, Washington never got a chance to collect any of that money.

"As soon as I started pounding my knees again, I could feel them going," he said. "I told Jack that if I was on the team, I might be able to play but there was almost no way I'd be able to practice most days. I knew that wasn't going to work for him or for me."

He retired again before the regular season began.

That winter he worked for his foundation and came up with one of his many "nutty professor ideas," as he called them. This one was for a weight vest like the one he had used in workouts since college.

In the spring he got a phone call from Tom Davis. Since his days as an assistant at American, Davis had gone on to great success as a college coach. He had been a consistent winner at Lafayette and then had moved on to Boston College, where he had taken the team as far as the final eight. He had left BC in the spring of 1982 to move to California and become the coach at Stanford. He had been there for two years when he called Washington, having heard he was interested in getting into coaching, to see if he might want to come work for him in Palo Alto.

"I had kept tabs on him after I left AU," Davis said. "When the incident with Rudy happened I was stunned. If we had a complaint about Kermit as a young player, it was that he was too soft. He never wanted to mix it up inside. There was no question about his strength once he got into the weight room, but he was about the last person I ever thought would be involved in something like that."

To most of the world the incident was the single most important thing one needed to know about Kermit Washington. To Davis it was nothing more than a blip, an out-of-character aberration. "I knew that wasn't who Kermit Washington was," he said. "I didn't hesitate to offer him a job, and no one ever said anything negative to me about it."

Washington was thrilled by the opportunity. He flew to Palo Alto to see Davis and go through the various interviews that were part of the hiring process at Stanford. He had gone out to dinner in San Francisco on Saturday night with friends and was flying back to Portland Sunday. He met with Davis on Sunday morning before he left, and the coach told him he was certain he was going to be able to hire him.

When the two men stopped in Davis's office before Washington headed for the airport, one of the assistants told Kermit his wife had called. Not wanting to be late for his plane, Washington decided to call Pat back after he got to the airport. At the airport, he called home. As soon as he heard Pat's voice, he knew something was terribly wrong.

"Where have you been?" she said. "I've been calling everywhere to find you."

Without explaining, Kermit, now terrified something had happened to Dana or Trey, said, "What's wrong?"

Pat paused, then took a deep breath. "There's no way to tell you this," she said. "Chris is dead."

"What happened?" he said, somehow finding his voice to get out two words.

"We're not sure," Pat said. "Something about a bank robbery."

It wasn't until much later that Kermit was able to piece together the details of his brother's death. His financial problems had apparently gotten worse after returning to St. Louis, and so had his marriage. He and Janice had split and, while she and Eric remained in the home they had bought when times were better financially, Chris had moved into an apartment.

Exactly when or why Chris made the decision to rob a bank, no one will ever know. But he did. According to the *St. Louis Post-Dispatch*, Chris committed his first robbery on December 12, 1983, six days after his divorce became final. The paper reported that he worked selling insurance briefly but lost that job. In April of 1984, he was late paying his apartment rent and he was apparently struggling to make child-care payments.

On May 4, a hidden camera took a photo of Chris during a holdup at the Clark Mercantile Bank in north St. Louis County. Police later told the newspaper that they were able to make a positive ID of Chris after looking at a newspaper photo taken in 1975 when he was working with the National Alliance of Businessmen in a program that helped find summer jobs for high school seniors who came from poor backgrounds—backgrounds similar to Chris and Kermit Washington's. In the photo Chris was wearing the same brown suit he was wearing when he robbed the bank.

The end came ten days later. Police and FBI agents surrounded the apartment building where Chris was living. According to the *Post-Dispatch*, when they ordered Chris to come outside and surrender, they saw him peek at them from behind curtains. A moment later, a muffled shot was heard. When police entered the apartment, they found Chris Washington with a bullet through his head, the shot apparently fired by a 9mm Smith & Wesson automatic pistol that appeared to be the same as the one photographed in the May 4 robbery. The police found one photograph displayed in the apartment: Chris in his Cardinals uniform.

Kermit did not fly to St. Louis for his brother's funeral. Shortly after he returned to Portland, he got a call from his father. Why, he wanted to know, didn't you take better care of Chris? How could you let this happen?

"It was all my fault, according to my father," he said. "I didn't know what to even say to him. I knew part of it was that he was hysterical, and I understood that. But I wasn't doing very well right then myself."

In fact he was doing very poorly. He decided not to go to the funeral because he knew that it would not go well between him and his father and his sister-in-law. He was angry: angry most of all that Chris was dead, but angry too that he was somehow being held responsible by his family. He knew he wasn't responsible, but the thought that he might have been able to do something, should have done something, ached inside.

Even now, when he talks about his brother, Kermit questions himself. "If only he had called me, just once," he said. "But I know he was hurt because I had told him I couldn't give him any more money. Maybe I shouldn't have done that. Maybe he would have called me if that hadn't happened. Even after he robbed the banks, I could have saved him. I could have flown there and gotten him a lawyer, and he would have gone to jail, but it wouldn't have been for too long. He never hurt anyone, never fired a gun, and he had a clean record up until then. It didn't have to turn out the way it did."

Although the two brothers had clashed and had grown apart in the last year of Chris's life, Kermit felt as if he had lost his best friend. Throughout those lonely years growing up in Washington, his constant companion had been Chris. It had been Chris he had sat with in the little bedroom on Farragut Street when they dreamed about stardom. Both had found it, in a real sense, beyond what they had dreamed. But it had never brought happiness to Chris Washington.

"I've had some tough times," Kermit said. "But I've also had some great times and a good life. It was never that way for my brother. Just when he really started to make it, he got hurt, and it was never easy for him after that. He was so smart when we were kids. He could have done so many things . . ."

His voice trailed off as he talked. Kermit Washington talks easily about his difficult boyhood and at length about how he has dealt with the Tomjanovich incident. He has long-winded opinions on everything from religion to politics to the current state of the NBA. But when he talks about his brother, his normally booming voice becomes very soft and the words, normally a torrent, become a trickle.

"I still miss him," he said. "He was my buddy."

Barbara Washington died that summer. Unlike Chris's death, her death was not a shock. She had been fighting cancer for months, and Kermit had known it was only a matter of time. "With Mom, there was sadness but also a sense of relief," he said. "She had suffered for a long time."

The good news was that he had a job that was keeping him busy. Being a college coach was brand-new to Kermit. He was learning as he went. The NCAA rule book might as well have been written in Greek as far as he was concerned. "It seemed as if every time I worked on recruiting a player I broke a rule," he said, laughing at the memory. "I did things that seemed innocent and then found out they weren't."

During that first summer, Kermit was watching a couple of potential recruits during a summer league game. In between games some of the kids asked him if he wanted to play a little pickup. Why not? "I was still in decent shape," he said. "I could play a little without hurting myself."

That wasn't the issue. The issue, according to the rule book, was participating with potential recruits. A no-no. When he mentioned to Davis that he had played pickup, Davis rolled his eyes. "We'll have to self-report to the NCAA," he told Washington. "Don't ever do it again."

Fortunately, because Stanford self-reported and because it was apparent to the NCAA that Washington simply didn't know the rule, Stanford was let off with a warning.

College coaching was a love-hate thing for Washington. He loved working with Davis, who he thought was a great coach and a wonderful man. "Tom Davis was so good he didn't need any assistants on the floor," he said. "He could teach, he could do anything and everything you needed to do. I never had a bad moment with him."

It wasn't quite that way with the assistants. Whether it was because they resented him for walking into the job without any training as a coach or because Washington refused to show them any respect is hard to tell. "What did they know about coaching?" he said. "They were never real players."

That is a familiar ex-jock refrain. If you didn't play the game, how could you know the game? Of course Davis was hardly a player of great renown, but that was different. Washington had no trouble seeing him as an authority figure, because he had first seen him in that role as a wide-eyed eighteen-year-old.

Washington enjoyed the players. They were bright and motivated, and when he worked with them in the weight room he could tell they respected him. With good reason: he could outlift them all.

At this point in his life, Washington was obsessed with weight lifting. He had worked out since the end of his playing career with body builders and was bigger than he had ever been. He enjoyed the weight room aspect of his coaching job so much that he began working with athletes from other Stanford teams, something the athletes liked and the strength coach hated.

"He thought I was treading on his territory," Washington said. "But I never went to the athletes. They came to me."

He was still sensitive, hypersensitive, to criticism. Davis remembers that he stopped asking him to officiate during scrimmages because he would get so upset whenever one of the players questioned a call. "It was like the days at AU when we figured out we couldn't yell at him," he said. "I remember one day he made a call in a scrimmage and one of the kids said something like, 'No,

Coach, you blew that one.' He took the whistle off, threw it on the ground, kicked a basketball across the court, turned around, and just left. He felt as if the kids didn't respect him as much as they should."

Most of the kids liked and respected Washington. They knew he had been a successful NBA player, and Davis often used him as an example of how much a player could improve from his freshman year to his senior year if he put his mind on it.

"I enjoyed it there," Washington said. "It wasn't perfect, but Coach Davis was great to me and I made a lot of friends among the athletes there. I didn't really like recruiting very much, and after a while I felt a lot of frustration. Part of it was that I really couldn't understand how a kid could have the chance to come to a place like Stanford and would ask questions like 'How often will we be on television?' The other part of it was that the kids we did get didn't really need that much help. In the weight room, sure, I could help them there. But these were smart kids, getting a Stanford education. They didn't need much guidance. I felt like there were other things I could be doing in places where I might be needed more."

Davis could see that adapting to the role of coach wasn't easy for Washington. "He was a good recruiter when it came time to close on a kid," he said. "Because it was impossible to spend time with him and not like him and be impressed by him. The earlier stages were tougher, because it takes a certain aggressiveness to get in with a kid [and] that just wasn't Kermit. I think it was tough for him as an ex-pro to adapt to doing some of the things you are asked to do as an assistant coach. But he worked hard at it and kept getting better. I think if he'd had the patience to stay with it, he could have been very good at it."

After Washington's second season, Davis accepted a job at Iowa, opting to return to his roots in the Midwest. He offered Washington the chance to go with him, but Washington turned him down. "I just didn't think living in Iowa was for me," he said. "And to be honest, I wasn't sure college coaching was going to be the right thing for me in the long run."

Instead he accepted an offer from Stanford athletic director Andy Geiger to stay on as a weight training coach, working with the basketball team and selected athletes in the other sports, staying clear of football, which was one area the other strength coaches guarded zealously.

"What made Kermit good was that he was willing to work as hard as you wanted to work," said Patrick McEnroe, who is now the U.S. Davis Cup captain but then was a member of the Stanford tennis team. "I remember thinking that if everyone had his work ethic, we would all be a lot better at what we did."

As much as he enjoyed the athletes, the politics of Stanford ultimately proved to be too much for Washington to deal with. He never seemed to find a niche with the other coaches in the department, to the point that he actually had to go to Geiger to get a key to the weight room. A year after Davis left, he left too. He wasn't exactly sure what he wanted to do next. But he had an idea in the back of his head.

Maybe, he thought, he could be a basketball player again.

While Washington was trying to find a comfortable niche, Rudy Tomjanovich was convinced he had found his. He had spent two years as a full-time scout for the Rockets. At the end of his second season—1983—Del Harris resigned as coach after another brutal, injury-plagued campaign had seen the team plummet to a 14–68 record.

One of the reasons for the team's awful record had been an off-season trade that sent Moses Malone to Philadelphia for Caldwell Jones and the Cleveland Cavaliers' first pick in the 1983 draft—which the Sixers had owned. With Malone almost certain to leave at the end of the season to be a free agent, Ray Patterson gambled that the Cleveland pick might be the number one pick in the draft, and that might give the Rockets the chance to draft 7-foot-4-inch superstar Ralph Sampson, who was about to be a senior at the University of Virginia.

The gamble paid off, but in the number three pick. The Rockets earned the number one pick on their own, first by going 14–68 and then by winning a coin flip with Indiana for the top pick. In those days, the teams with the worst record in each conference flipped a coin to see who got the number one pick. The Rockets took Sampson with the top pick and Rodney McCray, from Louisville, with the number three pick. Their college scout wanted to use the number three pick on Dale Ellis, a sweet-shooting 6-7 forward from Tennessee. But he was overruled by the new coach, Bill Fitch, who had replaced Harris at the end of the dismal season.

"I ended up loving Rodney as a player," Tomjanovich said years later. "He was a great guy and a very good player. But I loved Dale Ellis. I thought he had a chance to become something special." What he became was one of the great 3-point shooters in the history of the league, someone whose shooting skills kept him in the NBA for seventeen years.

When Fitch took over the team, he was given the authority to hire a second full-time assistant. The natural choice was Tomjanovich, so he moved to the bench with Fitch and Carroll Dawson for the 1983–84 season. That was the year the Rockets managed to lose 9 of their last 10 games to finish with the worst record in the Western Conference for a second straight year—though at a much-improved 29–53. Their swoon did two things: it gave them a chance to be part of the coin flip again, and it helped bring about the NBA lottery system for awarding the number one overall draft pick after several teams complained that the swoon had been suspiciously convenient for the Rockets.

Proving that their coin-flipping skills were peerless, the Rockets won again, this time beating the Portland Trail Blazers, who had

Indiana's number one pick. The Rockets used their pick on Hakeem Olajuwon, who proved to be one of the great players in the history of the league. Portland picked Sam Bowie, another 7-foot center, who did *not* prove to be one of the great players in the history of the league.

The Chicago Bulls had the third pick that year. They took a forward from the University of North Carolina who was listed at 6-6 but was really only slightly more than 6-4.

"You see, Houston and Portland knew what they were doing," explained Pat Riley, then the coach of the Los Angeles Lakers, one night that summer. "Olajuwon is going to be a great player, and Bowie is a seven-footer who can play facing the basket. This kid, oh, he's really talented, but he's not six-six, he's six-four. People in the media and fans don't understand how important that is, because they don't really understand the game."

The 6-4 kid in question was Michael Jordan.

"Who knows what would have happened in the league if we had taken Jordan?" Tomjanovich said. "We liked the twin towers concept [Sampson and Olajuwon], because Ralph was really too slender to defend inside. When I saw Olajuwon, I thought he had the potential to be a Bill Russell–like defender. In fact he ended up having much more of an offensive game than I thought he would. In the end, choosing him worked out very well for us. But if we're being honest, I don't think any of us really knew that Jordan was going to become Jordan. When I scouted him, I thought he would eventually be an All-Star, but I never dreamed he'd end up being the dominant player in the game."

The good news for the Rockets was that Olajuwon became Olajuwon. If the Rockets had lost the coin flip, they would have taken Jordan with the number two pick. Portland did not take Jordan with the number two pick, meaning it would go down in history not only as the team that once took the immortal LaRue Martin with the top pick in the draft, but the team that passed on Michael Jordan to take the oft-injured Sam Bowie.

The twin towers concept did work for the Rockets. In 1984–85, Olajuwon's rookie year, they won 48 games—a 19-game improvement over the previous season and a 34-game improvement over the 1982–83 season. They lost a disappointing best-of-five first-round series to Utah, losing the decisive fifth game at home. But a year later, after a 51–31 regular season, they made it back to the finals, shocking the Lakers in the Western Conference finals. They won the Lakers series 4–1, clinching when Sampson made a spinning, desperation buzzer-beater for a 114–112 victory in the Forum. Sampson released his shot no more than twenty feet from the spot where Washington had almost killed Tomjanovich eight and a half years earlier. Thus, one of Tomjanovich's happiest moments in basketball occurred in the same place where his worst moment in basketball had occurred.

The finals were not all that different from 1981. The Celtics were the opponent again, Bird was the biggest problem again, and Boston again won the series in six games. The difference was that the Rockets didn't feel as if this trip to the finals had been the product of a fluke or a hot streak. They thought it was part of a puzzle that was being pieced together and would lead to an NBA championship. They had two of the great young players in the game in Sampson and Olajuwon, and the future seemed to have no ceiling.

Only it didn't work out that way. Sampson's fragile body began to break down the next season, and he only played in 43 games. Olajuwon had emerged as the clear star of the team, but without Sampson the Rockets didn't have that double threat of two big men who could both score consistently. The team's record dropped to 42–40 in 1986–87, and they lost to Seattle in the second round of the playoffs. The following December, the team gave up on Sampson, trading him to Golden State for Joe Barry Carroll and Eric Floyd. The trade worked okay; the Rockets won 46 games, but they were beaten by Dallas in the first round of the playoffs. That was enough to cost Bill Fitch his job.

The new coach was Don Chaney, the same Don Chaney who had been Kermit Washington's teammate and close friend in Los Angeles and Boston, the same Don Chaney whose wife, Jackie, had placed the emergency phone call to Pat Washington on the night of the punch to warn her about what had happened. Chaney brought in John Killilea as a third assistant and scout, but kept Carroll Dawson and Tomjanovich with him as assistants. The new staff meshed quickly.

"You will never meet a better person to work with than Rudy," Chaney said. "We hit it off right from the start. Our daughters were close in age, our wives liked each other, and we had similar backgrounds. It was as if we'd grown up together almost. Rudy really enjoyed being an assistant coach. I think he would have been perfectly happy to just keep being an assistant. I never had the sense that the thought of being the head coach ever crossed his mind."

Chaney's sense was correct. Tomjanovich was extremely happy working with Chaney and Dawson. As a second assistant, he was rarely in the public eye. Almost never did he have to deal with the media. He just coached. There were still those moments in airports when that flicker of recognition would cross someone's face and he would hear, "You're the guy who got nailed." But that happened less often, especially since NBA teams were beginning to travel on charters at least some of the time by then.

In 1990–91, Chaney's third season, the Rockets were 52–30 and he was named NBA coach of the year. Even with that record, the team was only the sixth seed in the Western Conference and drew the Lakers in the first round of the playoffs. The Lakers won in a 3–0 sweep, but there certainly seemed to be plenty of hope for the future again in Houston. As it turned out, this was Magic Johnson's last season prior to his HIV-positive announcement, and the third-seeded Lakers ended up in the finals against Jordan's Bulls, who won the first of their six titles in the Jordan era.

Fifty-two games into the following season, Houston's hopes had soured. The Rockets hadn't played poorly, but they hadn't played as well as had been expected. At 25–20, they hit a skid, losing five of six. On February 18, they had a huge lead at home against the Minnesota Timberwolves and ended up blowing the lead and the game, losing 124–122 in overtime. It was one of those losses that keeps coaches up at night.

This was one of those nights. As he describes it in the opening chapter of his autobiography, he got a call at 3:00 A.M. from Robert Barr, the team's strength coach, who told him he had an eerie feeling that something was about to happen. Tomjanovich didn't want to hear it. He hung up and tried again to sleep, without success. He had never been a good sleeper since the punch, but this was a night when he didn't sleep at all.

The team had an 11:00 A.M. practice the next day. When it was over the coaches talked briefly about getting together later to discuss game planning for their next game, two days later against the 76ers. Chaney went upstairs to his office, while Tomjanovich and Dawson went to put together some tapes on the Sixers. Shortly after that, they received a phone call: Steve Patterson wanted to see the two of them in his office. Steve Patterson had succeeded his father as the team's general manager in 1989. Dawson and Tomjanovich looked at each other. Why would Patterson want to see the two of them and not Chaney?

The answer was obvious. "We need to go in there and fight for Don," Tomjanovich remembers telling Dawson. "This isn't right."

As it turned out, there was nothing to fight for. The decision had been made. Chaney had been told. He had gone from coach of the year to unemployed coach in a little more than half a season. The assistant coaches protested briefly, but Patterson held up a hand. "Guys," he said. "I know how loyal you are to Don. But it's over."

Patterson had tried to talk team owner Charlie Thomas out of the move already that morning. "I wanted to at least wait until the end of the season, see if Don could get things straightened out," he said. "But Charlie had made up his mind. If I hadn't made the move, he would have had someone else make the move."

Patterson and Tomjanovich were friends. Steve had worked for the team since 1984, but he had hung around the team since college, when his father first became general manager. Often he and Tomjanovich went to blues bars together. But this was business.

Patterson turned to the future. The logical move, in-season, was to hand the team over to Dawson, the number one assistant. But Dawson had serious blood pressure problems and had lost sight in one eye. Patterson was concerned that elevating him might escalate his health problems. "Which means," Patterson said, "that you're the guy, Rudy."

Tomjanovich was stunned. It *had* occurred to him that Chaney might be fired. It had *not* occurred to him that he would be sitting in a room being told he was the choice to run the team. In his book Tomjanovich wrote that Patterson said, "I'll give you guys a few minutes alone to talk it over." What he did not write was the last thing Patterson said before leaving. "Rudy, if you say no, my next call is going to be to Tom Nissalke."

Nissalke was out of coaching at the time, living in Houston and doing some of the Rockets' games on TV. The implication was clear: if Patterson called Nissalke, there was no guarantee that he wouldn't insist on bringing in an entirely new staff.

Patterson wasn't bluffing. He had already called Nissalke and told him he intended to offer the job to Tomjanovich but wasn't sure he would be willing to take it, knowing how loyal he was to Chaney. He wanted Nissalke ready in case Tomjanovich said no, because he had to name a coach that day.

Tomjanovich had very serious doubts about being the head coach. Part of it was feeling bad for Chaney; part of it was jumping from number two assistant to head coach. But the overriding reason was not wanting to become a truly public figure again. He had enjoyed life in the shadows as an assistant. He still remembered how tough the 14–68 season nine years earlier had been on Del Harris and on Harris's family. He was a popular, well-known figure in Houston, and moving up to being head coach would put him squarely in the spotlight again. Losing would not be easy if the team didn't do well, and he knew, just knew, that every single story written about his elevation would include the inevitable paragraphs about the punch.

In the end, though, there was really no choice. Nissalke might keep both him and Dawson on or he might not. He might want to keep Tomjanovich since he had twenty-two years with the organization and not keep Dawson. He couldn't risk that. When Patterson returned he reluctantly told him he would take the job.

"Good," Patterson said. "Take thirty minutes, clean yourself up. You look tired. Then we'll introduce you to the media."

Those may have been the words Tomjanovich was dreading most: introduce you to the media. He had lived very happily away from notebooks, microphones, and cameras for more than ten years. Now he was back squarely in front of them.

20

Finding a Niche

While Rudy Tomjanovich felt comfortable as an assistant coach from day one, Kermit Washington never felt that way. Whether it was having to be a recruiter, the politics of Stanford, or the sense that he cared more than a lot of the athletes did, it was never the right fit for him.

Which was why, after his third year at Stanford, he thanked athletic director Andy Geiger for keeping him around after Tom Davis's departure and resigned. He felt as if he had a few months to find a job because he would be spending the summer running Pete Newell's Big Man's Camp.

That was what it had evolved to by 1987—capital letters and all. Each summer, dating back to those torturous days in 1976, there had been more and more players showing up to work with Newell. Kiki Vandeweghe, while he was still in college, had been an early recruit. Then players like Jerome Whitehead and Kenny Carr had also joined in. Soon NBA teams, seeing the improvement in the players who were working with Newell, began encouraging their players to seek Newell out and ask him to spend some time with them.

By the time Washington retired as an active player, the camp had become a business. Newell had no interest in running a business, so he turned the organization of the camp over to Washington, telling him if there were any profits, he was welcome to them. Washington then brought his friend Stu Lantz in to help him put the camp together.

When Washington went to work at Stanford, the camp moved to Palo Alto. By now more than fifty players were showing up each year. Later, as the camp continued to grow, a college division would be added. Washington made arrangements for court rentals and made deals with local hotels to put up the players during the two weeks that the camp was run. Teams now had to pay to send players to the camp: $2,000 per week. Once expenses were taken care of, Washington and Lantz divided the money, since Newell did not want to be paid. Even so, neither man was getting rich.

"We probably made about fifteen thousand dollars apiece when all was said and done," Washington said. "That wasn't really why we did it, though. We did it because of Pete. I always felt as if I owed him because of what he'd done for me, not only all the work he had done on my game, but because of the way he stood by me after the Rudy thing happened. I'm not sure I would have gotten through it all if not for him and Red and Pat. They were my salvation when things were at their worst."

During the summer of 1987, Washington played a lot of pickup ball at the camp. He had never completely stopped playing basketball. During his years at Stanford he had actually played some rec league ball. He still enjoyed the feeling of being on the court and competing. Since he never played more than a night or two a week and never practiced, the pain in his knees and his back was almost completely gone. Then, in the summertime, when he played against good players in the camp, he found that he was still able to hold his own against NBA-caliber competition.

That's where the idea of making a comeback came from. The more he played that summer, the more certain he was that he could play in the NBA again. He felt healthy. He believed he was stronger than he had ever been, because he had spent so much time building his body up in the weight room. He was thirty-six, certainly not young, but there were players in the league older than that. What's more, when the summer ended, he didn't have a job to go back to or any specific prospect of a job.

He called the Trail Blazers and told them he would like to come to training camp and see if he could make the team. Ramsay had retired the previous season and been replaced as coach by Mike Shuler. Shuler told Washington he was welcome to come to camp as a free agent.

The experiment didn't last long—in Portland. As soon as Washington began dealing with the daily pounding of preseason practices he could feel his body starting to break down again. He was still convinced he could play, because when he did make it to the floor, he would play well. The problem was, he couldn't maintain it for any long period of time. He wanted to be part of the team as a 10–15-minute-a-night, off-the-bench role player. Shuler didn't necessarily have a problem with that, but he did have a problem with any player, especially one whose game minutes were going to be limited, who couldn't practice. It came down, finally, to that: Shuler told Washington if he couldn't practice on a regular basis, he couldn't make the team. Washington knew there was no way he could do that, especially over the course of an entire season.

Shuler and Washington agreed to disagree and Washington left camp. Before he even had a chance to think about what to do next, Washington got a call from Don Nelson, who was then the general manager of the Golden State Warriors. The Warriors were looking for experienced backup help in the frontcourt, a mature player to provide some leadership on a young team. Larry Smith was injured and Chris Washburn, who had been the team's number one pick in the 1986 draft, was headed for drug rehab. Nelson thought Washington could provide depth inside.

Washington jumped at the chance. He reported to the Warriors' camp and played well in several exhibition games, well enough for coach George Karl to tell him he would be in the rotation when the season began in Sacramento. Washington's knees still ached, but Karl was more flexible about his practice time than Shuler had been, and he still thought he had some good basketball left in him.

That feeling didn't last long. Washington played well on opening night, a blowout loss to the Sacramento Kings, but with each passing game, his playing time dwindled. It was apparent early that it was going to be a long season for the Warriors, and Karl didn't see any purpose in giving a lot of minutes to a player who clearly wasn't going to be around when the team became competitive again. Nelson was in the process of trying to shake up the team, a shakeup that would eventually lead to the trade with the Rockets that would bring Ralph Sampson to Golden State. Washington had played 30 minutes on opening night. It was less and less after that. And then, after six games, it dwindled to nothing.

"I could see what was happening," Washington said. "George was a good guy, I liked him, but I think it was Don who wanted me on the team, not George. When the team started badly, it wasn't as if keeping an old guy around made sense. It wasn't as if they were going to be fighting for a playoff spot."

Even if he understood it intellectually, Washington was still hurt when the end came in Atlanta. Karl called him in and told him they had made a decision to cut him. Nothing personal, but it was clear that the team needed to focus on younger players. Washington said he understood—which he did—but he was still unhappy.

"I think it came down to George not wanting Don to tell him who should be on the team," he said. "I mean, when I got to play, I played well. I could have helped teach their young big men along the way. But it didn't happen that way."

There was one sidelight to his brief time with the Warriors. Just prior to the start of the regular season, the team played an exhibition game in Sacramento. Tomjanovich was there doing some preseason scouting for the Rockets. Prior to the game, for the first time in the ten years since that fateful night in Los Angeles, Washington and Tomjanovich spoke.

The conversation was brief. Washington told Tomjanovich that he hoped he understood that he had never meant to hurt him the way he had, that the punch had been an instinctive reaction, nothing more. "Rudy, I didn't even know it was you," Washington said.

Tomjanovich believed him. He told him he had forgiven him long ago and that they both needed to just move on with their lives. It was in the past.

"But it's not in the past for me," Washington said. "People bring it up to me all the time. Even now, in this comeback, every story written about me doesn't talk about the good things I've done in my life, it talks about the punch. It still haunts me."

Tomjanovich didn't really know what to say. He didn't doubt anything Washington was saying, but he had to live with the looks and the comments too. And he had endured unbelievable physical pain. It was difficult, try though he might, to work up a lot of sympathy for Washington.

"I wanted to feel sympathetic," he said years later. "I understood what he was saying to me. I had always tried to follow Dr. Toffel's advice and not resent Kermit or feel animosity toward him for what he had done. I felt like I had done a pretty good job, mostly by just not thinking about him. But if I tried to feel sympathy, to really feel badly for him . . . back then, that was tough."

The two men shook hands that night. Tomjanovich told him there were no hard feelings. Washington wanted to believe that. So did Tomjanovich.

It wasn't easy for either one of them.

Like it or not, Kermit Washington knew the day he was cut from the Warriors that once and for all he had to stop thinking of himself as a basketball player and start thinking of himself as an ex–basketball player.

An ex–basketball player who needed a job.

He was in pretty good shape financially. He had finally sold his homes in California, and between the camp and Stanford, he had made pretty good money since retiring. He had invested his NBA money well, so he was comfortable living in Lake Oswego, a suburb of Portland, with Pat and the two children.

But he wasn't the kind of person who could sit around and hope his investments did well. He would continue to work the camp in the summer, but he needed more. He went back to the abandoned weight vest idea, trying to market it enough to make it profitable. "I ended up losing a bundle on it," he said. He also began contacting NBA teams about a job, to no avail.

In the process of trying to market the weight vest, he went on a local radio show in Portland. They wanted him to talk about his comeback, his years in Portland, basketball in general. He was still a very popular figure in the Portland area. Washington agreed to go on because he knew at some point the host would ask him what he was doing and he would get to talk about the vest.

The appearance went well, so well in fact that the radio station asked him if he wanted to do some part-time work cohosting a sports talk show. This was before stations all around the country were switching over to an all-sports format, so there weren't that many hours a week available. And the pay was a joke: $20 an hour. Washington accepted.

"I figured it was a chance to go on and promote the vest on a regular basis," he said.

The vest wasn't going to make money if he was given a twenty-four-hour-a-day infomercial on the station. Most people who work out don't want to run themselves into the ground doing it. The vest might help get an athlete with Washington's drive into better shape, but the average recreational workout athlete wanted nothing to do with it.

But while the vest wasn't selling, Washington was building an audience. He had the built-in advantage of being an ex-Blazer, someone most sports fans in Portland had fond memories of. Beyond that, he was good on the radio. He was articulate and quick, knew a lot about sports, and had plenty of opinions on anything and everything.

"I liked doing it," he said. "At first the money was ridiculous, but I wasn't doing it for the money. As time went on, I got paid more and I felt very comfortable on the air. Talking has never been a problem for me."

By 1990 Portland, like most cities in the country, had an all-sports radio station. Washington was hired as a host and eventually was paired with another former Blazer, Mychal Thompson, during afternoon drive time. By then he was making decent money at the radio station while continuing to work on the Big Man's Camp for and with Newell and Stu Lantz.

It was during this period that Washington changed the Sixth Man Foundation into Project Contact.

"I got very frustrated with dealing with kids in Portland," he said. "I would make an arrangement to get Nike to contribute five hundred pairs of shoes and we'd give them out someplace and kids would come up to me and say, 'Why can't I get a different color?' It just seemed to me that in our country, even the kids who don't have much feel entitled.

"I had done a lot of reading about Africa, about the wars over there. I remember seeing a TV special on Rwanda and thinking to myself that these were people who *really* needed help, that if you could help out there you would be making a contribution that went way beyond getting sneakers or basketballs for kids in Portland. I kept hearing and reading about the fact that there was no medicine and no doctors for people over there, and I thought maybe I could help with that."

That was how Project Contact came into being. Washington became the organizer: raising money, finding doctors and nurses willing to go overseas for up to two weeks at a time to set up free clinics that doled out medicine and helped people get treatment. He went first to Rwanda but found it so dangerous that recruiting people to go there was virtually impossible. He finally settled on Kenya, where the need was great but the dangers not quite so daunting.

"It was still dangerous," he said. "We learned as we went. We were, technically, carrying drugs into the country, which you aren't supposed to do. But for a hundred dollars you paid off the customs inspectors and they didn't look inside your bags. Then once we were there, we would find doctors and medical students who would help us out. We paid the doctors twenty-five dollars a day and the medical students fifteen dollars a day to augment the doctors and nurses who made the trip." Several people who traveled with Washington learned the hard way that taking malaria pills prior to getting on the airplane was a necessity.

Project Contact became Washington's magnificent obsession. Every time he went to Africa he could see that the work he and his people were doing was important. They would usually set up head-quarters inside a church and people would line up to see a doctor. Depending on how much medicine they could acquire prior to a trip, the doctors would see between 1,500 and 2,500 people on each visit.

Washington's goal was to make at least two trips a year. It wasn't always easy. The logistics were difficult to begin with, but so was raising money. Sometimes Washington would track down old NBA friends for help. Shaquille O'Neal had been in Newell's camp on several occasions, so Washington was able to get a couple of auto-graphed jerseys from him, which he sold to raise money. Vince Carter and Latrell Sprewell helped out the same way. Jerry West got him some Lakers memorabilia to sell. Once, when fund-raising was going badly, Washington sold a car to help finance a trip.

Clearly he put in the time and the effort because he is generous by nature, someone who has always been aware of those who are afflicted, perhaps because he grew up in difficult circumstances. But when he talks about Project Contact and the charity work he has done through the years, it becomes evident that the Tomjanovich incident is part of the story too.

"I know what most people think of me," he said one day. "Most people when they hear the name Kermit Washington think of what happened with Rudy and think I'm a thug. I know that. But I hope maybe when people understand the kind of work we've done in Africa, they'll understand there's more to me than just those five seconds. I would like it very much if people would think of Project Contact when they think of me rather than Rudy Tomjanovich.

"I really believe," he continued, "that if we could raise enough money, we could treat twenty-five thousand people a year, who knows, maybe a hundred thousand people a year. We could win the Nobel Prize if we got the proper funding."

One can almost hear Washington's thoughts at that moment: Maybe *then* people won't just think of me as the guy who slugged Rudy T.

Rudy Tomjanovich may have been dragged kicking and screaming into the job as Rockets' head coach, but once he had it he didn't want to give it up. He had been named interim coach on February 18, 1992, and Steve Patterson and team owner Charlie Thomas had told him that no long-term decisions would be made until the end of the season.

That was fine with Tomjanovich. Unlike most coaches stepping into a new job, the last thing he wanted the day he was hired was a long-term commitment—from him or from management.

But once he dug in and started doing the job, a funny thing happened: he liked it. Perhaps he was influenced by the fact that the team won five of the first six games it played after he became the coach. But it was more than that. Tomjanovich enjoyed the responsibility of being in charge; he liked thinking up ways to adjust the offense and the defense to make the Rockets a better team. He enjoyed the tension of the endgame, the chess match with the other coach, the adrenaline rush that came from having to make decisions under the gun and then the pleasure of seeing them work out.

"I was really into it right from the start," he said. "I was surprised, because I had never thought about doing it. The outside stuff really didn't bother me either. Most of the guys in the media are good guys, so I didn't mind that. The only problem I think I had was time management. There were just so many different things that I had to do as part of the job that I never felt as if I had a chance to come up for air."

With or without air, Tomjanovich knew as the season moved to a conclusion that he wanted the "interim" removed from his title, that he wanted to be the team's coach. Making the playoffs would go a long way toward getting that done, and with three games left it looked as if the Rockets would make postseason. But they lost all three games, the last two by 3 points each to Dallas and Phoenix (at home), and finished one game behind the Lakers for the eighth and final Western Conference slot.

Tomjanovich thought he had blown his chance, that Charlie Thomas would surely look elsewhere for a coach, and he would either have to go back to being an assistant or look someplace else for work. Neither of those scenarios made Tomjanovich very happy, and he spent a lot of time pacing around the house, wondering if the phone was ever going to ring with an answer.

It took a month. All sorts of rumors swirled. Steve Patterson admits now that there were people in the league who questioned whether Tomjanovich was the right choice to run the team. "I had calls from people who said to me, 'Do you really think he's smart enough or tough enough to be a head coach in the NBA?'" Patterson said. "I had no doubts. People get deceived by Rudy. They see him as this laid-back guy who just takes life as it comes. That's not who he is. He's smart, he's driven, he's tough. If he has a weakness it's that he's too tough on himself. I had no doubt he could do the job, but I knew Charlie was getting some pressure to find someone else."

Finally, on May 20, Thomas called Tomjanovich to his office and said simply, "Rudy, I think you're the guy for this job."

Tomjanovich was as relieved as he was happy. All the decisions he thought he might face about the future didn't have to be dealt with. He knew his family was concerned about the pressures that would come with the job—his daughters, who were now nineteen and sixteen, were especially concerned—but he was convinced he could handle it. He thought the Rockets weren't far from being a very good team again, and he thought his relationship with the players would become closer now that it was official he was going to be the coach for the long term.

He was right. The Rockets responded to their new coach the following season with the best record in franchise history: 55–27. They won the Midwest Division and tied for second in the Western Conference with the Seattle SuperSonics. Unfortunately, the Sonics were awarded the second seed based on having won three of four from Houston during the regular season. When the teams met in the conference semifinals, Seattle had the home court advantage. That proved critical, since neither team won a game on the other's court. Game seven was a gut-wrenching overtime affair, Seattle finally winning 103–100.

It was a tough-to-swallow loss, because the Rockets believed they were good enough to beat the Phoenix Suns in the conference finals. They didn't get the chance to find out, but Tomjanovich was convinced they were very close to being able to seriously contend for the NBA title. The Rockets had added players like Robert Horry and Otis Thorpe to go with Olajuwon in the frontcourt. Tomjanovich thought the team needed one more guard to give it some depth on the perimeter. Against the advice of a number of people, he took Sam Cassell out of Florida State late in the first round of that spring's draft. Little did he know that he had just acquired the final piece of the puzzle.

The Rockets were 58–24 in 1993–94 and again won the Midwest Division. That made them the second seed in the West, behind Seattle. But the SuperSonics were upset in the opening round by Denver, and that meant the Rockets would have home court advantage regardless of whom they played the rest of the way. It was the first time in the history of the team that had been the case.

They cruised to the finals, beating Utah in five games in the conference finals. Once there, they caught another break: Michael Jordan was in the midst of Retirement I: The Baseball Years, and with Jordan in Birmingham flailing at curveballs, the New York Knicks were finally able to get past the Bulls and were the Rockets' opponent. Not that the Knicks were a pushover by any means. They had their own great center to battle Olajuwon in Patrick Ewing. Guard John Starks was an All-Star, and Charles Oakley was the prototype power forward/enforcer. They played great defense, bruising, physical, beat-you-up defense, because their coach, Pat Riley, demanded it. They were convinced this was their year to be champions after running into the wall that was Jordan the previous three seasons.

The series ping-ponged. The Rockets, with Cassell playing brilliantly down the stretch, won game three in New York after the teams had split in Houston, to give the Rockets a 2–1 lead. But the Knicks came back to win the next two, sending the series back to Houston with New York up 3–2. Game five was played on that eerie Friday evening when NBC switched away from the finals to join the rest of America in watching a white Bronco ride slowly down California's I-405 with O. J. Simpson in the backseat and Al Cowlings behind the wheel, on the phone with the police.

"We all knew what was going on, because the scorer's table told us that TV had switched away from the game," Tomjanovich remembered. "It was strange, but you couldn't do anything except keep playing."

Game six in the finals had always been fatal to the Rockets. But this time they pulled out an 86–84 victory, as Starks's 3-point shot at the buzzer, which would have won the title for the Knicks, fell just short. That meant the championship would come down to one game and it would be played in the Summit.

There was nothing pretty about the game. Both teams were tight and the defenses, as had been the case throughout the series, dominated. Neither team came close to scoring 100 points in any game—the Rockets' 93 points in game three was the high-water mark—proving that Riley-ball had taken over the NBA. The minuscule TV ratings were evidence that the absence of Jordan and the absence of scoring weren't very healthy for the league.

The Rockets and the city of Houston didn't really care about any of that. All they knew was this was their chance for a championship, the city's first in any professional sport since the Houston Oilers had won the American Football League title in 1962. Riley was kind enough to stick with Starks in the fourth quarter, even though former All-Star Rolando Blackman was on the bench, while Starks missed eleven straight second-half shots. That was just enough to allow the Rockets to escape with a 90–84 victory and the title.

The entire city was euphoric. More than 500,000 people showed up at the victory parade. Every time Tomjanovich pulled up someplace at a red light, the person next to him started honking, then rolled down the window to yell, "Thank you, Rudy. God bless you, Rudy." Sometimes they would get out of the car and come over for a handshake or a hug or a kiss.

"It was great," Tomjanovich said, "but it was embarrassing sometimes."

Sitting in the building on the night of game seven, Steve Patterson felt proud and vindicated. He remembered the phone calls telling him it was a mistake to think Tomjanovich was smart enough or tough enough to be a successful coach. Calvin Murphy couldn't stop crying for joy—joy for his team, joy for his city, but most of all joy for his friend. Rudy Tomjanovich was on top of the world.

21

Troubles

Looking back, Rudy Tomjanovich and Kermit Washington might very well agree that the trouble began again when the Rockets reached the 1994 finals.

At that moment life for each of them was good. Tomjanovich had become a star in the coaching profession. Washington was doing well on radio, had started Project Contact, and had found a comfortable niche in Portland.

But the punch still lingered.

It was at halftime of game one or game two of the finals—she's not sure which game—when Sophie Tomjanovich walked into a room set up in the Summit for family and friends of the Rockets' players and coaches. All three of her children—twenty-year-old Nichole, seventeen-year-old Melissa, and eleven-year-old Rudy III, whom they called Trey—were with her. This was a proud week for the Tomjanovich family.

In the corner of the room was a television. Naturally it was tuned to NBC. Sophie remembers glancing over to see if the network was showing first-half highlights or an interview. The answer was neither.

"I looked up and there it was," she said. "All over again."

On the television screen it was December 9, 1977. There were Kermit Washington and Kevin Kunnert squared off, with Kareem Abdul-Jabbar trying to swing Kunnert away. And from the corner of the screen, Rudy Tomjanovich was running toward the fight . . .

"Let's get out of here," Sophie said to the children.

None of them had noticed what was on the TV screen, but Sophie could see people crowded around watching, as if at the scene of an accident. "Come on," she repeated. "Right now." Surprised, Nichole, Melissa, and Trey followed her out of the room.

"I couldn't stay another second," she said. "All I could think was, 'Why? Why do they have to do this? Why do they have to keep coming back to that? Hasn't Rudy accomplished enough that they can let him, let us, move on?'"

The irony, of course, was that Rudy's accomplishments were the reason the punch was back in the public eye. If he had still been the Rockets' second assistant, or if the team hadn't been in the finals, no one would have bothered bringing it up. But he was coaching in the finals, and the punch was part of his story.

It was no easier for Kermit Washington or his family to see the replay popping up on TV screens again. (NBC certainly wasn't the only media outlet to rerun the tape.) Every story chronicling Tomjanovich's success brought up the punch, what he had gone through, and how he had come back from near death to play again.

"None of the stories said, 'Kermit Washington, a good guy who made a mistake,'" Washington said, laughing. "They all said things like 'muscle-bound, hulking enforcer.' I remember thinking, 'My God, it's been seventeen years and here we go again.'"

Naturally Washington was often asked by callers to his radio show about the punch. It had come up early in his radio career and it continued to come up. Almost always the question was "What really happened that night?"

Washington would then go through his version of events. In that version, of course, the villain of the piece was Kevin Kunnert.

Kunnert had retired from the Trail Blazers at the end of the 1982 season, a few months after Washington's retirement, his knee too torn up to allow him to continue playing. Like Washington he had decided to stay in Portland. He liked the fishing and hunting in the area, it wasn't as cold in the winters as Iowa, and his family had come to love living there. He settled in Tigard, no more than fifteen or twenty minutes away from where Washington and his family lived.

On one occasion Kunnert happened to be listening when Washington was asked about the punch. What he heard made him so angry that he asked the station to send him a tape.

"It all began when I got the rebound," Washington began.

Right there Kunnert started to get angry. "*He* got the rebound?" he said years later. "He didn't get the rebound, I got the rebound. Why would he say that?"

Washington went on from there to describe the infamous and hotly debated two elbows. He then said, "I was confused. I was no fighter. I had never been in a fight."

"Never been in a fight?" Kunnert said. "Ask John Shumate or C. J. Kupec if he had ever been in a fight. He was no fighter? Check the tape and tell me if he looks like someone who wasn't a fighter."

Washington concluded by saying he never could figure out why the NBA took no action against Kunnert and that he was convinced the NBA kept "putting him on the same team with me so I wouldn't sue him."

Kunnert shook his head in disgust at that notion. "I signed with the Celtics as a free agent," he said. "Four of us went to San Diego in the swap. You think I was happy to be on the same team with him? Then Portland had the choice of Swen Nater or me and they took me—which was probably a mistake, given the condition of my knee, but it had nothing to do with the league."

Jack Ramsay confirms that fact: "We had a choice, our doctors looked at Kunnert's knee and said it was fine," he said. "I was the one who wanted Kunnert."

"The guy has created his own reality in all this," Kunnert said. "All you have to do is listen to that tape."

Washington has no memory of the specifics of what he said on the radio that day. "If I said I got the rebound, I made a mistake," he said. "I never did consider myself a fighter. Because of my role, I had to fight sometimes, but I don't think that makes me a fighter. Kevin can say what he wants about why we ended up on the same team, I think it's one hell of a coincidence, that's all I can say. He knows he threw those elbows. But I know he's never going to admit it."

Both men are equally vehement that their version of the truth *is* the truth. It helped neither one that they ended up living in the same city. If they hadn't, Kunnert wouldn't have heard that particular explanation on the radio and would not have been bombarded with stories about Washington in which he was repeatedly quoted as saying the fight was Kunnert's fault.

"I suppose I could have gone out and defended myself when he said all those things," he said. "But I always thought talking about it kept it alive. All I've ever wanted is for the thing to go away. But Kermit won't let it die. Every time I pick up a paper or hear him on the radio, there he is again telling people he didn't do anything wrong. He talks about how he thought about suing me. There may come a day where I sue him."

There is genuine animosity here, fueled by years of frustration on both sides. Washington honestly believes that Kunnert is responsible for what happened that night and for all the pain brought on by its aftermath. Kunnert is just as convinced that Washington has unfairly made him into a villain through the years and has created his own version of the truth to rationalize his actions.

The 1994 finals refocused public attention on the incident. Amidst the joy that came with winning the championship, Tomjanovich found himself being asked again and again about the incident and his recovery. When he picked up the commemorative issue of *Sports Illustrated* devoted to the Rockets' championship, he found a lengthy profile written by Phil Taylor about him. Late in the piece Taylor devoted four paragraphs to the punch, more as background information than anything else. Two years later, in his autobiography, Tomjanovich wrote that "after our first championship, *Sports Illustrated* included a story on the Washington-Tomjanovich incident. What did that have to do with our championship?"

There was clear frustration in those words and in the fact that four paragraphs would somehow stick in his head as being an entire story. To Tomjanovich, every mention of the punch was another piece of evidence that, no matter how much he accomplished, up to and including coaching an NBA championship team, he could not escape the shadow of that night.

"I was still the guy who got nailed," he said. "That was still who I was to most people. I felt as if I couldn't escape it."

One year later the Rockets repeated in remarkable fashion. Midway through the regular season, with a record of 30–17, they gambled, trading the very solid Otis Thorpe for the spectacular but aging Clyde Drexler, bringing a University of Houston legend home and reuniting him with Olajuwon, his college teammate. It looked for a very long time as if the move had backfired. The Rockets limped to a 17–18 record the rest of the regular season and went into the playoffs as just the sixth seed in the Western Conference.

They then put together two remarkable comebacks in the first two rounds. Trailing Utah 2–1 in the best-of-five first round, they won the last two games, including a 95–91 fifth-game victory in Salt Lake City, where the Jazz were considered virtually unbeatable. In the conference semifinals they faced Phoenix and quickly trailed 2–0 and 3–1. Somehow they rallied again, winning the last three games of the series, *two* of them in Phoenix. After that it was easy: a six-game victory over San Antonio in the conference finals and a sweep of the never-been-there-before, wide-eyed Orlando Magic in the finals.

They had won back-to-back titles. Houston had a new nickname: Clutch City. They were all heroes, and even though they hadn't faced Jordan, he had been in the playoffs, returning to the Bulls in March, only to have his team lose to Orlando in the second round. The Rockets were the kings of basketball, and their coach was now a big-time star. He may even have become someone other than the guy who got nailed.

It was a few days after the Rockets won their first title that Tomjanovich was stopped for driving under the influence. The charges were later dropped when a videotape refuted the policeman's charge that he had weaved across a double line. Tomjanovich was embarrassed by the incident but couldn't understand why he had been stopped. He had been drinking, sure, but he wasn't drunk. Or so he believed. When the incident occurred, no one who knew him was shocked. Those who knew him knew Tomjanovich drank—a lot.

"It got much worse after he became the head coach," Sophie Tomjanovich said. "He felt a lot of pressure, and he always felt as if he was under the gun in terms of time. It got to the point where he was doing two things: working and drinking. That was it."

Drinking had always been a part of Tomjanovich's life, from age fifteen on. He had never been a problem drinker, had never allowed it to affect his play or his work, and had never been an obnoxious drunk. "I was usually pretty quiet," he said. "I would just sit there and drink large quantities, then go home and go to sleep. I was never a problem for anybody. I just drank a lot." Without realizing it, he was becoming his father.

"I never knew that alcoholism could be genetic," he said. "I also didn't know how much I was drinking, because over the years I had developed the capacity to drink a lot without feeling affected."

Whenever Sophie tried to talk to him about how much he was drinking, he ignored her. "What did she know? She wasn't a drinker, she didn't understand." He smiled. "That's what we all say, isn't it, 'You just don't understand.'"

It was his daughter Nichole who got his attention first. They had gone out together one night, and after several beers Rudy switched over to hard stuff. "What in the world are you doing?" Nichole asked. "Do you realize how much beer you've had already?"

Rudy could see the concern in his daughter's face and eyes. Still, it couldn't be that bad. He felt fine at work, felt fine at games. Heck, he had coached *two* NBA championship teams.

By the end of the 1997 season, he was slowly understanding that he had a problem. "I would get depressed when things were going really well," he said. "I didn't know much about alcohol, but I knew it was a depressant. I didn't feel good a lot. I tried changing my diet, eating better foods, thinking that would help. Then I decided to try to cut down on my drinking. Instead of drinking every night, I drank every other night. But I could never do any better than that. Putting two or three nights in a row together without a drink was impossible."

Early in the summer of 1997, he drove to a park early one morning to take a walk before going into the office. He got back into the car, drove a short way, and passed out at the wheel. Fortunately he wasn't going very fast when he hit the tree. "I hadn't had anything to drink at all," he said. "I was never that kind of drinker."

Doctors tested him for anything and everything. They couldn't find a specific reason for the incident. Even so, after all the test results came back his doctor said to him, "Rudy, I think you need to seriously reconsider your lifestyle."

"Doc, I wasn't drinking."

"I know. I still think you need to reconsider your lifestyle."

More denial. More "what does he know, he's not a drinker." Okay, maybe he wasn't sleeping all that well and he was tired a lot. Maybe he was still dealing with the dream/anxiety attack in which he saw himself dead and could only see a black void. Maybe it had gotten worse.

Maybe he needed help. Sophie was almost pleading with him to do something, to seek help somewhere. "A lot of nights when he came home he was obnoxious," she said. "Never anything bad, just not enjoyable to be around. All of us [she and the kids] were concerned. But it is very hard to hear things from your family."

The phone call that changed things came from Robert Barr, the Rockets' longtime strength coach, who had been promoted to team vice president. He and Tomjanovich went way back, had spent long hours together. One day in the fall of 1997, he sat Tomjanovich down and said, "Rudy, Dr. Lowe is very concerned about you and wanted me to talk to you."

Dr. Walter Lowe was the team's orthopedic surgeon. He was around the team a lot and around Tomjanovich a lot. He thought Tomjanovich needed treatment. Barr was the messenger. "Why don't you just get this taken care of now, sooner rather than later," Barr said. "Dr. Lowe thinks you need to do it, and I agree with him."

Tomjanovich's initial response was the same as it had been with his family: What the hell do you know? "Robert wasn't even a drinker, so how could he possibly know if I was drinking too much?" he said. "But after we talked, I finally sat back and put it all together: my family thought I drank too much; a couple of doctors thought I drank too much; Robert thought I drank too much. I finally said, 'What the hell, let's just do it.'"

He checked into a treatment center in Arizona, in the desert outside Phoenix. Even then he didn't have a clear understanding of what he was dealing with or what he was getting into. "I went in thinking they were going to show me how to drink like other people drank," he said. "You know, have a couple and stop. Learn to leave a half-empty glass on the table without emptying it. I didn't see how anyone ever did that, but I figured they were going to show me how to do it."

That, of course, was not what the folks in the treatment center had in mind. For the first few days they gave him pills to help his body adapt to the fact that it wasn't receiving any alcohol. By the fourth day he was being weaned from the pills and he was miserable.

"I couldn't sleep," he said. "I was up all night one night, then again the next night, then a third night. The harder I tried to sleep, the more impossible it became. I couldn't stand it. No one had told me this was going to be about complete abstinence. I finally got up and called my doctor in Houston in the middle of the night and said, 'You gotta get them to give me something.'"

He did. A Benadryl.

"I was like, 'Are you kidding me?'" he said. "I finally got out of bed at six in the morning and went and sat outside the director's office and waited for him. When he came in, I told him I thought the place was great, I wanted to do this, I was committed to doing this, but I hadn't slept for three nights and I was going out of my mind and couldn't they just give me something so I could get some sleep.

"He looked at me and said, 'You know, when I was in here, it was a week before I could sleep. I understand what you're going through. But lack of sleep never killed anybody. You need to make sure you exercise a lot today, the earlier the better. Go to all your classes. You're in my class on spirituality today. That's really important. You need to understand your spiritual side more. You need to pray. You need to get closer to God.'

"I sat there looking at him, thinking, 'What the hell does prayer and God have to do with me getting some sleep? I don't need to pray, I need a pill or I need a drink.'"

He went back to his room, lay on his bed, and tried to read the Serenity Prayer, which was posted on the wall of each room in the center, as it is in many rehab centers. ("God grant me the serenity to accept the things I cannot change, courage to change the things I can, and the wisdom to know the difference"). He read it over and over, trying to find meaning in the words, trying to find something to grab on to.

Nothing.

He was seized with desperation. Maybe, he thought, I'll just get the hell out of here, find a way to get downtown, and get something to drink that will put me to sleep. He thought about that a little longer, then realized he had no car and the desert outside was full of rattlesnakes and tarantulas and coyotes and God knows what else. "They had warned us about wandering around out there," he said. "I'm a city boy. That wasn't for me."

He sat on the bed a while longer, exhaustion and desperation giving way to helplessness and despair. He had another thought: If he threw himself through the window (he was on the first floor) he'd be cut up and they would have to give him some kind of painkiller. "Then I thought about my face," he said. "I didn't want scars. Thank God I'm vain."

Finally, in complete despair, he prayed; really prayed for the first time since that awful night in the hospital in Los Angeles twenty years earlier, when he had prayed for the little girl in the coma. "I just gave in and accepted the fact that I couldn't do it alone, couldn't beat the system," he said. "I was in absolute despair and I asked for help. I didn't even really know how to pray. But I prayed."

It wasn't as if he stood up and was cured, or that the exhaustion and despair disappeared. But he did stand up feeling as if he could go on. He went to his classes that day, followed the advice to listen as hard as he could and to exercise. And that night he slept. Soundly. From that day forward, he felt better. He left the treatment center just prior to the start of training camp feeling like a new man.

"It was a wonderful feeling," he said. "As good as anything I'd ever felt in my life. The only problem was, I thought I had taken care of it, that I'd sort of checked it off my list of things to do. Okay, I'm done drinking, that's taken care of, what's next?

"Of course it wasn't nearly that simple or easy."

As he had been advised, Tomjanovich began going to Alcoholics Anonymous meetings when his treatment was completed. But he didn't really take it seriously. He went sporadically, and when he did go, he wasn't really listening to people. "I was sloppy about it," he said. "I went because they told me to go, not because I wanted to go or thought I needed to go. I thought I was done with the disease. I thought it was like going in for surgery. You get whatever needs fixing fixed, you recuperate, and it's behind you. Doesn't work that way."

He learned that fact the hard way the next summer. He was coaching the U.S. team in the basketball world championship tournament in Greece. The job was a major challenge because the NBA had locked out the players at the start of the summer, meaning no NBA players could participate. Tomjanovich had expected to coach a group of NBA All-Stars in the tournament. Instead he found himself coaching a collection of minor league players, Americans playing in Europe and college players.

"I enjoyed the hell out of the experience," he said. "The guys we had worked incredibly hard and played extremely well. I was proud of that team."

But somewhere, somehow, the pressure of trying to win the tournament (the United States ended up winning the bronze medal) got to him. Sitting in a beautiful seaside Greek restaurant one night getting ready to start the medal rounds, Tomjanovich heard himself say to a waitress, "Beer."

To this day, he isn't certain why he said it. "It was three o'clock in the morning," he said. "We'd had a great meal, and I was feeling great about things. I was drinking orange juice. The next thing I know, I'm asking for a beer. I woke up the next morning and thought, 'What the hell did you just do?' I had been dry for eleven months, I was coming up on my one-year anniversary of sobriety, and I just threw it all away just like that."

He got through the rest of the tournament without taking another drink, but soon after he got home to Houston it happened again. Another night out with friends, another slip. That made two. He was now officially frightened, because he now knew enough about the disease to understand what slips lead to. He called his sponsor and asked what to do.

"You need to get serious about AA, Rudy," he told him. "I know you haven't been until now, but that's where you need to turn. I don't mean just go to meetings, I mean go and *listen*."

Tomjanovich listened—first to his sponsor, then to those speaking at the meetings. Soon after he started attending on a regular basis, he found himself sitting next to a man who stood up and talked about sobriety. "I've been sober for a year," the man said. "I have lost my family and I've lost my job during that time. But my life is one hundred percent better now than it was a year ago. I know as long as I stay sober I'll be okay."

Tomjanovich found himself listening and looking into the man's eyes. "I could tell he meant every word," he said. "That's how important it was to him. Things like that made me understand that this wasn't an option, this wasn't something I should think about doing, it was something I had to do."

And so, finally, he did it. He began going to AA meetings virtually every day. On the road, he would find a meeting and go. He became close to members of his chapter in Houston. For the first time in his life, he began going to church—twice, in fact, every Sunday he was home.

"I like to listen to the preachers in both the churches," he said. "I like their messages. They're different, but they're both fascinating. I feel like I learn something listening to them, about life and about myself. I always come out of there feeling better than when I went in."

He became, in his words, a new person. Since he wasn't drinking, he felt better physically, but it went way beyond that. For the first time in his life, he felt at peace about who he was. No more self-doubts, no more beating himself up, no more having to prove himself over and over again. No more knots in the stomach. And no more anxiety attacks about death in the middle of the night.

"That went away completely," he said. "For twenty years I dealt with that and had really accepted it as part of my life, that I was going to always have to deal with these anxiety attacks. Gone. I feel totally different about myself now.

"Until I stopped drinking and got involved in AA, if you were making a movie on my life the musical sound track would have to have been the blues," he said. "That was always the way I felt about it. I always thought I had to outwork everyone because that was the only way to have success. Work, work, work, and nothing else mattered, because if you didn't succeed at your job you would be humiliated.

"That's not to say I don't get angry and I don't get frustrated. I do. But it's different now. I deal with it differently."

The difference is summed up in a rubber band he wears around his right wrist. It was suggested to him by a therapist as a reminder that when things start to go wrong, you stop yourself by "snapping back."

"I just snap the rubber band to remind myself, 'Hey, it's okay. I have a great life going here, and if something goes wrong I can handle it.' That's the difference now. I know I can handle things. I feel great not only about my life, but about myself."

The presence of the new Rudy has thrilled everyone in his family, although it isn't always easy for Sophie to understand the importance of AA in his life. "Sometimes she will say to me, 'Do you really need to go every day?'" he said. "And my answer is, 'Yes,

I do. I need to go every day.' Beyond that I *want* to go every day. It makes me feel good."

In 2001–02 the Rockets suffered through an awful 29–53 season. Murphy's Law was clearly in control even before training camp began, when the Rockets' most important off-season free agent signee, Maurice Taylor, ruptured an Achilles tendon and was out for the season. Early on, the team suffered through a 15-game losing streak, with leading scorer Steve Francis one of several players out with injuries. Through it all, Tomjanovich never flinched.

"It hasn't been fun losing," he said. "But if there's one thing I know now, it is that good things often come from bad things. We're going to make good things come of this. I guarantee it."

His tone was one of complete self-confidence. It was a long time coming.

22

No Peace to Be Found

When Rudy Tomjanovich won his first NBA title as a coach, in 1994, no one was happier for him than Kermit Washington. True, all the publicity generated by the Rockets' victory meant another round of stories about the punch, but Washington felt he could handle it. "I was," he said, "at a very good place in my life right then. And I was happy for Rudy. I really was. I always thought he was a good guy who deserved good things."

By the end of 1994 Washington was a successful radio talk show host in Portland. He had Project Contact up and running. His finances were good enough that he had bought into a sports bar, LeSlam, in a Portland suburb. Dana was in college; Trey was in high school. The only real disappointment he had suffered through had been his split from Pete Newell and the Big Man's Camp.

That had happened the previous summer. The camp had continued to grow steadily throughout the 1980s. Washington even put together a video on the camp, in part because he knew Newell would enjoy it, in part because it was another of his "nutty professor" moneymaking schemes. "I was figuring every college or high school coach in the country would buy it," he said. "A lot did, but not enough. I took a bath."

After Washington left Stanford, the camp moved back to Los Angeles. But with so many players attending, the logistics of finding court space and hotel rooms had become difficult. Newell and Washington decided they needed to move it someplace where the locals might be willing to work with them.

Newell wondered if Las Vegas, being a town always looking for tourism, might work. Washington suggested Hawaii. He thought there would be fewer distractions for the players in August in Honolulu than in Vegas. Newell had a contact in Hawaii—Merv Lopes, the ex-Chaminade coach whom he had come to know through the years when he had gone to Hawaii on scouting trips. Through Lopes, Newell and Washington were able to make contact with someone in the governor's office and the deal was done. The camp was moved to a 2,500-seat high school gym in Honolulu, and the government helped secure hotel rooms at a cut rate and transportation around the island for the players and counselors working at the camp.

"It was Kermit's idea to go there," Newell said. "But it was Merv who really got things done once we decided to go over there. We couldn't have made the move without Merv."

Washington was still very much involved in the camp at that point. He was (and is) very proud of the fact that he had gotten Shaquille O'Neal to start going there.

"I worked the phones on that one," he said, smiling. "I kept calling Shaq's people, telling them that *Sports Illustrated* was coming over to do something on the camp and that he needed to be there. Then I called *Sports Illustrated* and said, 'You need to come to the camp, even Shaq's coming.' In the end, they were both there."

But the move to Hawaii eventually led to Newell and Washington splitting. Washington believes to this day that Lopes and the other locals in Honolulu cut him out of the loop. Newell insists that isn't the case.

"Kermit got involved with other things," he said. "Which is fine, I want him to have success. He wanted his daughter to take over a lot of the work he had been doing, but that really didn't work. Dana was young and didn't know the people in basketball the way Kermit did. I would call Kermit because something needed to be done and I couldn't find him. By then he had the radio show and Project Contact. I told him if he couldn't become more involved, he needed to not be involved, because the logistics were getting too big for me to handle."

Both men still speak warmly of each other, and no one is more vehement in his defense of Washington when the subject of the punch comes up than Newell. "The only thing I can tell you for sure," he said, "is that it was not an act of malice. Kermit Washington's just not built that way."

But there is hurt in both their voices when they discuss the split over the camp. Washington thinks Newell trusted people he should not have trusted instead of trusting him. Newell thinks Washington lost interest and tried to blame Lopes and company for his leaving the camp.

"I love Pete Newell," Washington said. "If not for him and Red Auerbach, I never would have had any kind of career in basketball after the Rudy incident. He stood up for me when no one else would. I just wish he hadn't listened to other people about the camp."

The camp had provided a nice chunk of income for Washington, especially since Newell has never taken anything more than expenses for his involvement. "He would always say to Stu [Lantz] and me at the end of camp, 'You guys keep the money, just give me enough so I can take care of my plants back home,'" Washington said.

But when the camp went away, Washington was on solid ground financially even without it. That was why he decided to invest in the restaurant. "I was a little bit bored," he said. "I thought it would be fun, it would be different. I was right about one thing: it *was* different."

But not successful. Looking back, Washington can point to the purchase of the restaurant as the beginning of a slide that took his life in a bad direction after several years in which it had gone in the right direction. LeSlam was located adjacent to an upscale health and fitness club. Washington was convinced they would get a lot of business coming out of the club in addition to business from people shopping in the nearby mall. For whatever reason, it never worked out.

"I was naive," he said. "I thought, first of all, that people in Portland wouldn't let me fail at something like this. I had always been popular here, and there's so much interest in the Blazers that I thought people would come because it was my place. I was wrong about that. Also I just didn't understand how hard the restaurant business is. You have to be very lucky and very good and get the right people working for you to be successful. Even if you do get all those things going for you, you still may fail."

The restaurant was bleeding money. Washington tried different menus, different chefs. He put money into marketing. Nothing seemed to help. He was working, it seemed, all day and all night, between the radio show and the restaurant. He tried saving money by cutting staff and working extra hours himself. He began opening in the mornings to save money and closing at night because he came to believe that someone on his staff was stealing from him. Pat and Trey both worked in the restaurant to try to save money. Pat could see the failure and the hours weighing on her husband.

"Pat begged me to sell, to get out," he said. "Of course, she was right, I should have sold it within a year of buying it. I would have saved myself a lot of heartache and a lot of money. But I was stubborn. I wasn't going to let the damn restaurant beat me. I was going to get it right if it killed me."

It didn't kill him, but it killed his finances and probably played a role in killing his marriage. "He was never home," Pat Washington said. "He was always tired, and the way the restaurant was going made him very uptight. Kermit always has to be busy, but this went too far. Between the radio, the restaurant, and Africa, I never saw him."

The words come in a torrent when Pat Carter (she now uses her maiden name) talks about her ex-husband today. "Kermit's whole life, from the first day I met him, has been devoted to *being* someone. I didn't understand that for a long time. When we were in college, I could see it, and I knew it came from all those years of feeling as if he was nobody, of being told he wasn't any good in his own home. He felt worthless; he wanted to feel worthy. I thought if I loved him enough, after a while that hunger would go away, or at least dissipate.

"It never did. Even after he was a star in college, even after he made it in the NBA. Maybe—maybe—if the Tomjanovich punch hadn't happened and his career had continued to go forward, there would have come a time when he would have been satisfied. But honestly I don't think so. He needed so much reinforcement. He needed to know he was someone, that he wasn't the little kid who grew up homeless in his own home. Then later he needed to know that he wasn't just the guy who threw the awful punch. He will tell you he knows he is more than that, but deep down, he doesn't. He's still trying to convince himself that he isn't just that person.

"I knew he wasn't just that person. His children knew it. We loved him. But that wasn't enough. It was just never enough."

Kermit denies none of this. He admits he was, and is, driven to show the world he isn't just the person seen through the years on that one piece of tape. The work in Africa is to help others, but it is also to help him; not financially, but emotionally.

"The sad part of it all is I had everything you should want," he said. "I had a good job, I had a great family. I lived in a community that accepted me. But I couldn't see that I had it all, and I kept pushing, whether to prove myself the way Pat says or whatever the reason. And I crashed and burned."

It didn't happen all at once. The restaurant started the financial slide. Then came the marriage. He met Mimi Nguyen at a fitness club. She was young, attractive, and smart, a commercial real estate broker in Portland at the time. Washington makes no excuses for what happened. Two years later, on November 25, 1998—"Ten-thirty at night, to be precise," Pat remembers—he told Pat the truth, that there was someone else in his life.

"Unless you have been in love with someone, you can't imagine the hurt I felt," she said. "Even then I told him if he would give her up, I would try to make the marriage work, try to fix it. I told him I'd work in the restaurant day and night if that's what we needed to do. But it was too late."

Washington began 1999 with his marriage blowing up and the restaurant careening toward bankruptcy.

That summer Pat moved to Las Vegas, where she had found a teaching job in an elementary school. Kermit moved in with Mimi. Dana Washington was so hurt by the breakup of her parents' marriage that she didn't speak to her father for most of the next two years. Even today she finds it difficult. Trey Washington remained with his father, working in the restaurant even after Kermit finally was forced to sell.

By then he had lost $500,000. He made no money on the sale, only able to get an agreement from the new owner to assume the considerable debt attached to the place. Meanwhile, he had also lost his radio job. New management came to the station and broke up Washington's partnership with Mychal Thompson. Shortly after that, Thompson moved to another station. Washington didn't like his new on-air partner, and their lack of on-air chemistry meant the station had to choose between them. Since his partner was the program director, Washington wasn't likely to win that battle. He didn't.

The comfortable life he had settled into in the midnineties had crashed. His marriage was over. Instead of being comfortable financially, he was in debt for the first time in his life. Getting a job for most ex–NBA players, especially one who is articulate, college-educated, and willing to work hard, usually isn't difficult. But if you are Kermit Washington, it will never be easy. There is no margin for error.

He had first thought about coaching in the NBA after leaving Stanford in the late eighties. He thought his skills were more suited to the NBA. Recruiting at the college level was too much like being a door-to-door salesman. That wasn't him. But getting out on the floor and working with big men, teaching them the things Newell had taught him, or working in the weight room, *that* was him. And so he began to send out letters every year to NBA teams. Most, he says, went unanswered. Others were answered with form letters. Occasionally, someone he had known would call to talk to him. Always the message was the same: "I just can't."

For a long time Washington shrugged off the rejections. This, he decided, was the burden of being who he was. It hadn't prevented him from being a success. If he couldn't work in the NBA, that was disappointing, but it was okay.

Now, though, he was out of work. It wasn't so okay anymore. Coaching in the NBA was something he knew he could do. If he couldn't get radio work in Portland, where he was well known and had been popular, then he wasn't likely to get that sort of work anyplace else. Coaching, it seemed to him, was the logical route to follow.

"After all," he said, "all I needed was one guy willing to take a shot."

He couldn't find that one guy. He began writing letters to anyone he had ever met in basketball who worked for an NBA team or might have a contact with an NBA team. He continued raising money for Project Contact, but without the platform of the radio show it became more difficult. His résumé traveled more than most circus performers. But it never got Washington anywhere.

Washington is convinced that two words not mentioned in his résumé make it impossible for him to get hired in the NBA: Rudy Tomjanovich. After years of rejection, he came to believe there was a conspiracy to keep him out of the league, that he was being blackballed. "They know if I get hired, the whole thing will come up again," he said. "All the questions, all the issues. They don't want that. I've had coaches in the league whom I know tell me very honestly, 'Kermit, I just can't hire you.'"

Early in the year 2000, Washington decided he needed to take aggressive steps to try once more to cleanse his reputation and to force the hiring issue with the NBA. Just sending out résumés wasn't getting anything accomplished.

First he took a lie detector test. He called Dr. Stanley Abrams, a clinical psychologist in Portland who has been a polygraph expert for almost forty years. Most of Abrams's work is done with accused murderers. "Most of my referrals come from defense attorneys," he said. "They want their client to take a polygraph test privately, so that if the results don't come out well, they can't be forced to turn them over to a prosecutor. If a client tests well, then the attorney will usually ask for a police polygraph for his client. About eighty-five percent of the referrals I get are people who are not found to be truthful on the test."

Abrams knew who Washington was when he called because the two men had sat next to each other on an airplane twenty years earlier. "He didn't remember it, but we were on a cross-country flight together and he had told me his whole life story for hours," he said. "I remembered thinking then that this guy had lived a very tough life. But I didn't say anything to him about that conversation when he initially called me."

On April 27, 2000, Abrams tested Washington. The average lie detector test takes two to two and a half hours and usually consists of a handful of key questions asked in the midst of dozens of others. Usually the examiner will start out with questions like "Is your name Kermit?" "Do you live in the state of Oregon?" In the case of a murder, he will work his way up to things such as "Did you ever wish to see anyone dead?" or "Are you afraid I'm going to ask a question you aren't prepared for?"

According to Abrams the crucial part of the test normally consists of nine questions, a couple of them completely irrelevant, a couple used strictly for comparison, and finally the ones that relate directly to the issue at hand. The key questions on Washington's test were: "Were you struck by Kevin Kunnert on December 9, 1977, before you struck him?" and "After you were fighting with Kunnert, did you feel threatened by Rudy Tomjanovich?"

According to Abrams, Washington's responses were "almost miraculously high" in truth content.

But like most lie detector results, Washington's high scores are not likely to exonerate him in the court of public opinion. To begin with, there are the usual suspicions about lie detector tests. Abrams, who is considered one of the top practitioners in the field, says there are ways for people to "beat" the test, although he does not believe Washington did that. But even he concedes that lie detectors are imperfect, which is why they are not admitted as evidence in court.

More important perhaps is that Washington's being found to be truthful changes little about the incident: Kunnert readily admits that he swung an elbow in the direction of Washington's shoulder after Washington grabbed his shorts. So no one, even Kunnert, disputes that he struck Washington first. Further, everyone agrees that Washington reacted instinctively to the sight of Tomjanovich coming up from behind him. The question is, did he need to react the way he did, or, as Calvin Murphy has said, should he have defended first and swung second?

Even so, Washington believed the test strengthened his case, that it proved he wasn't just making up a story to cover his actions. Armed with the results, Washington wrote to the *New York Times*, saying he wanted to tell his story in the newspaper. The *Times* has a page called "BackTalk" in its Sunday sports section, for stories just like the one Washington was proposing. Neil Amdur, the *Times* sports editor, read Washington's submission and decided it would be worth running in "BackTalk."

On May 14, 2000, Washington's story, headlined "A Sudden, Violent Moment That Still Haunts a Life," appeared in the *Times*. In the story Washington again described the moments leading to the punch, again insisting that Kunnert's two elbows were the reason the fight started. "After being attacked by Kunnert, I did not think Rudy's intentions [when he saw him coming from behind] were good either," he wrote. "I just saw someone running at me and reacted. My punch landed on his face and he fell. As Rudy Tomjanovich fell that night, so did my basketball career and a lot of the rest of my life."

Washington went on to say that the media had turned on him after the incident, and he described his suspension as being for three months. He didn't get the number of months wrong on purpose. In telling his story later, he repeatedly said the suspension was three months long. Only after being shown newspaper clips that said the suspension was two months did he believe it was that long. Through the years, the suspension, in his mind, had become three months.

In the story he continued to describe the aftermath of the punch:

> My nightmare was just beginning . . . I was public enemy No. 1. In 1977, racial diversity was almost nonexistent; racial slurs about me became everyone's favorite. I was humiliated. I was an embarrassment to myself and my family. Not even the university I had attended wanted anything to do with me. Everyone who was once so proud of me could not even say my name in public.

He did, at this juncture, mention the support of Red Auerbach and Pete Newell. Then he continued:

> Since then, I have applied for various coaching jobs from high school to the pro level, but have always been turned down because no one wanted to be associated with my

reputation, or with me. My name stood for violence and bad publicity. I was blackballed everywhere. . . . Schools were hesitant to let me speak because all the kids ever wanted to hear about was the famous fight. . . .

Over the last 23 years, the clip of my hitting Rudy is played every time there is any type of violence in sports. I can't count how many times it ran during the Sprewell incident [when Latrell Sprewell choked his coach, P. J. Carlesimo, during practice]. . . . Everything I've ever accomplished in my life is overshadowed by this incident.

There were exaggerations in the story. Washington had been hired twice: by Tom Davis at Stanford, who had then offered to take him to Iowa, and by the Trail Blazers as a part-time strength coach in 1988. He did do speaking in schools under the aegis of the GTE (now Verizon) speakers' bureau, a group he became part of after being elected to the GTE Academic All-American Hall of Fame in 1994. He had applied for the athletic director's job at American Univeristy in 1995—and had been turned down because the school's administration felt that, given his lack of experience, he should break in as an assistant and work his way up. In that role, AU would have been very interested in bringing him back.

"I didn't see why I couldn't be the AD so they could use my name out front and then have someone with more experience be my assistant," he said. "They didn't want to do it that way."

Certainly it isn't accurate to say the school is ashamed of him. Two pages of the 2002 media guide are devoted to his accomplishments, and Tom George, who was hired at the start of the year as athletic director, says Kermit Washington is more than welcome to be a part of AU anytime he wants to come back.

But the crux of the story, that the Tomjanovich incident had shadowed his life and overshadowed everything he had ever accomplished, was true.

The *Times* piece brought on a spate of publicity. But the phone wasn't ringing except occasionally when people who had read his story or heard him speak wanted to make contributions to Project Contact.

No job offers.

One person who wasn't the least bit pleased by the new round of publicity was Kevin Kunnert. He was especially unhappy when his youngest daughter came home from school the day after Washington appeared on Jim Rome's syndicated radio show and told him that one of her teachers at school had heard the interview. "Hey," he told her, "I never realized it was your dad's fault that Rudy Tomjanovich got beat up the way he did."

Kunnert was outraged. "It's been almost twenty-five years now," he said. "And the guy still won't face up to what he did. If that's the case, so be it, but it isn't fair to keep dragging me and now my family into it. I didn't do anything on that court that night to deserve to hear this stuff about myself all these years later.

"Look, I'm sorry if the guy hasn't been able to find work, but it's not *my* fault. I've heard he's done good work with his charity, and I think that's all great. But it doesn't give him the right to keep telling this fairy tale about me. If the guy would just deal with what he did, I think he would be a lot better off.

"But he won't, and maybe he can't. So my family and I have to keep living with it."

Still searching for something—vindication, validation, most of all, work—Washington went in a different direction. He had a Portland lawyer, Mark Lindley, draft a letter and send it by certified mail, return receipt requested, to David Stern. The letter began by detailing all the publicity Washington had been receiving. It then went on to discuss Washington's charity work with Project Contact, mentioning that the NBA had denied requests from Washington to make a contribution to Project Contact.

After that, Lindley wrote:

Kermit feels that the NBA manipulated the situation when it occurred in 1977 for public relations purposes and worked against Kermit with NBA team owners to make Kermit the scapegoat and make the NBA look better to Kermit's detriment. As a result, Kermit's ability to flourish as an NBA all-star was undermined and any future opportunities with the league and in the basketball world in general were ruined.

Until recently, people have not heard Kermit's side of the story. A story that has been validated by the results of a voluntary lie detector test that Kermit subjected himself to earlier this year. Kermit found himself in the middle of an altercation initiated by Kevin Kunnert, saw Rudy Tomjanovich running at him, and hit Rudy Tomjanovich because he was threatened by turning and seeing someone running at him. Kermit is not a violent man. Kermit has never been arrested for possession of a weapon, has never been cited for driving under the influence, and has never choked an NBA coach. As a matter of fact Kermit does not even drink or smoke and never has. Kermit made a mistake in judgment twenty-three years ago, and he is still paying the price.

Because of the false light that the NBA has cast Kermit in, every time an incident involving violence in sports comes up, Kermit's involvement in the Tomjanovich incident and his subsequent suspension are repeatedly established by the NBA as a benchmark. It is our understanding that the NBA released footage of the incident and continues today to cast Kermit in a false light. Kermit certainly does not fit in with today's superstars with their long arrest records and erratic behavior that is condoned by the league.

Kermit believes that he is entitled to compensation in the amount of five million dollars ($5,000,000.00) for the difficulty that he has faced for the last twenty-three years as a result of the actions of the NBA. Kermit has tried to maintain a good relationship with the NBA, but the poor treatment that he has received has pushed him to this point. Five million dollars ($5,000,000.00) is a small amount for the NBA to pay for the injustice that Kermit has dealt with for the last twenty-three years. . . .

In the event a favorable response is not received by this office prior to the end of this month, this firm will proceed to take more formal action.

The NBA responded with what the league describes as "a lawyer letter." In sum, the letter said that while the league sympathized with any difficulty Washington had encountered through the years, it was not responsible. No check would be forthcoming, for $5 million or any amount.

Washington did not take any further legal action. "Mark told me it would cost me thirty thousand dollars just to get them in a courtroom," he said. "I didn't have that kind of money to gamble at that point in my life." But he did keep pursuing the league's charity office about giving money to Project Contact. "I kept telling them that they had taken a lot of money from me in fines in 1977, not to mention the lost salary involved, and since they always use fine money to contribute to charity, why couldn't they give some of their fine money today to my charity?" he said. "They could check out the charity, see that it was legitimate and doing good work, and then make a contribution."

Eventually the NBA did just that. It contributed $4,500 to Project Contact in the spring of 2001. The contribution was made at almost the same time that Bryant Gumbel was putting together a piece for his HBO series *RealSports* on the Washington-Tomjanovich incident. The NBA says the timing of the contribution was coincidental to the Gumbel piece. Washington, of course, thinks differently.

"No one there ever returned my phone calls until HBO got involved," he said. "Then, after HBO calls, all of a sudden they want to be my friend."

Coincidence or not, the $4,500 helped him fund a trip to Africa in May of 2001. Clearly the work he does with Project Contact gives Washington great satisfaction. The people he works with enjoy his company and respect him for what he is doing. "When

I'm in Africa," he said, "no one sees me as the person who punched Rudy Tomjanovich. They just see me as someone who is bringing them help they desperately need."

It is when he returns home that he again finds heartache. In the summer of 2001, after Maurice Cheeks was hired as the new coach in Portland, he interviewed Washington for a potential job on his staff. The last thing he said to Washington was, "I'll be in touch."

Washington never heard back from him.

Brothers

On a hot midsummer afternoon in Houston, Rudy Tomjanovich sat in his living room, legs stretched out in front of him, looking both tired and relaxed.

The NBA draft had taken place that week and he was convinced the Rockets had stolen a great player in Eddie Griffin. The hours spent preparing for the draft were evident in his eyes, but the satisfaction he felt registered in his smile.

He swirled a glass of ice tea in front of him, frowned, and pulled out a pack of cigarettes. "My goal this off-season," he said, "is to quit."

He lit a cigarette and leaned back. Like every room in the house, the living room has a fifteen-foot ceiling, custom-designed for a man 6-foot-8 to feel as if he has plenty of space. The house, which the Tomjanoviches have lived in for three years, was designed by Sophie, and it is elegant and tasteful. It is located in the River Oaks neighborhood of Houston, or, as the Houston papers describe it, "the fashionable River Oaks section."

That description makes Sophie Tomjanovich a little bit crazy. "We lived in the same house for twenty-one years," she said. "It isn't as if we inherited the house or any money. Rudy worked very hard for a very long time before we moved into that house."

Regardless of the cost or how fashionable it may or may not be, Tomjanovich feels comfortable here. The ceilings are high, the kitchen has plenty of space, and there's a swimming pool in the back. He has come a long way from helping his dad bring home welfare food in Hamtramck.

The HBO piece on Kermit and Rudy had recently aired and the subject came up. "Didn't watch it," he said. "They sent me a tape. I haven't watched."

The only time he ever watched the tape of the punch was in 1979, when he was preparing for the court trial. Not before. Not since. No need. No reason to remember something he is happy he can't remember. He was talking now about Kermit Washington.

"It took me a long time to get to the point where I could think about him without feeling some resentment," he said. "Right from the beginning, I think I knew that to recover, I couldn't afford to hate him, that if I did, it would be like taking poison and hoping someone else would die from it. I worked consciously at that for a long time. I just tried not to think about him. That was the best way.

"But I would get asked about him. So I would just say that I forgave him. My emotions about him were a lot more mixed than that. I remember him telling me that the incident ruined his life. I didn't want it to ruin his life. But I also didn't want to go through what I went through and I had to go through it.

"I see it differently now. Since my sobriety, since I started looking at life differently, I really do feel differently. If he called me today and asked for my help, I'd give it to him if I could. I know he didn't want to be involved in this thing any more than I did. Who hasn't made a mistake in life? Am I perfect? What's the statute of limitations on what he did?"

He smiled. "You know, the funny thing about it all is this: I barely know the man. We've never really sat down and talked to one another. We just both had the misfortune to cross paths that one night. And now, all these years later, I feel like I've been married to him for twenty-four years. He's been a part of my life the entire time."

John Lucas sat in front of a bowl of corn flakes and strawberries, talking about his friend Kermit Washington.

"I love Kermit, I really do," he said. "I've known him since college, used to play with him in the summertime. I've never sat down and talked to him about what happened that night. It's amazing how clearly I remember it all. I can see it, I can hear it, I can feel it.

"I know what happened. I know he had no idea who it was coming up from behind and he reacted. I know he could coach in the NBA." He laughed and leaned back in his chair. "I can hear it now if I hired him. 'There goes Father Flanagan again, trying to resurrect another life.'" Lucas, who works with troubled youth at his clinic in Houston, laughed again. "The guy worked with Pete Newell. He was one of the first guys in the league to know how to really work with weights. You telling me he couldn't help some team's big men? Of course he could."

His face turned serious. "But you know what I wish? I wish he could just say, 'I'm sorry. I screwed up.' All the years, all I've heard over and over again is, 'I'm sorry, but . . .' Sometimes in life, you make a mistake and there's no buts and no explanations. If I had been there after it happened, knowing the things I know about life now, I would have said to him, 'Go see the man.' I would have told him if he had to, fly to Houston, drive to Houston, hitch to Houston. Take ten bodyguards if you have to, but go see the man. Look him in the eye and tell him how sorry you are.

"It would have been the right thing to do for Rudy. And it would have been the best thing to do for Kermit. There's no peace in 'I'm sorry, but.' You can't find peace until you truly understand that the only thing to say is, 'I'm sorry,' period.

"I hope someday he says it—and means it. Maybe then he can have peace. With himself. Which is all that really matters."

On a rainy Portland night like most other rainy Portland nights, Kermit Washington was dropping a passenger off at his hotel. Sitting behind the wheel, the engine running, he was talking about the future.

"I hope I'll get to coach," he said. "I think I could help people. I know the game, and I know the ups and downs of life pretty well too."

He was preparing for another trip to Africa. He had been chasing, although not ardently, another of his nutty professor ideas—track down Charles Barkley and offer to help him get in shape for the NBA comeback he has been threatening. As it turned out, he would get into coaching late in 2001—in China. A longtime friend who works placing players and coaches overseas would find him a job coaching in the Chinese professional league. He would jump at the chance, figuring he had to start someplace. The job would last four months, until the Chinese team ran out of money. Washington would come home to Portland convinced he had found a future NBA player on his team, but nonetheless looking to start all over again.

He was living in a rented two-bedroom condo near the river in downtown Portland because he had rented his house in Lake Oswego in order to find some extra income. Trey, who was still working at LeSlam, was staying with him.

"He sleeps in every morning," Washington said, laughing, sounding very much like a father. "He has no idea what it's like to have it tough. He's never had it tough a day in his life."

He rambled on, sitting in the hotel's driveway, about Africa and the NBA; about his kids and his dog; about HBO and Jim Rome and the *New York Times;* about Pete Newell and Red Auerbach.

Finally, as always, he began to talk about Rudy. He never refers to him as Tomjanovich or Rudy T. Always it is Rudy. As if, as Tomjanovich says, they have been married for all these years.

"He is a good, good guy," he said. "I know that. You know what's funny? Under different circumstances, I believe we would have been the best of friends. Everything I've ever seen or heard about him tells me that.

"I hope he's doing well. I really do. He didn't deserve what happened."

"When you talk to him," he said softly, "tell him I said I hope he's okay. I really hope he's okay."

It is early in the year 2002. Rudy Tomjanovich has endured a miserable, injury-filled half-season with a Houston team that began the year with high hopes, only to watch them crumble because of injuries, much the way the 1977–78 team's hopes crumbled. In today's NBA, where coaches are discarded like socks in the midst of virtually any losing streak, he is about as secure as one can be. In his tenth full year with the Rockets, he is now second only to Utah's Jerry Sloan in tenure, and with two years left on his contract at the end of the season, he isn't the least bit nervous about his job security, even after a 15-game losing streak.

"In a lot of ways this has been a great experience," he said. "Our young guys have learned a lot, even though they've learned it the hard way. In the long run, we're going to be a lot better because of this. And if someday they come to me and say they don't want me to coach anymore, that's fine. I think I can deal with whatever happens and be happy. I don't worry about the future the way I used to. I'm just happy with where my life is right now."

He glanced at the rubber band on his wrist and twirled it. "Whatever happens, I'll be okay," he said. "More than okay."

He asked about Kermit Washington. "China, huh?" he said. "I'll bet that's fascinating."

A pause. "I hope he does really well."

Because, he is asked jokingly, they're still married after all these years?

"Because," he said, "we're brothers."

Acknowledgments

Often I have trouble figuring out where to begin when writing acknowledgments, because each book I write requires the cooperation, help, and patience of so many different people in my life. In this case, though, the starting point is both easy and obvious.

Kermit and Rudy.

This is their story, and it is not an easy one for either of them to tell or to relive. One might make the point that Kermit Washington had more to gain from cooperating with me since his reputation has been sullied so greatly by those ten awful seconds, but he was fully aware of the fact that I planned to track down everyone involved in the story and that there were going to be people who were not going to say nice things about him. Even so he never blinked.

Rudy Tomjanovich had every reason not to talk, to simply ask me to go away and leave him alone. Not only did he not do that, but once we began spending time together he was open and honest and talked candidly about the incident and his life, including his battle with alcoholism, knowing full well that talking about it was likely to bring about a spate of headlines in his hometown.

348 · JOHN FEINSTEIN

I will be forever grateful to both of them for allowing me into their lives and for their willingness to relive in detail a chapter both wish they could forget but know they never will.

The same is true for many others I spoke to, most notably Kevin and Mary Kunnert, neither of whom can understand why they still have to keep living with this story twenty-five years after it happened. When I literally knocked on their door (having been able to track down only an address, but not a phone number), Mary Kunnert, who would have been perfectly entitled to tell me to get lost in a hurry, not only invited me into her home, she sat and talked to me for close to an hour and promised to pass a note to Kevin—who was out of town—for me. Later Kevin spent hours in that same living room going over in detail what I know are painful memories.

Calvin Murphy hadn't talked about that night since 1979. He talked at length, emotionally and patiently. So did Mike Newlin, John Lucas, Tom Nissalke, Ray Patterson, Steve Patterson, and Jim Foley. Kareem Abdul-Jabbar, Tom Abernethy, Jerry West, Stu Lantz, and Chick Hearn also spent considerable time re-creating their memories of that night, as did the two referees, Bob Rakel and Ed Middleton. In the NBA office, I thank Commissioner David Stern and Deputy Commissioner Russ Granik, with special thanks to Russ for tracking down the referees' reports of that night in the archives. Thanks also to the ever-patient Brian McIntyre, who often seemed to have answers before I asked the questions.

Thanks also to the following for being so generous with their time: Jack Ramsay, Brent Musburger, Dr. Stanley Abrams, Mark Lindley, Don Chaney, Tom Young, Tom Davis, Joe Boylan, Donald Dell, Michael Cardozo, and Dr. Paul Toffel, who took a great deal of time to try to explain what Rudy went through in terms a non-doctor could understand.

Others must be singled out, most notably Sophie Tomjanovich and Pat Washington. As with their husbands, talking about everything that has occurred since December 9, 1977, was anything but fun for them. Both not only did so, they answered my questions in great detail without ever snapping or rolling their eyes—responses both would have been entitled to on more than one occasion. I cannot thank them enough.

I also owe a debt of gratitude to Pete Newell and Red Auerbach. Both are in their eighties now and remember *everything*. If I had any doubts about Newell's memory, they were quickly dispelled when he easily ran down the San Diego Rockets' first *eight* draft picks in 1970. Auerbach is equally amazing. Both are also great storytellers, a reporter's dream.

As is almost always the case, I received considerable help from my colleagues, notably Tommy Bonk, Ted Green, and Rich Levin. Levin has gone straight—he is now publicity director for Major League Baseball—but all three shared their vivid memories of that night and their impressions of the people involved. Bonk was also heroic in helping me track down archival material at the *L.A. Times,* as was Bernie Miklasz at the *St. Louis Post-Dispatch.*

Josh Rosenfeld deserves special mention, not only because his memories of Kermit Washington's AU years were so vivid, but for convincing Abdul-Jabbar to talk to me. Thank you, Josh. Thanks also to J. C. Whipple for digging into the archives at AU on my behalf.

As mentioned in the introduction, there is not enough I can say here about Tim Frank. He kept the idea alive in my head when a lot of PR people would have been more than willing to let it die, and he tracked down every piece of minutia I asked for, not to mention phone numbers—often multiple times—and archival material in Houston. I was especially touched by the Comets media guide he sent me. Thanks also to Dan McKenna, Tracey Hughes, and Nelson Luis of the Rockets' PR staff.

Several other NBA PR people provided invaluable help: John Black and his staff with the L.A. Lakers; Jonathan Supranowitz of the Knicks; Bob Price of the Cavaliers; Tommy Sheppard of the Rockets; Karen Frascona of the 76ers; and Maureen Lewis of the

Wizards, who may have been relieved that I was the only reporter who came into her building in the last twelve months without asking for time with Michael Jordan. Wes Seeley should be on the friends list, but as always his research talents were invaluable. And he *loves* Army basketball.

Thanks also to Jim Rome, for being smart enough to book Kermit on his radio show after reading the piece in the *New York Times*, and to his producer, Travis Rogers.

My friends and family always put up with my rantings and ravings throughout these projects, though I'm not sure why. I'm fortunate that the list of those people is as long as it is. So, thanks again to: Keith and Barbie Drum; Bob and Anne DeStefano; David and Linda Maraniss; Tom and Jill Mickle; Jackson Diehl and Jean Halperin; Bill and Jane Brill; Terry Chili; Tate Armstrong; Mark Alarie (who may show up again someday); Pete Teeley; Bob Novak; Al Hunt; Andy Dolich; Mary Carillo; Doug Doughty; David Teel; Beth Shumway; Beth Sherry-Downes; Erin Laissen; Jesse Markison; Bob Socci; Pete Van Poppel; Frank Davinney; Andrew Thompson; Joe Speed; Jack Hecker; Jim Cantelupe and Tiffany Bauman (mazel tov, Jim); Derek and Christina Klein; Bob Beretta and Mike Albright; Frank Mastrandrea; Roger Breslin; Scott Morse and Phil LaBella; Glenn Hofmann and Jim Marshall; Todd Newcomb and Jon Terry; Mark Maske; Elissa Leibowitz; Michael Wilbon; Tony Kornheiser; Bob Edwards; Ellen McDonnell; Tom and Jane Goldman; Ken and Christina Lewis; Bob Zurfluh (nice job on the parking, Zurf); Mr. Reliable, Bob Morgan; the immortal Hoops Weiss; and, of course, Norbert Doyle, who has inspired each and every one of my books. Send all complaints to him.

Dave Kindred and Ken Denlinger were my role models twenty-five (gasp!) years ago. They still are. George Solomon was my boss twenty-five years ago. God help us both, he still is.

Through all the bullying and blackmailing by the Thugs in Bristol, Joe Valerio has remained a steadfast friend. So has Rob Cowan. I miss Dick Schaap.

Basketball people: All my old Patriot League pals—and they know who they are: Tommy Amaker, Mike Brey, Gary Williams, Mike Krzyzewski, Mike Cragg, Doug Wojcik, Billy Hahn, Skip Prosser, Dave Odom, Roy Williams, Rick Barnes.

Golf folks: Paul Goydos and Brian Henninger (still my guys), Dan Forsman, Mike Muehr, David B. Fay, Frank Hannigan, Mike Purkey, Jim Frank, and Glenn Greenspan. John Morris was one of the gutsiest people I've ever known, second perhaps only to Kitty Morris.

Swimmers: Jeff Roddin, Tom Denes, Penny Bates, Carole Kammel, John Craig, Dan Rudolph, Paul Doremus, Dave Harmon, Mary Dowling, Jeri Ramsbottom, Susan Williams, Amy Weiss, Doug Chestnut, Peter Ward, Warren Friedland, Marshall Greer, Margot Pettijohn, A. J. Block, Danny Pick, and Mark Pugliese. Special kudos as always to Shelley Crist, for surviving another year with Jason. And, of course, my fellow FWRH's (twice!), Clay Britt, Wally Dicks, and Michael Fell.

The China Doll gang: Red Auerbach, Morgan Wootten, Jack Kvancz, Aubrey Jones, Sam Jones, the always gentle Hymie Perlo, Pete Dowling, Bobby Campbell, Stanley Copeland, Alvin Miller, Rob Ades (get off the phone!), and Zang Auerbach, whom I can almost always set my clock by.

Thanks also at Little, Brown to Shannon Byrne, Heather Fain, Heather Rizzo, Michael Mezzo, and Stacey Brody. Extra thanks to Ryan Harbage, who ran down every request, no matter how ludicrous. Holly Wilkinson has patiently dealt with me for almost eight years. If she thinks retiring to raise her family will allow her to be rid of me, she has another think coming. At ICM, Jack Horner and Judith Schell put up with me for a long time, and now Andy Barzvi and Christine Bausch are doing the same.

I usually end with my family, but I am going to change that tradition this time around, not because they mean any less to me. Mary and Danny and Brigid make everything else in my life worthwhile, and we are all fortunate to be surrounded by members of our families: Jim and Arlene; Dad and Marcia; Margaret, David, and Ethan; Bobby, Jennifer, Matthew, and (the newest arrival) Brian; Kacky, Stan, and Annie; Annie, Gregg, Rudy, Gus, and Harry; Jim and Brendan.

And finally (applause all around) a few more words on Michael Pietsch and Esther Newberg. To call them an editor and an agent, even though accurate, is entirely misleading. They are friends I rely on constantly. They have dealt with my foibles and eccentricities for years and listen patiently when I come up with crazy ideas. Most important, when I *really* didn't know what the hell to do in January of 2001 and was feeling guilty and confused about abandoning a project I knew they both wanted to see happen, they were 100 percent supportive. I am so damn lucky that they are a part of my life, both professionally and personally.

—John Feinstein
Bethesda, Maryland
June 2002

Index

A note about the author

John Feinstein is the author of several bestselling books, including books on basketball (*A Season on the Brink, A March to Madness, The Last Amateurs*), golf (*A Good Walk Spoiled, The Majors, Open: Inside the Ropes at Bethpage Black*), football (*A Civil War: Army vs. Navy*), and other sports. He is a commentator on National Public Radio and an essayist for CBS Sports. He is also a columnist for America Online and *Golf* magazine and a contributor to the *Washington Post* and the *Wall Street Journal*. He lives in Bethesda, Maryland, and Shelter Island, New York.

Look for these other bestselling books by
John Feinstein

The Last Amateurs
*Playing for Glory and Honor
in Division I College Basketball*

"Feinstein's descriptions of the games are intense and exciting."
— Conrad Bibens, *Houston Chronicle*

"There are numerous behind-the-scenes anecdotes that keep the pages turning." — Larry Platt, *Wall Street Journal*

"You'll be glued to the page. . . . Feinstein makes you care."
— Bruce Fretts, *Entertainment Weekly*

A March to Madness
*The View from the Floor in the
Atlantic Coast Conference*

"A basketball junkie's nirvana."
— Charles Hirshberg, *Sports Illustrated*

"A meticulously detailed account of a season of college basketball. . . . Full of insider's jargon, the drama of personal rivalries, the melodrama of hard-fought contests. . . . Fans will find everything in this book." — Richard Bernstein, *New York Times*

BACK BAY BOOKS
Available in paperback wherever books are sold

Look for these other bestselling books by
John Feinstein

A Good Walk Spoiled
Days and Nights on the PGA Tour

"The golf tour's true heart. . . . Feinstein gets it right."
—*New York Times Book Review*

The Majors
In Pursuit of Golf's Holy Grail

"The ultimate insider's account. . . . Feinstein examines the hearts and minds of the best players in the world to find what it takes to win the game's most prestigious events." —*Golf Tips*

"Another major triumph for John Feinstein. . . . If you want to know how touring pros think, this is the book."
—Dave Anderson, *New York Times Book Review*

Open
Inside the Ropes at Bethpage Black

Coming in paperback in spring 2004

"When it comes to detailing the life of the professional golfer, there is none finer than John Feinstein."
—Everett J. Merrill, *Philadelphia Inquirer*

BACK BAY BOOKS
Available in paperback wherever books are sold

Look for these other bestselling books by
John Feinstein

A Civil War: Army vs. Navy
A Year Inside College Football's Purest Rivalry

"An excellent book. . . . With Army-Navy, you always get your money's worth." —*Wall Street Journal*

"Not only entertaining but also inspiring."
—Henry Kisor, *Chicago Sun-Times*

"Compelling. . . . A fast-paced account full of insights and interesting characters." —Jim Shea, *Hartford Courant*

"Highly readable. . . . Feinstein is an outstanding chronicler of the game as a game." —Clay Reynolds, *Houston Chronicle*

"A winner for everyone who is a fan of college ball."
—Frank Donnini, *Newport News*

BACK BAY BOOKS
Available in paperback wherever books are sold

Coming in spring 2004

Caddy for Life
The Bruce Edwards Story
by John Feinstein

An extraordinary account of teamwork, loyalty, and professionalism in the front ranks of the PGA—the compelling and inspiring story of Bruce Edwards, recently diagnosed with Lou Gehrig's disease, who has been Tom Watson's caddy for more than three decades.

Published in hardcover by Little, Brown and Company